FULL
OF
BULL

(Updated Edition)

FULL
OF
BULL

(Updated Edition)

*Unscramble Wall Street Doubletalk to
Protect and Build Your Portfolio*

Stephen T. McClellan

Vice President, Publisher: Tim Moore
Associate Publisher and Director of Marketing: Amy Neidlinger
Executive Editor: Jim Boyd
Editorial Assistant: Myesha Graham
Operations Manager: Gina Kanouse
Digital Marketing Manager: Julie Phifer
Publicity Manager: Laura Czaja
Assistant Marketing Manager: Megan Colvin
Cover Designer: Alan Clements
Managing Editor: Kristy Hart
Project Editor: Lori Lyons
Copy Editor: Cheri Clark
Proofreader: San Dee Phillips
Indexer: Erika Millen
Senior Compositor: Gloria Schurick
Manufacturing Buyer: Dan Uhrig

This book is sold with the understanding that neither the author nor the publisher is engaged in rendering legal, accounting, or other professional services or advice by publishing this book. Each individual situation is unique. Thus, if legal or financial advice or other expert assistance is required in a specific situation, the services of a competent professional should be sought to ensure that the situation has been evaluated carefully and appropriately. The author and the publisher disclaim any liability, loss, or risk resulting directly or indirectly, from the use or application of any of the contents of this book.

FT Press offers excellent discounts on this book when ordered in quantity for bulk purchases or special sales. For more information, please contact U.S. Corporate and Government Sales, 1-800-382-3419, corpsales@pearsontechgroup.com. For sales outside the U.S., please contact International Sales at international@pearson.com.

Company and product names mentioned herein are the trademarks or registered trademarks of their respective owners.

Printed in the United States of America

First Printing June 2009

ISBN-10: 0-13-702312-X
ISBN-13: 978-0-13-702312-7

Pearson Education LTD.
Pearson Education Australia PTY, Limited.
Pearson Education Singapore, Pte. Ltd.
Pearson Education North Asia, Ltd.
Pearson Education Canada, Ltd.
Pearson Educación de Mexico, S.A. de C.V.
Pearson Education—Japan
Pearson Education Malaysia, Pte. Ltd.

Library of Congress Cataloging-in-Publication Data

McClellan, Stephen T.
  Full of bull : unscramble wall street doubletalk to protect and build your portfolio/ Stephen T. McClellan. — Updated ed.
      p. cm.
  Includes index.
  ISBN-13: 978-0-13-702312-7 (pbk. : alk. paper)
  ISBN-10: 0-13-702312-X (pbk. : alk. paper) 1. Stocks—United States. 2. Investments—United States. 3. Investment analysis. 4. Wall Street (New York, N.Y.) I. Title.
  HG4910.M3696 2010
  332.63'220973—dc22
                                    2009006072

To Elizabeth,
my love, my bride, my friend

Contents

Acknowledgments

This book was materially enhanced by input from a few trusted Wall Street veterans whom I have known for most of my career. They reviewed the manuscript and made worthy suggestions. My old friend Peter Anastos spent his career in the mutual fund industry and the past several years before retirement as head portfolio manager of the Alliance Capital technology fund. Jim Lee was an institutional salesman at the small firm where I started in 1971 and worked as an investment manager over the years. He is an astute observer of the Street as well as investment trends. Over the decades, he has seen it all, from the buyside perspective. George McDougall, a friend since first grade, helped me find a title and aided in the editing. John Korvin, a golf partner who skins me regularly, and Mike Walsh, a comrade involved in technology market research, gave me valuable suggestions. Jim Boyd at FT Press guided the publication process. WT Blase & Associates and The Hendra Agency assisted in marketing promotion.

The foremost person assisting in the preparation of this book was Joyce Padua. She works with me as my personal assistant. We slogged every morning—me buried under copious notes on one side of my desk, she sitting across in front of the computer. She did her share of editing, too. Now she thinks she is an expert investor. Another valuable contributor was my freelance editor, Kathryn Crim, who brought order and clarity to my jumbled prose.

Then there is my progeny. Laurel Almerinda remembers the labors of my first book. As an artsy, creative, and driven USC film school alum, she is pursuing a career as a screenwriter and as a chef in Los Angeles. Justin McClellan toiled for his engineering degree at Boston University and is now employed in the aerospace field while eagerly working to master the ropes of managing his own portfolio of stocks. They constantly offer unsolicited parental advice to keep me in line.

While the first edition of this book was in midstream, I fell in love with my bride Elizabeth Barlow, an artist who spent her career in the opera and ballet. Her feline, Figaro, came along with her and promptly took over as master of the house. Several times Elizabeth overheard me casually giving practical, and what I thought was obvious, investment advice to someone. She usually reacted by reminding me that what was intuitive to me as a professional insider was enlightening to outsiders, and would inquire if I had addressed that in my book. Amazingly, in many cases, I had not. So I immediately jotted the suggestion into the book. Elizabeth helped me visualize investing from the eyes of a nonprofessional outsider.

About the Author

Stephen T. McClellan was a Wall Street investment analyst for 32 years, covering high-tech stocks as a supervisory analyst. He was a First Vice President at Merrill Lynch for 18 years until 2003, and ranked on the annual *Institutional Investor* All-America Research Team 19 consecutive times, *The Wall Street Journal* poll for 7 years, and has a place in the *Journal*'s Hall of Fame. From 1977 to 1985, he was a Vice President at Salomon Brothers and before that held a similar position at Spencer Trask for 6 years. Before commencing his Wall Street career, he was an industry analyst with the U.S. Department of Commerce. From 1964 to 1967, the author served as an operations officer aboard the USS Suffolk County (LST-1173) in the U.S. Navy.

Mr. McClellan has a Chartered Financial Analyst (CFA) designation, is a member of the New York CFA Society and the CFA Institute, was President of the New York Computer Industry Analyst Group, and was President and Founder of the Software/Services Analyst Group. He has made television appearances on Bloomberg TV, FoxBusiness News, CBS, CNN *MoneyLine*, CNBC, and *Wall Street Week*. He has conducted several radio interviews on such programs as Bob Brinker's *Moneytalk* and given presentations to numerous organizations, at conferences, and to companies. Mr. McClellan has published articles in the *Financial Times*, *The New York Times*, *Forbes*, and other publications. His MBA in Finance is from George Washington University and his BA is from Syracuse University.

The author's speaker's bureau is Leading Authorities, Inc., in Washington, DC. His website is www.stephentmcclellan.com.

Preface

This book is for the individual investor. It is all about investing, not trading, because investing is the way to make money in the stock market. Unfortunately, transaction-oriented Wall Street tends to discourage and even hinder proper investing. Broker investment advice can be misleading, even contradictory. Professional insiders know better than to take the Street literally. You need to take the same approach. This book will show you how to avoid Street pitfalls, circumvent inappropriate research guidance, correctly interpret Wall Street commentary and opinions, properly assess statements by corporate executives, and put news media reports in their proper context. It will provide you with an understanding of the confusing ways of Wall Street so that you can make more profitable long-term investment decisions.

Full of Bull was first published in hardcover in late 2007, and slight revisions were made for the second printing released at the beginning of 2008. In early 2009, I made extensive updates for this paperback version. I also added a new chapter discussing bear market investing. During 2008, one of the worst bear markets since the Great Depression gripped investors. Those who did not react by preserving capital—my foremost investment strategy—lost as much as 30% or 40% in their stock market holdings. I was frequently asked, "What should I do now?" The new Chapter 4, "Investment Strategies to Survive in a Bear Market," familiarizes investors with bear markets, the economic influence, and the role of Wall Street, and makes suggestions on how to invest during such a period.

Life sometimes shifts in unforeseen directions. For 32 years, I was consumed by my job as a securities analyst on Wall Street. My plan in late 2002 was to continue grinding away for a couple more years before hanging it up. I had no compelling new venture or life plan that I was anxious to embark on. As the stock market bubble deflated in 2000 and 2001, the economics of brokerage firm research were permanently altered. The discrediting of analysts, elimination of investment bank research subsidies, and shrinkage in commission fees ushered in an era of parsimonious research budgets. Senior analysts were no longer being paid the vast sums of the past. At the Four Seasons Resort on Hawaii's Kona Coast, as I sat by the pool after my fifth mai tai, it hit me: I could add a couple more years of adventure to my life if I opted out. In early 2003, I tossed in the towel and concluded a long career as an analyst.

On my first day of retirement, when depression might have ensued from the new void in my life, I headed off to Utah to ski with my son and attend the screening of my daughter's new short-subject movie at the Sundance Film Festival. This marked the first time in over three decades that I boarded a plane without bringing along a carry-on bag full of work. I was savoring the prospect of perusing the newspapers and maybe reading a history book, when a guy in a suit plopped down next to me and inquired as to my business. Upon learning that I had stock market expertise, he began firing off a series of simple investment questions. After more than three decades of analyzing, researching, writing, and talking about stocks, the last thing I felt like doing on my first trip free of Wall Street was to chat about investing—especially to educate a naive, nettlesome passenger probing me for silver bullets. I quickly wriggled out of the conversation. Then a jarring realization hit me: There was a whole world of individual investors out there, struggling to make money in the stock market with little knowledge of how the Wall Street investment game is really played.

Over the following two or three years, I filled up a notebook with observations and insights that might be useful to an individual investor. My previous book, *The Coming Computer Industry Shakeout,* which I wrote in the early 1980s, concluded with a brief chapter on basic principles for individual investors. Although rudimentary, it made a splash with readers and the press. This time, with *Full of Bull,* the entire book is devoted to such investment maxims. My style is opinionated, forthright, and direct. My views may be controversial, but I try to emulate the revered sportscaster Howard Cosell and "tell it like it is." These are my own conclusions—acquired during my decades on Wall Street.

I grew up in Wilmette, Illinois, ran track at New Trier High School, and tooled around in a jeep delivering newspapers each summer. I was initially intrigued with the stock market and Wall Street in college at Syracuse University, so I buttressed my liberal arts economics major by taking additional business and finance courses. When I heard that a two-person stockbrokerage firm in Chicago might be in need of summer help, I leaped at the opportunity. Morton D. Cahn was an octogenarian and the most senior member of the Midwest Stock Exchange. His halcyon days had been the 1920s, but in the 1960s, he still kept a tiny one-room office running and spent his days on the exchange floor doing maybe a dozen trades a day. All summer in that office, I devoured every facet of the business—calculated commissions, messengered securities around the city, took transaction orders over the phone, studied a text on bonds during my downtime, and handled the office all alone when the old-line office manager was away on vacation. By Labor Day, I knew my career would be on Wall Street.

Some of the paychecks I collected from that stint were destined to be invested. I was eager to become an honest-to-goodness stockholder myself. My dictatorial father, who was springing for my college expenses, vetoed the idea. But I was adamant and put in a buy order for five shares of Union Carbide at $91. When I divulged my "shareholder" status to him, he was furious. But I was unyielding. I guess I was coming of age and beginning to stand up for myself. Every day during my senior year at Syracuse, on shirt cardboards, I recorded Union Carbide's opening, high, low, and closing prices and its trading volume. I cared. You cannot imagine the satisfaction I felt every three months when I received my dividend check for $6.25. And the next summer, I sold the shares for over $109—my maiden investment had produced an inspiring capital gain!

In those college days, New York City was our venue during Thanksgiving vacations for jazz clubs, hockey games, and other cavorting. But I spent Friday (the market being open) wandering around Wall Street as an anxious outsider wanting to become an insider. I haunted the New York Stock Exchange, the American Exchange, Trinity Church, the streets, bookstores, and even brokerage lobbies. My buddies were dumbfounded that I would waste a day of our precious, exciting school break in Gotham trolling the canyons of Wall Street. For me, though, it was Priority Number One.

Later, as an operations officer in the Navy, aboard a ship based in Norfolk, I devoured *The Wall Street Journal* when in port, scrutinized *Forbes* magazine while on watch, compiled a notebook of research, and planned my strategy to reach Wall Street. I had a meager few hundred dollars invested in one or two stocks. Shortly before mustering out of the military, while preliminarily knocking on Wall Street doors, I received some emphatic counsel from a Merrill Lynch personnel-department interviewer. He told me I needed an MBA degree if I hoped to get a job in the business (as if I could run across the street, grab a graduate degree, and be back that afternoon!). The prospect of three more years in school before reaching the Street was daunting.

So, during the late 1960s, as the Vietnam War raged, I donned my uniform, interviewed, and was rubber-stamped at George Washington University Business School, where my dad had earned his law degree in 1929. Upon settling in Washington, D.C., I landed a position with the U.S. Department of Commerce. There, I assisted the existing office equipment industry analyst, a senior veteran who called me his amanuensis. He showed me the basics of how to write research publications. I was immersed in tracking and publishing reports on the rising computer industry. Three years later, MBA in hand, I blanketed Street brokerage firms with letters seeking interviews. With no clue as to what specialty I preferred—institutional sales, trading, investment banking, or research—I haphazardly tossed around my glossy résumés. One boutique firm, Spencer Trask, a small, respected, research-focused brokerage, noted my computer-industry expertise and ushered me upstairs to the research director. His offer to hire me as a junior analyst was the only one forthcoming. I took it instantly, starting at an $18,000 annual salary. The MBA turned out to be irrelevant; familiarity with the data processing field was the trigger. Life is strange.

My debut day in 1971 was eons removed from my walk-off in 2003. The first six years on Wall Street was a massive learning experience. At Spencer Trask I was mentored by the electronics analyst who hired me, Otis Bradley; soon I became a full-fledged analyst myself and enjoyed a coddled existence at this old-school, genteel, white-shoe firm. In 1977, I made a leap to Salomon Brothers, an aggressive, trading-oriented, highly profitable firm endowed with stellar professionals and a recognized, confident élan. It was a cauldron, but it introduced me to the changing real world of Wall Street. After 8 years, I slid over to Merrill Lynch and stayed there for 18 years. At the time I was signed, Merrill was becoming a heavyweight in

research, a household word, a leader on Wall Street, and a good place
to be as an analyst. At Merrill I achieved #1 status in *Institutional
Investor* magazine's analyst rankings for several years, moved to the
West Coast in 1991, and operated from San Francisco for the remain-
der of my career.

Once, after I was retired, a casual investor mentioned to me,
before a round of golf at our club, that he was about to purchase a
particular stock in the aerospace-defense sector. His justification was
something like "nine Wall Street Buy recommendations and only one
Neutral, all the favorable Street opinions have been in place for a year
or longer, and the consensus price objective is some $18 above the
current level." He obviously believed all this Street talk, having no
idea that, given precisely the situation he described, perhaps he
ought to be *avoiding* the stock.

As a Street professional, I interpreted the situation such that the
one lonely Neutral stance was really a Sell indication (probably
insightful and timely) and should be given more credence. Street analysts use the terms Hold or Neutral to subtly indicate a negative view.
I also thought that all the Buy opinions were likely growing stale, so
there might be more downgrades ahead shortly. My golfing partner
was late to the party and had undoubtedly missed the big gains in the
stock. Furthermore, I assumed that those analyst price targets probably had been boosted a couple of times already to justify the continued Buy ratings. My skeptical assessment was probably shared by
almost everyone on Wall Street, but my golf bud, being a typical individual investor, misinterpreted the situation. From all my years on
Wall Street, I understand that the key to superior investing is in
decoding the Street's confusing (if not misleading) doubletalk and
ignoring and sometimes even defying its advice. Nevertheless, most
investors fall right in line like true believers.

My golfing friend and I, when it came to investments, did not
speak the same language. Wall Street directs its advice to the managers of big mutual fund portfolios and hedge funds. Similar to a
baseball manager talking to his players or other league officials, the
Street assumes that other professionals in the business understand
the nuanced manner in which the game is played. It knows that they
are able to use research material appropriately (that is, not take it literally), and it expects insiders to react in a certain manner.

The individual investor is often misled by Wall Street's ambiguous ways. What investors are missing is the knowledge necessary to deal with the Street. Individuals need to put the deluge of stock information in the proper perspective and make their own investment decisions. It is not enough to tap into the Internet, tune into CNBC, scan the financial section of the newspaper, devour magazines like *Money*, listen to a broker, or even read the typical book on how to invest. Keeping in touch with all these sources helps, but the information must still be utilized effectively. The misleading actions of Wall Street must be taken into account. What should you make of a Street recommendation upgrade from Sell to Hold or Neutral? If a stock is downgraded from Buy to Neutral, should you hold it or sell it? After a stock-price target is reached and the target is raised, the Street tells the investor to continue buying. Wasn't the initial target real? And if so, should not the investor be told to Sell when the objective is achieved? You get the picture. You do not have a chance unless you can decipher all the confusing, unpredictable, and often counterproductive Wall Street babble.

The purpose of this book is to expose the puzzling and deceptive behavior of Wall Street that so disadvantages individual investors, tripping them up in their attempts to invest properly and rationally. It unscrambles the confounding practices of the Street in terms a layperson can comprehend. The reports by securities analysts are highly useful as background research. Analysts are steeped in company and industry expertise; they can provide helpful commentary in reaction to events and news; and they publish earnings estimates. But an investor needs to know what to discount in Street research—how to separate the wheat from the chaff. An individual investor must grasp how the system works and be able to factor it into his or her investment approach. Once armed with an insider's understanding of all the Street's subtleties, you can be your own investment analyst. My strategies will equip you to evaluate companies, select stocks, and take advantage of your position, one free from the many constraints that inhibit professionals.

To stay abreast of my current stock market investment views, go to my blog at www.stephentmcclellan.com. There you can also read articles and interviews and browse my appearance schedule.

Stephen T. McClellan
February 2009

1

Decoding Wall Street's Well-Kept Secrets

As a securities analyst for 32 years, I am amazed that naive investors can be so misled by Wall Street doubletalk. You can be an astute investor only if you fathom the puzzling and often deceptive nature of the Street. Wall Street operates in strange, ambiguous ways that it would prefer to keep secret. Do what Wall Street does, not what it says. Do not take the Street literally. Its research cannot be trusted. Corporate executives react to Street sentiment, attempt to influence their own stock prices, and also deter objective investing. The individual investor is an afterthought, mostly neglected by analysts and broker-dealer research departments. The Street cannot be ignored. But if you understand the research game to the same degree that professional portfolio managers do, the playing field will be more even. By unscrambling Wall Street doubletalk and decoding the confusing, cryptic Street practices, you can unlock the handcuffs that inhibit superior investing, to protect and build your portfolio.

Wall Street brokerage firms focus first and foremost on themselves, and after that on institutional clients such as mutual funds and hedge funds. One of the most important profit centers is the trading desk, transacting myriad trades each day as a principal (generating profits for the house account). In his *Forbes* column, Laszlo Birinyi, Jr., who heads a financial/investment consulting firm, expresses the concern that the Street "serves itself rather than its clients...at the expense of individuals and mutual funds." He states that "an awful lot of short-term trading profit [is] swallowing up money that in the past would have ended up with long-term investors." The only way for the individual investor to offset this disadvantage is to hold stocks long-term and be aware of the Wall Street system to the same degree as the insiders.

In mid-1985, I decided to take a new job with Merrill Lynch, but first I had to sit tight for ten days. I was scheduled as Louis Rukeyser's guest under the Salomon Brothers moniker and could not resign gracefully until off the set of *Wall Street Week*. I was already feeling edgy when I arrived in the remote horse country of Owings Mills, Maryland. After I'd cooled my heels a couple hours in the studio, Lou, who had not finished writing his commentary, was still not ready to tape the show at the normal time that Friday evening, an hour before it aired on PBS. So my appearance was one of his infrequent programs that went on live—adding pressure and more time to stew. Seated just off the set for the first half of the program with a pitcher of water, I was told to be still or the viewers might see the movement of my shadow. Nervously, I consumed most of the jug and badly needed relief about the time the hostess grabbed my arm to strut me out to the couch in front of the cameras and panelists. My bladder bulged as we wheeled into camera view and the hostess whispered to me, "Do not trip on the platform—three million viewers are watching."

Analysts like me are not accustomed to being grilled. We normally have the upper hand. At least we are good at faking aplomb and we rarely come unraveled. I sank down into the gigantic soft sofa, feeling like a midget looking up at Rukeyser, who towered over me in his high-perched chair. All my hours of practiced answers flew out of my head. I was babbling. It was like truth serum, but I survived. This book puts you in Rukeyser's shoes. It unravels Wall Street security analysts and their research. And it will give you investment strategies to counter the Wall Street bull.

What Is a Wall Street Securities Analyst?

To comprehend Street research, you must first be familiar with the function of a securities analyst. I am talking about an analyst at a brokerage firm investment bank, not an in-house stock analyst at mutual funds, banks, or investment management firms that cater only to the portfolio managers within his or her own firm. The job function of brokerage analysts is to conduct research on companies and industries and "sell" it to the brokerage institutional clients and secondarily to individual investors. A typical Street analyst heads a small team of associates, is situated in New York (I was in New York for 20 years and then relocated to San Francisco for the last 12 years of my career), has maybe a dozen years experience, and is in the 30-to-40 age range. The ideal analyst has an MBA degree, should be a Chartered Financial Analyst (CFA), and is adept at reading and interpreting financial statements, understanding and building complicated mathematical earnings models on a computer, writing research reports, talking and interviewing, and selling/marketing. This is a wish list, because rarely do analysts have all these qualifications.

The primary requisite of any analyst is to be an expert on a particular industry sector and group of companies therein. There are analysts covering areas such as high-tech semiconductors or software, retail specialty stores, the oil and gas industry, biotech, airlines, utilities, and banks. I began covering the entire computer industry in the 1970s when it was small, gravitated toward focusing on software and computer services in the 1980s, and then covered only computer services starting in the 1990s (companies such as EDS, Automatic Data Processing, and Accenture). Analysts conduct research on and rigorously track a limited number of companies in their chosen industry area. They must understand the dynamics, influences, and underpinnings of the industry, and be exceptionally familiar with as much detail on each company as possible—elements such as the financials, products, competitive position, management, strategies, and research and development. Analysts must be able to judge executives; assess the impact or effect of any number of influences, such as competitor pricing or a demand falloff on a company; have the vision to see the big picture amid tumultuous current pressures on a stock; and analyze a company's outlook with incomplete information in an unclear situation.

It is common for analysts to have worked in the industry they are covering before starting on Wall Street. Analyst industry expertise is more important than a background in securities, investment, or finance. I became savvy about the computer industry while employed at the U.S. Department of Commerce tracking the sector there. Wall Street recognized my knowledge of the area and hired me for that reason, not because of my MBA degree.

The second-most-important analyst qualification is an understanding of the stock market, investment, and securities (stocks, bonds, options, convertibles, and so on). This is basic stuff, things such as listed versus NASDAQ-traded securities, bid and ask spreads, stock buybacks, dividends, share issuances, stock options, debt (bonds), and all the mechanical aspects of the stock market. Sometimes this knowledge is obtained while earning an MBA degree, or on the job, in the business, as a junior start-up analyst; and it is enhanced in the process of acquiring the professional CFA designation. I did both but was further ahead of the game due to my college summer job at a small brokerage firm in Chicago, when I first began reading financial newspapers/magazines and books, investing on my own, and following the market for years before I landed on Wall Street.

Street analysts also need to have some grasp on the economy. My undergraduate degree was in economics. Several economic factors impact stocks and company fundamentals. Analysts should be conversant with elements such as interest rates, employment, GDP, inflation, recessions, government spending and borrowing, foreign currencies, and international trade. An MBA degree is a key source to absorb background in economic disciplines.

The securities analyst's role is to determine the industry and individual company outlook in the sector covered, conclude whether the stocks are attractive investments (a Buy opinion) or likely to perform poorly (a Sell), write up these findings in research reports, and monitor all this on a continuing basis. A key mission is to then verbally communicate this research to the brokerage firm's institutional investor clients and other key audiences, such as the in-house sales force and traders on the desk and the outside media. Notice I left out retail individual investors. Analysts do not deal with them directly. Analysts on Wall Street must sell their research, that is, market their product and views. To be proficient at this so-called marketing, analysts must be outgoing. No shy types. They make presentations to single portfolio managers or a room full of institutional investors. Analysts need to be convincing on the telephone and over their firm's squawk box. They must have conviction; be strong, opinionated, and confident; and come across as cool, intelligent, and balanced, similar to a 747 airline pilot during a turbulent thunderstorm (my worst nightmare). This requires personality, charm, and a colorful and engaging character. (Of course, I was all that and more—did I mention humility?)

The brokerage institutional salespeople cater directly to the portfolio managers, traders, and analysts at the firm's institutional clients—mutual funds, hedge funds, pension funds, banks, and other financial institutions. All day long, they carry the analyst's research message to these institutions, in person, on the phone, or by e-mail. Salespeople might cover a half dozen such institutions and talk with perhaps five or ten key contacts at each one. They also help sell to these big clients initial public offerings (IPOs) and secondary share issuances their firms are underwriting, and set up meetings between their analysts or corporate executives and these institutional customers. Traders execute sizable buy and sell orders on behalf of major clients and attempt to make money for the brokerage firm's own account by trading stocks. Investment bankers deal with corporations, governments, and other entities in need of such financial services as selling stocks or bonds, doing mergers and acquisitions, and structuring complicated financial/investment transactions.

What is a typical day in the life of an analyst? During the latter portion of my career, I was located in San Francisco, where the stock market opens at 6:30 a.m., so my hours were on the early side. My firm's morning conference call, where research analysts present pertinent new views or updates, commenced at 4:15 a.m. I rolled out of bed at 4:10 a.m., tossed on my sweats, and jumped on the horn. Because this live broadcast went out to hundreds of offices worldwide, it was critical to not fall asleep or screw up. Then, after donning slacks and a sweater, I drove through dark streets, grabbed a giant coffee, cream, and sugar, and was at my desk by 6 a.m. Things were now happening full blast because it was 9 a.m. in New York. The sales force was on my case to call key institutional clients to add color to the comments I made on the earlier morning call. My stock screen was racing with price changes, news stories, and other information. E-mails by the dozens pleaded for responses, opinions, scheduling, and all sorts of other matters. My team was just outside my office door, wanting to chat or discuss research. No help from my administrative assistant, who waltzed in at about 7:30 a.m., and worked fairly normal hours. At some point, I hustled a couple blocks over to a local hotel for a breakfast meeting with a mutual fund portfolio manager.

Back in the office around 9 a.m. *The Wall Street Journal* called. An executive from a company I covered was in town and showed up at my door mid-morning. We discussed his firm's business outlook for an hour. My 16-ounce takeout coffee got cold, but I was still sipping it. I had to scrutinize, in advance, a detailed computer earnings model of a company that was to report its results at 1 p.m. this particular day, after the market closed. Soup at my desk for lunch, the first thing I had eaten all day. The earnings results hit the tape. We did instant analysis, prepared questions, and tuned in to the company's 2 p.m. investor conference call. It was over at 3 p.m., and after a few minutes of pondering and quick analysis, I ground out a research report. Maybe about 5:30 p.m. I waved goodbye to the garage attendants, who gave me no credit since I did not top a 12-hour day. Alongside me on the front car seat was a portfolio of material to review during the evening with a bowl of ice cream and the baseball game quietly on TV in the background.

Abnormal events in the day of an analyst are normal. I was summoned to a pay phone while atop the High Sierras in Yosemite by Ross Perot (the other campers were impressed) and was detained by passport control officers at an Italian border the night Aldo Moro was assassinated. I have broadcast my research comments over the squawk box system from aircraft carriers and jumped on the box from phone booths in Vienna cafes. Sometimes I had the opportunity to take advantage of the firm's Chicago Cubs Wrigley Field courtesy suite up behind home plate, squeezing in an occasional night game where I had misspent the bulk of my youth in the bleachers. I have witnessed Michael Jordan in the NBA playoffs, gate-crashed the Cannes Film Festival, bumped into Queen Elizabeth exiting a London theater, sipped cocktails at Raffles bar in Singapore, and basked on Waikiki Beach. But there are dodgy scenarios, too. The Kansas City car service driver that I had used for years on client visits there turned up as a fugitive when the police found multiple homicide victims in his home. This mild-mannered chauffeur was on the phone with our Chicago sales desk apologizing that he was not available for the next assignment, while law enforcement was in pursuit. He was later apprehended, convicted, and given five life sentences.

And then there was September 11th. Jenny Dugan, a junior analyst on my team, and I were in New York to conduct a day of one-on-one meetings with investors. Two clients had requested the 8 a.m. lower-Manhattan-area time slot, Fred Alger Management and another bigger mutual fund, which ended up getting the nod. Jenny was meeting with the latter client in the World Trade Center tower at 8:50 a.m., while I was uptown. The first plane hit one floor below the Fred Alger offices where our meeting would have been were it not for that other request. Tragically, no one at that firm survived. She and her group found the stairwell overcrowded and exited via the elevator. To this day she is reticent to discuss her experience that morning. She has hidden away her WTC-2 security building pass issued that morning revealing her photograph and the September 11th date.

The greatest reward a securities analyst can obtain is to be brilliantly correct on a major investment recommendation. I discovered Fiserv as an emerging stock early in the late 1980s, constantly pounded the table with a resounding Buy, and watched it rise steadily in price for more than a decade. A more established company, Computer Sciences, had been a lackluster performer for years when its prospects gradually started to improve. I was the earliest analyst on the Street to recognize the metamorphosis, and my favorable opinion shift proved to be an insightful call. It was a winner for years. Conversely, the worst nightmare for an analyst is having a recommendation go wrong. All analysts vividly remember their bad picks.

The perks of an analyst's job are not bad either. The best place on earth for golf is Augusta National in Georgia, the site of the Masters tournament. Even for Tiger Woods or Jack Nicklaus, that place is sacred. The ghosts of legends like Bobby Jones and Ben Hogan haunt the fairways. So you might imagine the awe that Augusta inspires in a mediocre duffer like me. When the chairman of an Atlanta-based software firm, John Imlay, part owner of the Falcons NFL football team, inquired about my availability to take in a game from the owner's box, loiter in the locker room, and chat with the coach on the field, I could barely get the yes word out of my stammering lips. And while that was rolling off my tongue, he mentioned as an aside that we would also be motoring to Augusta afterward for a couple days of golf there.

Magnolia Drive, the Butler cabin, dining in the clubhouse, each of the 18 holes that I was so familiar with from TV coverage—the entire venue was a dreamy, mystical ecstasy. Caddies handed us the golf club we were supposed to use, not the one we could hit best given our ability—normal people cannot hit a two-iron. I maxed out my credit card in the golf shop, was told "those green jackets on that rack are for members only," swiped all the logoed stationery from my room, and feigned a nonchalant demeanor the whole time. My game was atrocious. What do you expect playing on hallowed ground as if in the presence of Divinity? Well, you can see the outing was a highlight in my life, and it was not a bad locale to chat up management.

The most trying aspect for securities analysts on Wall Street is dealing with a sense of vulnerability to anything that might impact the stocks they cover. The fear stems from realizing that at any time during a business day, a company under coverage might announce dramatic, surprising news, such as a shortfall in earnings or loss of a major contract. An analyst in this circumstance must scramble to assess the situation, then jump on a conference call, and respond to an avalanche of inquiries from the sales force and investors. This is difficult enough if the analyst is in the office with all necessary resources at hand. It is a disaster if it happens when the analyst is on a tightly packed all-day client meeting trip, on an airline flight, vacationing on a cruise ship, or on the golf course. Analysts can never relax on days the stock market is open. Even on holiday in August, we monitor our Blackberries or iPhones and call in periodically every business day, just like a doctor on call.

After you appreciate the basic function and role of Wall Street investment analysts, you need the rest of the story—the reality and well-kept secrets of Street research. To be effective, investors need to comprehend how Wall Street operates, to work around it in some cases, and to take advantage of it in other situations. You will be able to invest on a par with the professionals after the strange, deceptive ways of Wall Street are demystified.

Wall Street Analysts Are Bad at Stock Picking

It might be shocking but stock picking is not the analyst's job. Until recently, brokerage firms did not even track the accuracy of their analysts' opinions. It is just not an important part of the analyst's job description. Wall Street analysts are supposed to pursue information about the companies and industries they cover, evaluate and gain insight on the future prospect of those companies, assess their investment value, and form opinions on the outlook for their stocks. We are required to assign investment ratings such as "Buy" or "Sell" to indicate a net overall evaluation. And that is where the real issues start to surface. Professional qualifications, incentive compensation, and the main audience—*institutional* investors—do not stress this function of stock picking.

It is not just opinion upgrades, or Buys, that are unreliable; downgrades, or Sells, are also frequently unavailing. In December 2007, a major brokerage firm lowered its Buy rating on Countrywide Financial, a company in the crosshairs of the subprime mortgage debacle, to Neutral after the price had already plummeted from $40 to $9.80. Another high-profile firm underscored its $110 price objective for Bear Sterns while the shares were trading in the $50s, three days before the stock plummeted to under $3 in a JPMorgan Chase bailout. In May 2008, the high-profile oil analysts at a leading firm forecast the price of oil to reach $200 in the ensuing two years. By September the revised forecast was $148 after the price had sunk to $80, and in October the estimate was cut to $86, always following several steps behind the plummeting oil prices. (Oil had cratered to $40 by December.) There were several Buys on Fannie Mae the day it capitulated to $1 a share. Thank you very little! Such calls are all too typical.

An *Institutional Investor* magazine survey in the fall of 2008 asked the buyside institutions—mutual funds, banks, pension funds, and hedge funds that buy and sell stocks through the brokerage firms—to indicate the most important attributes they sought in sellside (brokerage) Street analysts. Of 12 factors ranked in order of priority, stock selection placed dead last. Industry knowledge was the key quality that institutions wanted in analysts.

The best analysts, as ranked in the October 2008 *Institutional Investor (II)* magazine poll, offered some of the worst recommendations over the past year: A leader in covering brokers and asset managers recommended Bear Sterns in January at $77. Eight weeks later it was selling at $2. The number one–ranked insurance industry analyst reconfirmed his long-standing Buy opinion on AIG in August and retained his favorable view until the federal seizure at $3 a share in mid-September. The top-rated analyst in consumer finance pounded the table, enthusiastically endorsing Fannie Mae and Freddie Mac right up until their government takeover below $1 a share.

When stocks have several Sell recommendations, there is nowhere else for that stock to go but up. When the fourth or fifth Sell opinion is issued on a stock, it is probably ready to recover. Analysts are usually late and are also copycats. For years, *The Wall Street Journal* published a quarterly dartboard contest. The expert stock selections made by analysts and portfolio managers did no better than those picked randomly. A website featuring a newsletter called the "Paradox Investor" assessed the performance of all Sell- and Hold-rated stocks on the Street for a two-year period ending in the fall of 2003. This portfolio of negatively viewed stocks gained 53.5%, more than 75 percentage points better than the market.

Mutual fund money managers are no great shakes either. In the 2007 *Barron's* Roundtable, which brings together 11 leading Street stock experts, only four had more than half of their top choices outperform the market. Daunting. In 2008, some 56% of the 72 total picks outperformed, though only 32% showed a gain in absolute terms, and half of those were currencies, commodities, and other nonstocks. More than one-third of the selections collapsed by at least 50%. Quite a statement on the ability of Wall Street to pick stocks.

If that is not enough proof, Charles Schwab rates stocks A to F. From May 2002 to October 2003, its F-rated names, those deemed to have the poorest prospects, performed the best of any category, ahead 30%. In another survey, *The Wall Street Journal* reported that *Investars.com* ranked Street research firms by how each one's stock picks performed compared to the S&P 500 over a one-year span ending in May 2005. You have probably never heard of four of the top five: Weiss Ratings, Columbine Capital, Ford Equity Research, and Channel Trend. The major brokerage Buy-rated stock results were strewn farther down the list. Pretty much the same pattern held true when performance was evaluated over a four-year term. The Street pushes analysts to emphasize institutional hand-holding and marketing, not research and stock recommendations. No wonder the record stinks.

Insightful research analysis has little bearing on the accuracy of Buy or Sell recommendations. Brokerage analysts are usually good at providing thorough, informative company and industry research. But their investment-rating track record is mediocre. The system encourages this by compensating analysts for profile, status, clout, and industry/company knowledge rather than for their investment opinion accuracy. The extreme influence and impact of analysts can result in great damage when investors are misled. Jack Grubman is the poster boy example here. As a telecommunications analyst with more experience than most of the green Internet analysts, he should have known better than to engage in overt cheerleading of his banking clients. Apparently he did not, as evidenced by his statement in a *BusinessWeek* quote about his actions: "What used to be conflict is now a synergy." He shunned his fiduciary duty to be relatively unbiased as an analyst. Grubman's incestuous investment banking behavior destroyed his research credibility. Several of his top recommendations were advocated almost all the way into Chapter 11—Global Crossing, MCI WorldCom, and others. He is now permanently barred from the business.

Analysts' compensation, often more than one million dollars annually, is unrelated to the performance of their stock recommendations. A portfolio manager's investment record can be tracked daily in the mutual fund listings. But analysts are not paid for the accuracy of their stock opinions. Their income depends on institutional client polls, overall eminence and influence, institutional sales and trading evaluations, aid in doing investment banking deals (there is still involvement here), and overall subjective judgment by research management.

Opinion Rating Systems Are Misleading

Even if the Street's investment opinions were credible, investors still would be unable to determine exactly the meaning of the recommendation. Sometimes Buy means Sell. Brokerage firms have differing stock-rating terminology that can be highly deceptive. Analysts are often forced to hedge as their investment opinions attempt to straddle dissimilar audiences. Although most firms have contracted their stock opinion format from four or five different gradations to three, there is still excessive wiggle room. The famous Neutral or Hold monikers are merely a way for analysts to hide and save face, since after the fact they can usually argue that they were accurate, however convoluted the claim. Investors have no clue what to do with such a Hold opinion. Only the highest rating in any firm's nomenclature, usually Buy, Strong Buy, Overweight, and so on, indicates that the analyst has a favorable view on a stock. Or does it?

In the latter part of 2006, according to *Barron's*, a Morgan Stanley analyst initiated coverage of Toll Brothers with an Overweight rating, the stock trading above $29. Sounds positive, doesn't it? Well, the price target was $23, indicating his expectation of a major drop in price. Apparently, that firm's rating meant only that the stock would do better than its counterparts in the home building industry. This was no help to investors who might have believed the opinion called for purchasing the stock for its appreciation potential. Confusion reigns.

Analysts use lower-level ratings, such as Accumulate, Above Average, Hold, Neutral, and sometimes even Buy (if the firm has a superior Strong Buy in its system), as rubrics to convey a negative stance to their key client base, institutional investors. They avoid the more pessimistic classification levels such as Below Average, Underweight, Underperform, or Sell, in order to dodge the flack from corporate executives and those institutional investors who own big positions in the stock. It is also a way to massage investment bankers. Accumulate opinions were once referred to euphemistically as a "Banker's Buy." Sounds positive, but in reality it is negative. It helps the analyst save face.

The current almost-universal three-level investment rating scheme is fraught with confusion and disparities among different firms. Investment recommendation jargon needs to be clearer and more consistent throughout the Street. Does Overweight mean Buy? *The Wall Street Journal* asked, in an article discussing a National Association of Securities Dealers (NASD) study, how ratings were applied: "Is an *underperform* stock in an *outperform* industry more attractive than an *outperform* stock in an *underperform* industry?"

Recommendations can be absolute or relative. Analysts can cite accuracy with a positive opinion if it outperforms an index or the market, even if the stock declines and investors lose money. An absolute term like Buy might portray an indication that the stock might rise anywhere from 10% to 25% in the next 12 months. According to the *Journal* article, at Bear Stearns an Outperform implied that the stock would do better than the analyst's industry coverage. At Smith Barney, a Buy connoted an expected total return of more than 15%. A Buy at UBS Warburg meant it would rise 15% or more over prevailing interest rates. Thankfully, some firms have finally gone to just one investment rating time frame, eliminating the near-term and long-term tandem that was often a conundrum. But there is a long way to go to get the industry's investment rating systems on a similar page.

In mid-2008, a major brokerage firm shifted its policy to help bring some balance to its universe of ratings. To encourage more negative opinions, it started requiring its analysts to assign an Underperform to 20% of all the stocks under coverage. At the time only about 5% of all Street recommendations were Sells. But confusion persists since the firm's definition of Underperform is "the stock will either fall within 12 months or rise less than competing companies with higher ratings." This means the stock might either go up or go down—not very enlightening.

It is impossible to determine the level of an analyst's enthusiasm or skepticism from the published rating. Recommendations vary in degree of fervor. Sometimes a Buy is a rather wimpy, weak, low-key endorsement. Other times a Buy might be a table-pounding, jump-out-of-your-shoes, immediate-action indication. A Hold can be fairly positive, say when the analyst is in the process of gravitating toward a more favorable stance, prior to an upgrade to Buy. Or a Hold could mean the analyst thinks the company's outlook and stock prospects are terrible, but he is hesitant to upset vested interests with the dreaded Sell word. The latter is usually the case. The Street normally interprets Hold opinions negatively. So should the individual investor.

Any stock rating below the highest level connotes an analyst's pessimism or cautious stance. An analyst opinion change from the top level is tantamount to a literal Sell recommendation. Maintaining the top long-term classification while reducing the near- or medium-term view is another decisive communication of a gloomier opinion. And one should totally disregard all "long-term" ratings. They represent another analyst dodge.

Wall Street investment advice is further blemished by being risk adverse. Obfuscating is pervasive, stemming from a mortal fear of being wrong. Sometimes analysts have a Neutral short-term view (this means negative) but a slightly more positive Accumulate or Above Average long-term opinion. This is equivocating. In a simpler system, the analyst might carry only the Neutral recommendation. That way, he can dodge responsibility no matter how the shares perform. If the stock spirals lower, you will hear, "I was not really recommending it." Conversely, if the shares climb, there will be nothing but silence. Even Strong Buy ratings carry different degrees of enthusiasm. If the analyst has six or eight companies with the same optimistic opinion, credit will be taken for those stocks that ascend. A ready excuse is offered for any of those whose prices meander, that the name was not among the top two or three best picks.

The ideal rating system would be a two-pronged scheme to push analysts into one camp or the other. This could be positive/negative, outperform/underperform, or overweight/underweight. Notice that my terms for bad stock prospects are less harsh than Sell but indicate essentially the same thing. They aid the analyst and brokerage firm in saving face, and at the same time in pacifying relationships with institutional holders and corporate executives. Forget using Buy/Sell— too crass, politically unacceptable. Under such a simple system, the analyst view on the stock would be more clearly communicated, and the accuracy more readily tracked. But do not expect this to ever happen. Wall Street would never deign to be that accountable.

For the sophisticated institutional audience, I would go a step further, and remove investment ratings altogether. Portfolio managers and buyside (institutional investors) analysts draw their own conclusions and make their own investment decisions. Sellside (brokerage) analyst stock opinions are an annoyance to these investors. Analysts can deliver the same value-added investment research to institutions without this distraction. Research quality and objectivity would improve if analysts could lower an opinion without incurring the wrath of big holders and corporate executives.

Street investment opinions are also tarnished in other respects. Wall Street loves stocks that are rising now. There is no patience to wait for future upside. It is difficult for an analyst to upgrade a depressed, languishing stock even though it might have value. It could take too long to move. Once a stock has appreciated and "looks good on the chart," it is much easier for analysts to get all the necessary committee approvals. Such a recommendation is more readily accepted by institutional clients, and there is less risk for the analyst. As a result, upgrades are usually late, missing much of the rise in the stock. Boosting an opinion requires clear catalysts, evidence, and precise forecasts, all difficult to spell out early. Thus, Buys are rarely value-oriented. They are momentum-driven. Committees that oversee recommended lists refuse stock suggestions when the price is bumping along the bottom and shows no upside momentum. As a washed-out value, it runs counter to the mentality of the committee. Investors can outwit the Street by seeking stocks that are out of favor and not being widely recommended, that represent value, and that might eventually attract opinion upgrades.

Research Never Contains an Analyst's Complete Viewpoint

Because reports are in the public domain and are read by all the analyst's disparate audiences, particularly negative or controversial content is watered down, or modulated. The degree of our skepticism, aspects of a company that are unclear but highly suspect, untrustworthy management, lack of confidence in estimates, anything edgy, doubtful, any wariness—none of this gets put into an analyst's research report. If it did, legal compliance would edit it out anyway. Reports get such scrutiny that analysts are careful; they hold back and reserve the touchier, conjectural content for direct conversations when they can tailor it to a specific institutional client. An analyst's body language or subtle leaning on a stock is never revealed in writing. Although analysts are no longer legally able to have a stance that conflicts radically with the one portrayed in the report, there is much left to be read between the lines.

Wall Street Has a Congenitally Favorable Bias

Think of Wall Street as if it were the auto industry. Automobile companies make cars and trucks. Through their dealers, they sell these products aggressively. Given their vested interest, auto dealers recommend "buy." You have never heard them tell consumers to "sell." An article by Clifford S. Asness in the *Financial Analyst Journal* makes a similar comparison. He accurately states, "A large part of Wall Street's business is selling new and used stocks and bonds, which strangely they do make recommendations about."

The Street rarely espouses bearish views on the very products it wants to sell to clients. No matter how deep the bear market or how clouded the outlook, brokerage firms want investors to continue investing in stocks. A leading firm emphasized in its February 2009 magazine to investor clients, "Defensive investing does not mean staying out of the markets. Look for conservative opportunities." John C. Bogle, founder of the Vanguard mutual funds, claims: "Our financial system is driven by a giant marketing machine in which the interests of sellers [Wall Street] directly conflict with interest of buyers [investors]." Fifty percent of all trades are sales, by definition. Yet more than 90% of all research is directed at buyers, positive Buy recommendations, or Holds.

The press also leans heavily to the optimistic side. Entering 2008, amid the worst bear market since 1931, the leading financial magazines featured cover stories such as "Your Comeback Year—2009," "Get Your Money Back—A Six-Step Plan to Rebuild Your Savings," and "Yes, Things Are Grim, But Here's Your New Plan to Emerge Stronger." Even the venerable *Barron's*, in advertising the debut of its new newsletter, emphasized that it would present an "investment idea each day...90% of the calls will be bullish." Wow, 225 Buy recommendations a year—one every business day! And almost all Buys, even in a bear market. That same publication features an annual market forecast by 12 leading Street investment strategists. At the outset of 2008, the panelists' S&P 500 predictions for the year ranged from 1525 to 1750. The end result was an astonishing miss from the actual 903 at year's end. The dozen 2009 forecasts for the S&P 500 were again universally bullish, from 950 up to 1250, despite the bear market scenario.

Wall Street is totally oriented to a rising market and upward-moving stock prices. The common terms used to describe stock market conditions are heavily slanted toward the positive. When the stock market drops and you lose money in your stock holdings, it is called a "correction." When the market rises, the Street does not call it a "mistake." "Volatility" and "turbulence" are other terms that often surface to describe a falling market. Isn't a surging market just as volatile as a declining one? A plummeting market finally bottoms out, and it is seen as "stabilizing," a favorable description. But if stocks are soaring, the market is never portrayed as being unstable. When the economy dips into recession or the employment level falls off, it is termed "negative growth." The government is the same way. When Ben Bernanke testified before Congress, he refused to use the R-word (recession), instead referring to a "contraction" of the economy.

The Street just keeps trying to sugarcoat or neutralize the situation even when stocks are diving, as during the 2008 bear market. As *Barron's* described, its attitude is like the federal government's: "Fundamentally everything's fine...not to worry, it'll soon get better." Or "Wall Street...enjoys singing in the rain without an umbrella, hoping to lift investors' spirits—and, just coincidentally, brokerage commissions and positions—by pretending to espy nonexistent rainbows, accompanied, of course, by their obligatory pot of gold."

Most institutional investors hold stocks, long positions, and rarely sell short or bet on a decline. Analysts are given incentive to issue Buy opinions by the favorable feedback that flows from major institutional owners of the stocks and from corporate executives. They are discouraged from expressing negative views by the adverse reaction and often disparaging remarks that follow from these constituencies. In fact, when organizations are holding several million shares of a stock, you can imagine their reaction to a Street downgrade that drives the price several points lower. These organizations have portfolio managers who make stock selections; they do not need Wall Street analysts for that purpose.

A *Wall Street Journal* study in early 2004 found the positive bias to be most glaring at smaller brokerage firms that still seem to be in the rut of hyping a lot of Buy recommendations. Even the ten major firms that agreed to several research reforms in a 2003 industry settlement with the New York Attorney General averaged about twice as many Buy ratings as Sells. The ratio was almost seven times more Buys at smaller firms. In a mid-2006 *CFA* magazine article by Mike Mayo, it was noted that of the recommendations on the ten biggest market cap stocks in the U.S., there were 193 Buys and only 6 Sells. Systemic bias? Analysts' opinions are swayed by vast brokerage investment banking opportunities with these major corporations. The system is stacked against negative recommendations.

Analysts have a tendency to fall in love with the companies and stocks that they are advocating. It is like identifying with your captors. Human instinct. Their bias is ineffaceable. Some of this insanity was eliminated when subservience to investment banking was reduced. But do not think for a second that full objectivity has been restored. The percentage of favorable Street recommendations still far outweighs negative opinions, at least if you take published ratings literally. In early 2001, ten months into the precipitous market slide that followed the Internet bubble, Salomon Smith Barney had only one Underperform and no Sells among the nearly 1,200 stocks it was covering. According to Zacks Investment Research, of the 4,500 stocks it tracked in the fourth quarter of 2005, amid the ongoing bull market, 42% were rated Buy or Strong Buy. Only 3% carried Sell or Strong Sell recommendations.

At the end of 2007, after a notable stock market drop, the distribution of Wall Street research opinions was 49% Buys, 46% Neutrals, and only 5% Sells. During 2008, the number of hedged, unhelpful Neutral or Hold Street opinions skyrocketed as stock prices nosedived, but Sells remained scarce. By the end of January 2009, some 16 months into the bear market, according to Bloomberg data, there were still less than 6% Sell recommendations on the Street, compared to 58% Neutrals and 36% Buys. In randomly glancing at a February 2009 research report on a healthcare company, I noticed the analyst carried 17 Buy ratings on the 28 companies covered, more than 60% favorable views despite a bear market. This is typical. The major brokerage firm that altered its opinion rating system in 2008 required its analysts to rank at least 20% of the stocks under coverage as Underperform (Sell). That led to 31% of all the stocks covered by the firm being rated as Sell, an admirable balance compared to the rest of Wall Street; but it still left 69% of the coverage universe with ratings of Buy or Neutral during perhaps the worst bear market since the Great Depression.

A study by UCLA, UC Davis, and the University of Michigan reveals another form of skewed recommendations. Independent stock research opinions are more accurate than those of analysts from brokerage firm investment banks. The record is about equal during bull markets when Buy ratings are prevalent. But independents stand out in bear markets such as 2008, when they promulgate more negative views. Brokerage firms are reluctant to downgrade investment banking clients. Gee, why am I not surprised? A brokerage analyst invariably maintains a closer relationship and has more access to executives of an ongoing banking client. Studies prove that the analyst at the brokerage that leads a company's initial public offering provides noticeably more affirmative coverage than analysts at firms unaffiliated with the deal.

Downgrades Are Anguishing, Arduous, and Rare

Analysts are reticent to downgrade opinions, fearing institutional holder retaliation. Buyside analysts and portfolio managers are most generous in voting commission allocations to the sellside analyst firms who help tout their stocks. These institutions vent their fury and banish brokerage analysts who downgrade ratings on the stocks they own. This anticipated punishment is a critical constraint when pondering an opinion reduction.

When reducing ratings, analysts come under so much criticism that our argument must be airtight. It is discomforting to reduce an opinion after the stock has already started to fade. This creates more hesitation. Like the monkey that sees no evil, we close our eyes to initial negative developments. By the time the weight of negative evidence is exceedingly compelling, most of the damage to the stock has already been done. When analysts finally capitulate and go to a full-blown Sell opinion, the stock has likely already hit rock bottom.

Although patience might be required, there is usually more upside potential in the shares at that juncture for an individual investor than further downside vulnerability.

Brokerage firms have made the procedure of altering an investment rating hugely more complex for the analyst because of regulatory and legal issues. That was a consequence of the pathetic stock recommendation record after the 1990s bubble burst. Investment research committees meet at certain intervals, require burdensome reports and documentation, and grill the analyst, and then after all that, legal compliance gets involved. There is a lot of second-guessing and attention paid to current stock price trends, rather than a longer-term investment time horizon. Changing an investment opinion is a frustrating exercise. And the analyst needs to be ensconced in the office to jump through all the hoops—forget being on the road. It is just easier to do nothing. Opinion changes are hardly worth all the effort. Analysts thus resist upgrades and downgrades. Ratings that might be inappropriate remain intact out of inertia.

Early stock opinion downgrades are infrequent. Taking a negative stance and lowering an opinion is like a divorce—it might be necessary, but it certainly is unpleasant. But such dramatic calls are telling, if coming from a veteran analyst highly credible in covering the stock. After more than 16 years of superb execution and fabulous stock performance, EDS laid an egg in 1996, almost immediately after regaining its independence in a spinout from General Motors. The company's quarterly earnings results ran across the newswire, vastly below Street expectations. My instinct told me something was terribly amiss, and my reaction was immediate. In this case, there was no prolonged torment, no deliberations, committee meetings, or soul-searching. I summarily downgraded it with no time to ponder the consequences. It was an emotional, traumatic situation, and, given my reputation and prolonged bullish view on the stock, it had a incendiary impact. The company and its shares performed pathetically over the ensuing three years. This rating drop happened so abruptly that it was actually easier to effect than most reductions. But even this good call was after the fact; the bad news had already hit. That was more than ten years ago. In this new era of heavy compliance oversight, such a quick reaction and opinion change is rare or impossible.

Sell opinions, especially if in the minority, put us on an unpleasant hot seat. If an analyst shifts an opinion to Sell, only a portion of the relatively few owners of the stock might take the advice, pull the trigger, and generate a commission. The majority of other investors do not care. An upgrade to a Buy, on the other hand, can be marketed to virtually all investors, and the potential to create transactions is expanded by orders of magnitude.

Most Downgrades Are Late; the Stock Price Has Already Fallen

Most opinion reductions are "me too," the fourth or fifth such recommendation on the Street, and all copycats after the dismal outlook has been highly evident for some time. The shares have usually already fallen 25% to 50% or more, and have fully discounted the plethora of bad news. In 2008, such belated, useless downgrades happened over and over with Lehman Brothers, Bear Stearns, AIG, Fannie Mae, GM, and countless other dogs. Almost all downgrades are late and represent the final capitulation. After most of the ratings have been downgraded, it might be a good buying entry point for a patient investor. After most Street analysts are pessimistic, the share price has only one way to go—back up.

Buy and Sell Opinions Are Usually Overstated

Analysts cheerlead their Buys and disparage the Sells. The Street tends to overdo its enthusiasm on stocks being fervently recommended, effectively pounding the table to entice investors to amass major positions. This ardor is self-fulfilling. Research analysts are overconfident. The more proficient analysts that are in this endeavor, the higher the stock climbs, and the better our call looks. We promote these favored ideas way out of proportion to the reality. As a result, the stocks can ascend to artificially high, unsustainable levels. The opposite is true for infrequent Sell opinions. We exaggerate the negatives, diss the company at every opportunity, and basically pile on an already troubled, depressed stock. This is to help push the shares lower and make our negative view all the more correct. In both situations, analysts overstate their positions. Stocks swing in both directions far beyond what is warranted, because analysts overstress their stances. Investors should sell when analysts get overly enthusiastic and likewise avoid unloading (maybe even buy) when an analyst has derided a company too long.

Wall Street Has a Big Company Bias

Another bias on Wall Street is an ongoing emphasis on big companies. Analysts have a tendency to concentrate their coverage on stocks that have the highest market capitalizations. These names are more actively traded and widely held, with the most institutional investor interest. Big companies are where most investment banking business is derived and where investment firms generate most of their equity business profits. The bulk of phone calls and press attention pertains to such companies. They are over-covered and over-analyzed, and the price valuations of their stocks tend to be more efficient, fully reflecting all known factors. Technology, telecommunications, and healthcare are the most over-researched and covered by the most analysts. Wall Street tends to add analysts in sectors where it does the most banking and trading business, not necessarily in areas representing the best investments. According to a study by Doukas, Kim, and Pantzalis referenced in *CFA Digest* in mid-2006, there is a clear relationship between excess analyst coverage and stock premiums. The same study showed a direct correlation between low analyst coverage levels and stock price discounts.

Executives and board members have a similar preference for bigness—they hesitate to do spinoffs, love acquisitions, and are obsessed with company size, enjoying the status of being a part of the S&P 500. But mass usually indicates mediocrity. And megamergers never work. Most analysts at major firms get attention and make their reputations by emphasizing big cap recommendations. Brokerage revenues are decidedly boosted by outstanding calls (a rare event) on broadly held stocks, not small caps.

Individuals can benefit by making an astute, early investment in smaller companies not already picked over by Wall Street. Mutual funds and other institutions need to take sizable positions in stocks. Though they might invest in some smaller cap stocks, even a spectacular winner will have minimal influence on a fund's total performance. Therefore, when analysts pound the table on a thinly traded company that proves to be a fine idea, the overall impact is muted. Even if a table-pounding Buy recommendation causes a small cap stock to soar in price, the analyst gets little recognition for being an advocate. Small companies have few shares outstanding and thus only a scant number of investors own the stock and benefit from its appreciation. There are meager economic payoffs for a brokerage firm in recommending small stocks, whether for trading, banking, or commissions. Small stocks thus present the individual investor with a better prospect of undiscovered value and the potential to achieve greater prominence in the future as their market caps expand.

Brokerage Emphasis Lists Are Not Credible

Most brokerage firms sport their top stock picks in a high-profile emphasis list. Carrying titles such as Focus List, Alpha List, and, my favorite, Americas Conviction Buy List, these exalted rankings are really just amateur hour. Although Street firms often flaunt statistics showing that their Buy collections outperform the market, these "best" recommendations do not perform materially better than all the other favorably rated stocks lacking such lofty status at that firm. Such comparisons are glaringly absent in brokerage research because they are too embarrassing. *Barron's* quantifies the brokers' model portfolio performance every six months using Zacks Investment Research statistics. The record is not pretty. In 2006, the average brokerage-recommended list underperformed the S&P 500. The leader was Matrix USA, not exactly one of the biggest firms on the Street. Over a five-year period, they lagged again, ahead only 44% on average, compared to the S&P 500 equal-weighted total return of 69%. The five-year winner was a firm that has no in-house fundamental research analysts—Charles Schwab!

In mid-2007, the results were still dismal. The brokers' lists lagged the S&P 500 again during the previous 12-month span. In the rankings for all of 2007, five brokers' best Buys outperformed the market while nine lagged. During the first half of 2008, seven firms outperformed while six underperformed. The focus lists of all but one declined in absolute terms, so you would have lost money with their best recommendations. A roll of the dice probably would have had superior results.

Like a zephyr, emphasis list ideas blow in and out. Selection committees can be a charade. If a new name is needed to add to the exclusive list of best recommendations, the technical chartist might suggest those Buys that have good charts. Analysts in the firm are called and possibilities are trial ballooned. Their decisions are often surprising. The lists are maintained in a rather frivolous manner. Assuming a one-year investment time horizon, panic and anxiety can strike these committees when a stock moves a few points. Hip-shooting is common; emotions and stock price charts rule the day. There seems to be no consistent, longer-term, investment-oriented approach. An analyst's best recommendation can be yanked despite protest after falling a few points. Even if it recovers, the name is long gone from the list.

Stock Price Targets Are Specious

Analysts are now required to include price targets on research reports, with attendant justification, which can involve a formal model to calculate fair or intrinsic value. But this also means predicting the future, encompassing influences such as overall stock market trends, the economy, war, and interest rates, all of which are far beyond an analyst's presumably good insight into company and industry prospects. In the bubble years, the Internet analysts pulled absurd, astronomical triple-digit price objectives out of the blue, and naive investors actually gave these goals credence. It still happens, as in the case of the excessive expectations for the Google stock price in 2007 and even in 2008.

In current sober times, the guesses might be a bit more tempered but are still unrealistic, or at least unbalanced. Stock price estimates are utilized to emphasize Buy or Sell ratings. Analysts put too high a goal on stocks for which they have favorable opinions to help justify their view, and to assist in marketing to hype the story. The price-point forecast is artificially low for companies on which analysts are negative. When such a target is hit, it can trigger a downgrade in analyst opinion. That impacts the stock price and has adverse short-term influence on long-term investors. Opinion changes that are based on the stock achieving a published price target should be taken lightly. Price objectives are just plain fiction.

The Street Orientation Is Extremely Short-Term

The modern era of research transformed security analysis and investing—all of Wall Street, really—to a shorter, briefer length for everything. Investors can exploit this tyranny of the short-term and enhance portfolio performance by thinking long-term and being more patient and value-focused. Institutions are trapped on the treadmill of quarterly performance evaluations. Their investment time horizon has shrunk drastically. If a stock recommendation lacks upside potential in the current quarter, a professional portfolio manager's eyes glaze over. Analysts have succumbed to this same frenzy of near-term expectations and demands. Attention spans are telescoped, so research reports are shriveled in size. Corporations are subsumed by the same trend. Quarterly earnings results are the paramount milestone, a critical influence, and the subject of intense analyst emphasis. Annual earnings estimates are highlighted by expectations for the existing quarter. And it is this shortsightedness that gives the individual investor an opening. As an individual, you can invest and hold stocks for at least two or three years to improve performance results, because you are not being judged on a quarterly basis like the Street.

Wall Street analysts are supposed to be investment analysts doing investment research. This means that their conclusions, findings, views, and recommendations should be investment-oriented, looking ahead at least a year or two. Yet most institutional clients, particularly the biggest commission producers like hedge funds, are short-term trading-oriented. The same goes for the key intermediaries that analysts deal with constantly, institutional sales teams and the brokerage firms' trading desks. Mutual fund performance is tracked daily and measured against the competitors every quarter. Analysts are torn between two conflicting goals. Earnings estimates, price targets, and other prognostications on the companies that analysts cover extend a year or more into the future. But intense pressures mount from institutional clients, traders, and research management for a recommendation to prove out in a period of just days or weeks, months at the longest. And this influence pushes analysts' research to be oriented myopically on immediate results. Analysts cater to a market of traders rather than a market of investors, so they put out trading research. Most Street research is unsuitable for the true, long-term investor.

Research reports and brokerage stock rating systems indicate a one-year investment time frame. In reality, opinions are based on how analysts think the stock might do over the next one to five months, at the maximum. If analysts do not believe that the stock will take off within the next couple of months, there will be no opinion upgrade. The key institutional investor audience seeks instant gratification and is impatient, like the rest of Wall Street. A question I constantly heard was, "What is the catalyst that will move the stock?" When raising an opinion, the Street always stresses the immediate expected development that will drive the price higher. Do not ever think any recommendation is based on how the stock will perform over the next year or two. We analysts get criticized if our stock recommendation stagnates for even two or three months. Patient investors can outmaneuver Street insiders by a willingness to buy early and hold for a couple years and not be whipsawed by temporary influences.

Wall Street's short-term time frame necessitates speed. Analysts are compelled to stress quickness over quality or thoughtfulness. The qualitative side of a company's business is more difficult to evaluate. Quality security analysis is scant since it takes too long, and analysts are normally in a reactive, hurry-up mode. Immediate interpretation of news or events is demanded. After it's put forth, the inclination is to stick with that stance, even if later evidence or assessment indicates a different conclusion. Erroneous instant reactions have a way of manifesting over time.

Analysts Miss Titanic Secular Shifts

Another consequence of a short-term viewpoint and the herd instinct is that analysts miss titanic secular shifts. Broad industry trends last a while. Major movements such as a new technology, a different manufacturing process, or changes in consumer habits that are catalysts for a sweeping industry move are often identified by the Street only after they're in place and obvious. The theme is then underscored as the key underpinning of ongoing recommendations. The problem is that Wall Street always espouses the view that this overwhelming industry change will endure for the foreseeable future. Inevitably, a critical turning point is reached when the trend begins to subside. But it is subtle. And because analysts are momentum oriented, they rarely see the shift until it is too late. They are too narrowly concentrated on details and do not heed the bigger picture. Analysts are so consumed with marketing, telephone calls, meetings, conference calls, publishing short blurbs, traveling, and reacting to daily events that there is no time for studied, overall macroassessment. They might be good at evaluating the trees, but they fail to have enough vision to see the forest.

Analysts rarely take seriously the emerging companies that are pioneering a new wave. They are similar to executives who play a defensive game to protect their turf. Established companies rarely create new technologies that will render their existing products obsolete. Analysts likewise become fixed in their coverage and views, and are predisposed to defend a favorable ongoing opinion of a recognized industry leader. They fail to give proper credence to up-and-coming companies that represent a disruptive market leapfrog. Analysts are uncomfortable with any thinking that might run counter to their long-established point of view. They often miss the boat when a new force emerges.

The rise of PC software in the late 1980s brought a surge of IPOs, including Microsoft, Lotus Development, and Borland. A friend I'd known since elementary school, then an orthopedic surgeon in Ohio, inquired innocently whether he should pick up a few Microsoft shares when it started trading. I thought that it and myriad other companies—each specializing in spreadsheet, database, operating system, and other PC software—were only a speculative flurry and a risky proposition that investors should avoid. Bill Gates's company

seemed just like the rest of the bunch and not that special. So I dis-
suaded my school chum. He could have retired earlier were it not for
my foolish advice. These new companies were challenging the
entrenched, established software for larger computers. I paid only
passing attention to this new PC software age. My counterpart at
Goldman Sachs, Rick Sherlund, did the Microsoft initial public offering (IPO) and was the early axe in that stock—that is, the most
informed analyst covering the name. Within a few years, Microsoft
had vaulted to the most important and thriving firm of all software
and computer services. And Sherlund displaced me as #1 in the
vaunted *Institutional Investor* rankings. I paid the price for my oversight.

Street Research Is Unoriginal; Opinions Conform

Everything the Street publishes or communicates is excruciatingly
reviewed for approval by legal compliance. Research is hamstrung,
emasculated, and diluted. Pithy or controversial content is often eliminated from the research. Analysts run in packs—they herd, imitate
each other, and find it uncomfortable to stand alone. The Street tends
to have similar opinions on most stocks. Analysts identify and underscore the macro industry trends in the stock groups covered, which
puts them all in the same boat. If the sector is in favor, almost all of us
recommend just about every stock. We love a stock when fundamentals are healthy, regardless of excessive valuation. The same is true on
the negative side. After major disappointments or shortfalls, we all
belatedly change over to negative views.

Further diminishing the relevance of brokerage investment
research and opinion ratings is the fact that research reaches individual investors late. Analyst contact priorities are first the sales force
and traders, then the press. Stocks react when events occur and news
breaks. The analyst immediately jumps on the squawk box and makes
comments to the sales force. Traders get a call about the same time.
(They are not supposed to be first, but sometimes they are.) After
phone calls are returned from institutional sales, the next priority is
the press. We love to see our remarks running across the Dow Jones

newswire—and Bloomberg, Reuters, and the next day's *New York Times,* too. Then we might start chatting with the key institutional clients like Fidelity. By the time most investors hear of or read our research views, it is way too late. Its tardiness renders it worthless for near-term trading. Individual investors are low in the analyst's pecking order and need to treat Street research accordingly.

Analyst Research Is Valuable for Background Understanding

Street security analysts are good for something. Their reports are useful for understanding the business fundamentals of companies and industries. Research reports detail numerous aspects of a company and provide good background for an investor, such as the earnings outlook, profit forecasts and earning models, business operations, the market, competition, issues and challenges, management, and finances.

Analysts are highly knowledgeable on the industries they cover, especially if they have tracked a particular company for a number of years. They attend briefings for company investors, participate in management conference calls with the Street, and periodically talk with company executives, such as the chief financial officer (CFO) and director of investor relations (IR). On conference calls, available to all investors to listen in on, analysts ask probing questions, flush out the real story, and expose critical elements. Because analysts have active contact with executives, they are completely familiar with the company party line, its goals and objectives, and its management style. Individual investors are rarely privy to this type of information directly, but this color can sometimes be obtained in research reports.

Analysts are good at identifying how particular events and influences could impact a company's outlook. When news breaks or an event occurs, Street analysts can provide detached, cool-headed, informative commentary. A leading competitor in an industry sector has a negative earnings or order rate shortfall. A big acquisition is announced. A blockbuster new product development comes to light. A hurricane or other natural disaster takes place. All these types of news can affect the stock prices of a number of companies. Analysts normally issue reports that shed light on and explain such circumstances. Although such research is often rushed and tends to be a short-term interpretation, it is still useful for getting the gist of the situation.

Earnings estimates are another valuable tool contributed by analysts. These are normally accompanied by comprehensive earnings models that forecast revenue, operating profit margins, tax rate, cash flow, return on equity ratios, and other such quantitative measures. Earnings projections are both quarterly and annual, and are helpful in assessing the stock price valuation based on the price-to-earnings (PE) ratio. The anticipated rate of growth in profits is an important element in the overall outlook of a company. But the best use of these numbers is in comparing actual results. Stock prices react each quarter to the slightest shortfall or overachievement in results. And they can respond precipitously to modifications in analysts' earnings forecasts. Sometimes a minor rise indicates materially improving prospects. A trivial reduction can signal noticeably eroding business conditions. The stock price reacts accordingly. Earnings estimates are a good way for investors to get a handle on Street expectations and the general magnitude of earnings growth.

A Lone Wolf Analyst with a Unique Opinion Is Enlightening

There is true value added in a unique perspective that is contrary to the crowd. An analyst shift to a negative stance that is all alone is a noteworthy signal. Other analysts might maintain their favorable views and pooh-pooh the dissenter's conclusion. He might be castigated, dissed by executives, and attacked by major institutional holders of the stock. These repercussions are anticipated, and that is why a dramatic rating slash is always brutal for the analyst. Often there are no hard numbers or evidence to clearly indicate cracks in the surface. When an analyst is so courageous and willing to stick his neck out with a minority viewpoint, he is displaying a certain conviction. The view is enlightening.

Richard Bove at Rochdale Research has had a 26-year career as an objective, often contrarian analyst covering the banks and investment companies. His firm is not a major investment banker for that sector, so Bove seems to have free rein to tell it like it is. A lone wolf, he was vociferously negative on the group before the collapse in 2008. In a *New York Times* story he was quoted as saying, "I do not give a damn about what the company thinks. I can say what I want about Citigroup, when I want, as long as I am honest. I was convinced that the financial industry was out of control. It just smelled, it looked, it felt like this thing was going to crash. And we kept pounding on it." An observer mentioned in the same article, "He is amongst the best pure security analysts, quite frankly, that I have ever met. He does not mince words, but his comments are founded on strong analysis." Unfortunately, the Wall Street system in the main prevents such forthright, unbiased research.

The Best Research Is Done by Individuals or Small Teams

Individuals and small teams concentrate on a modest range of stocks or a limited sector. They do not attempt to cover the waterfront, but rather do focused research on a select number of companies. Small teams tend to emphasize quality research rather than quantity. The tendency with big research teams is to generate a deep level of detail, extensive earnings models, the nth degree of information, and a plethora of reports. It is overkill. Investors, the sales force, traders, and all the other audiences are unable to absorb this amount of trivia. With big teams analysts get sidetracked, bogged down in all the fine points.

Although senior analysts should be freed up to ponder bigger picture trends, instead they spend most of their time marketing, meeting, and calling on institutional clients. Senior analysts are distracted by all the oversight, review, coordination, and supervision. Junior, inexperienced analysts are conducting the research. Analysis is a mile wide and an inch deep. Small groups or individual analysts avoid these pitfalls and their research is superior.

Analysts might be error prone if they are not concentrating on a narrow industry segment. During my eight-year span at Salomon

Brothers in the mid-1980s, I covered the entire computer industry. Instead of specializing, I was attempting too broad a reach. I did not think to specialize in computer services and software until three years after the establishment of a separate category for that sector in the preeminent annual *Institutional Investor (II)* analyst poll. After I made the shift, I immediately vaulted to a #1 ranking and retained *II* All-America team status for 19 straight years.

Overconfident Analysts Exhibiting Too Much Flair Are All Show

Arrogance, showbiz, flair—analysts are noted for these characteristics. They display excessive confidence to the sales force and important institutional clients to demonstrate the strength of their convictions. Any hesitation is interpreted as doubt and impacts credibility. We learn quickly to be accomplished actors, even bluffers. We talk fast, connoting a (false) air of assurance.

The amplitude of our conviction in stock recommendations, forecasts, and assessments varies widely, but our audience would never know it. We have such extensive knowledge of the companies we cover and are expert at faking answers to questions, if necessary, to preserve our omniscient image. This is a pernicious practice. Investors can be readily swayed, even when analysts are spectacularly wrong. This is how analysts led investors astray during the 1990s Bubble Era.

It should now be clear that the Street is not a reliable source for objective stock recommendations. Sure, the Street acts as though it can provide investment advice and financial counsel. But that is not really its job. It is structured to trade securities, perform securities transactions, distribute and sell securities as a dealer, and do corporate finance deals. Wall Street is not suited to be an investment manager, financial advisor, or stock selector. These services are a conflict of interest with the bedrock brokerage and banking functions. The Street does not intentionally mislead—there is no deceit—it is just the way the business operates. Do not take the Street's directives literally; be familiar with its shortfalls, and invest with the awareness of a Wall Street insider.

2

Understanding Wall Street's Misleading Practices

After digesting the ambiguous doubletalk and often deceptive ways of Wall Street discussed in Chapter 1, "Decoding Wall Street's Well-Kept Secrets," investors need to be aware of the more subtle detrimental influences of the Street. Now that you have been introduced to some of Wall Street's secrets, you need the graduate course in comprehending Wall Street's misleading practices. Individual investors cannot invest properly until they discount the research directives from the Street. Beyond filtering out incessant Street noise, you must put Street research in the proper perspective. With a superior investment strategy, you can outmaneuver even institutional portfolio managers while exploiting the Street on a proactive basis.

Street Research Came Full Circle During My Career

I was fortunate to evolve as a securities analyst during the 1970s, an era when Street research was just beginning to emerge. At that time, it took years for an analyst to establish credibility and make an impact on institutional investors. I arrived at Spencer Trask, a small boutique brokerage firm, in 1971 and began trudging away. My firm sent me to public-speaking training sessions. Over a three-year span, requiring intensive reading, studying, and an annual all-day exam, I obtained a Chartered Financial Analyst (CFA) designation. It was de rigueur for a career analyst in that era. My director of research was a Yale English major, so my reports at first were heavily edited. They finally became readable, intelligible. My nickname was "Hound of the Baskervilles." I am not sure why, maybe because it implied tenacity and assiduity. We analysts did everything ourselves: meetings, reports, executive interaction, analysis, client contact, and sales-force dialogue. I was a one-man band. There were no teams. It made me into a complete analyst.

The brokerage firm that I joined was typical of the dozens of flourishing, stock-focused, research-based partnerships then so prevalent in the business. Our office was located a few doors down from the New York Stock Exchange, like all other brokerage head-quarters, in the heart of Wall Street. Since then, most of the firms have moved Uptown. Spencer Trask was classy, genteel, professional, and quiet, having been in business since 1853. I found the cadre of research analysts there to be intelligent, probing, thoughtful, and pro-ficient writers. They spent most of their time conducting research, talking to executives, visiting the companies they covered, and com-posing in-depth reports. There was little financial or mathematical analysis, and only modest attention was paid to detailed modeling in that pre-PC period.

Most firms like mine did no investment banking and no trading. Research alone generated the revenue. It was not beholden to multi-ple, conflicting constituencies. Analysts were objective and the research was credible. Securities analysts were not prominent figures in the media, but rather more akin to surgeons or professors. Individ-ual retail clients paid fat commission fees for their stock transactions, so at weekly research meetings some of the commentary addressed individual investment concerns. By today's standards, the pace of activity was leisurely—we arrived for work at 9 a.m. and departed at 5:15 p.m., with long client lunches and sometimes dinners.

Individual clients were taken seriously by the firm, but I quickly found that institutional clients received most of the analysts' attention. Another revelation I did not have before reaching the Street was that stocks were assessed based primarily on the future earnings prospects. And corporate executives were inclined to woo analysts for favorable opinions. This was often done by extending perks, such as IT&T's annual all-expenses-paid analyst trip to Paris with spouses to hear management briefings. (Largess like this is no longer allowed due to changes in securities regulations.) Compensation was miserly by later standards. Established senior analysts averaged $50,000 to $100,000.

The stock market was in the doldrums during much of the 1970s, tanking for almost three straight years during 1972–1974 and remaining dull for most of the rest of the decade. Until 1975, there were excessive, fixed commissions that paid for research without the help of other brokerage income sources such as trading or investment banking. And research was not that costly for investment banks; I did not achieve the $100,000 income level until 1980. My daughter Laurel was born during my first few years on the Street, I had a mortgage, and my son Justin showed up six years later. Finances were tight. Those were lean times for a junior analyst.

The research process included spending chunks of time questioning and having discussions with company executives. Certain executives were just unavailable to analysts. H. Ross Perot, the founder of EDS, was one such figure. So it was a privilege to be the only Wall Street representative at EDS's October Monday-night annual meeting in Dallas in the early 1970s. It was a friendly audience of employees and spouses. Information flowed. But the highlight was dinner later at Perot's house for the management team. I was invited along and got to meet his children, ogle his Monets, and schmooze with all the other executives and their wives. One year, the NFL Monday Night Football game featured the Cowboys at home at the same time as the annual meeting, a scheduling crisis for most of the EDS executives who were season ticket holders. That pushed the gathering to a Thursday-night slot the next year.

My firm merged with a mid-size wire house in 1977, Hornblower & Weeks, a brokerage that catered mainly to retail individuals with essentially no interest in research. The good analysts fled to other firms. Salomon Brothers, a prestigious, high-profile, aggressive, institutional firm at that time, hired me as their computer industry analyst in 1977. My honeymoon as an emerging analyst was over. The pro-tected, cozy camaraderie I had been used to was now a quaint mem-ory. The floor traders in "the room" (the biggest brokerage trading floor on Wall Street) ran Salomon Brothers, and I immediately learned to tether myself to the head equity trader, feeding him trad-ing angles on the computer stocks a couple times a day. Most firms had not yet thought of having their analysts aid traders. This trading-floor aspect is colorfully portrayed in Michael Lewis's book *Liar's Poker.* I soon began to bolt out of analyst meetings in mid-session and run to the pay phones to reach our traders when I sensed news aspects that might impact a stock. That was before cell phones.

The research department at Salomon started to gravitate toward conventional stock coverage. I was the first there to publish a com-pany report, as opposed to industry analysis, a breakthrough at the firm. Henry Kaufman was Salomon's noted economist in the early 1980s. He had a worldwide following and the clout to move markets with his interest-rate forecasts. Kaufman led the entire stock market out of the 1970s doldrums with his dramatic prediction of an interest-rate shift in 1982. He was a senior player at Salomon, but took the time to tediously monitor my groundbreaking initial report on a com-pany called Sperry Rand, a bold tactic for that trading firm.

When I arrived, Michael Bloomberg, the head equity trader, had just moved off the trading desk to a position of back-office tech sup-port. He soon developed sophisticated bond data tracking terminals and software. When Salomon merged with another trading firm, Phibro, Bloomberg left to start his own company. Bloomberg L.P. developed into a household name on the Street and his financial data service became ubiquitous. He chuckled all the way to the bank. I ran into him on the beach in the Hamptons once, and his first question was, "McClellan, are you still writing all that bullshit?" He got some comeuppance years later when we both flew in F-16s with the Air Force, both of our stomachs going through convulsions. Afterward, he, like me, was green and staggering. He is now the mayor of New York City.

The early 1980s was about the time that all Street analysts started to become more involved with the investment banking function, eventually leading to the downfall of objective research in the 1990s.

A sweeping management shift at Electronic Data Systems (EDS) launched Mort Meyerson as its driving force under H. Ross Perot. Over the next few years, I made several trips with the EDS management team to meet with institutional investors. My association with EDS was mainly research related, and not the blindly biased cheerleading role that became prevalent in the '90s Bubble Era. But Salomon was instrumental in EDS's acquisition by General Motors, and I was engaged in numerous investment banking deals with EDS over the years. This was the dawn of the analyst role in banking.

While at Salomon, I got the idea to write a book about the computer industry, its future prospects, the companies, the managements, and my views. This was a crazy concept because if I was forthright, a tumult of controversy would follow, and dwarf the consequences of a negative research report. A book carries greater validity than reports and its impact is more powerful. And so it was with *The Coming Computer Industry Shakeout,* which hit the bookstores in June 1984.

I went about interviewing the CEOs of the 50 leading computer industry companies, starting with John Opel, Chairman of IBM. Doors swung wide open when CEOs were informed I was undertaking this book project, which was an advantage for an analyst covering the industry. I labored in my basement starting at 4 a.m. each workday, scribbling in longhand on yellow pads, before heading to the office at 6:30 a.m. On the weekends, I started at 6 a.m. I started drinking coffee for the first time in my life. The heat was on to publish before my material became obsolete. Upon getting my hands on the first printed copy of the book, I had an emotional reaction: I had just given birth.

The book was conceived in the library of the *QE2* on a Caribbean cruise. I presented the finished product to the captain in a reception line a year later on another *QE2* voyage. Our dining room waiter handed me a note the next morning, inquiring whether we would like to switch to the Captain's table for the duration. I asked who might also be sitting there, and at the next meal another scribble arrived with the names Stan Musial, Brooks Robinson, and a couple other Baseball Hall of Famers. The English waiter asked, "Who are those people?" As a lifelong baseball fan, I almost passed out in delirium.

Shakeout made more waves than I expected. It hit some best-seller lists and was favorably reviewed in *The Wall Street Journal*, *The New York Times*, and other papers. TV interviews ensued, and this was when I was a guest on Lou Rukeyser's *Wall Street Week*. One marketing-oriented CEO purchased three dozen books, had me sign notes to him in each, and bestowed them on his best customers, claiming that each was his own personal copy. At the same time a storm of contention arose from the companies in the book on which I made negative or critical comments. Two or three even threatened legal suits.

Security analysis progressed in the 1980s to what is recognized today as institutional research. The research became more sophisticated, detailed, specialized, focused, prolific, and timely, and began to emanate from teams of analysts rather than stand-alones. Analyst coverage narrowed in order to be more thorough. This evolution coincided with the trend toward dominance of institutions and their insider advantage. The research game became complex, dominated by institutional investors, and individual investors were abandoned by analysts.

Research Is Centered on Institutional Clients, Not Individual Investors

For almost two decades now, analyst attention has been directed to institutions, not individual investors. Retail clients are a low priority on Wall Street, mostly neglected by analysts and research departments. Research for individual investors is tepid. In many instances, reports are simply repackaged, abbreviated, and watered down—which makes it difficult to glean the nuances of an analyst's thinking by reading research reports. An analyst's ultimate judgment on stocks is communicated verbally in a tailored manner to portfolio managers, but seldom, if ever, directly to individual investors. Analysts rarely talk to the office managers or the biggest retail brokers at their firm, and almost never do they have contact with registered reps in branch offices. Most analysts totally avoid these financial consultants' calls. Traders, institutional sales, press, institutional investors, corporate executives—all precede individual clients in analyst priority. Most investment ideas are shopworn by the time a report is read by an individual investor.

Private individual investors, served by the financial consultant sales force or brokers, want unbiased, black-and-white, definitive, opportune Buy and Sell opinions. They want the analyst to be a stock picker or a portfolio manager. They expect to be able to follow analyst investment ratings literally, believe that the stock price targets are credible, and trust that the analyst's research is oriented to their objectives. This wish list is nice, but it is only a pipe dream. Most of an analyst's time is spent marketing, not doing research; that is, communicating investment views and information in direct conversations with portfolio managers and analysts at the mutual funds, banks, insurance companies, hedge funds, pension funds, and other institutions. The practice got the Street into trouble after the 1990s bubble finally burst. Private retail clients had been misled by taking analysts' stock opinion ratings too literally. They thought a Buy rating meant the analyst really viewed the shares as attractive. Wrong. This situation has not improved materially since that time.

You need to know that your place as an individual investor in the Wall Street pecking order is at the bottom. Outside of the brokerage firm, institutional clients hold sway. Analysts are beholden to these giant investment pools, and because these institutions are the brokerage firms' prime clients, they have titanic leverage over the Street.

Analysts spend double or triple the time on institutional client contact compared to research analysis. And the institutional audience gets essentially 100% of an analyst's marketing attention compared to individual investors. Analysts play almost exclusively to institutions such as Fidelity, Putnam, Wellington, Waddell & Reed, T. Rowe Price, Alliance, American Express, Capital Research, and to the hedge funds that trade so actively. These organizations allocate vast commission dollars to the brokerage firms for analyst research to support their portfolio managers and own in-house research. The time devoted to institutional marketing detracts enormously from doing research. Traveling to curry the favor of these mega-institutions takes analysts not only to major cities around the globe, but also to Des Moines, Topeka, Salt Lake City, Vancouver, Portland, Madison, Lansing, Raleigh, Tallahassee, Montgomery, Indianapolis, Chattanooga, Nashville, and Memphis.

Institutions make constant demands on analysts, insisting we bring managements of the companies we cover to their cities for meetings, requiring exclusive one-on-one executive meetings at our conferences, and pressing us to call them first with insightful tidbits and subtle opinion shadings. Their every whim is our priority. Fidelity or a huge hedge fund gets one of the earliest calls from the analyst after he hangs up with his in-house trader and a couple of institutional salespeople. Institutional power sucks analysts into a vortex. Commission revenue and transaction flow influence the brokerage firms' profits, the trading-room-floor activity, and investment banking IPO and other financing deals.

Mammoth institutional investor clients demand preferential Street treatment. The big enchiladas on the buyside insist on telephone calls to glean the nuances from an analyst who puts out a new pronouncement or observation on the morning sales-force conference call. The institutional sales desk usually hits the analyst with key priority call assignments to discuss such research assertions. These gorilla clients have the economic power to obtain the best executive one-on-one time slots at brokerage conferences, special conference call briefings to their portfolio manager teams, preferred meetings with analysts during a day of marketing in their city, and the analysts' aid in scheduling calls and meetings with top corporate executives. They commonly ask analysts about which stocks they are "becoming more excited about" or "starting to get more concerned about." This can be in the company of a brokerage firm's heavyweight salespeople who can influence analyst compensation with their year-end evaluations. The pressure is extreme to give privileged insight and treatment to these institutions at the expense of the small individual investor.

My arrival at Merrill Lynch in the mid-1980s coincided with a major new emphasis and expansion of research by the leading brokerage firms all over Wall Street. The leading firms started hiring analyst all-stars. The importance of the *Institutional Investor* poll rankings skyrocketed. I reached the #1 slot among my competitors in my sector of coverage and was involved in taking Oracle, Fiserv, First Data, Accenture, and other such companies public. Securities analysts started having more widespread impact on stocks, as well as contributing more heavily to brokerage profits. But they were not yet media darlings, not recognized household names.

In the early 1990s I shifted my location to San Francisco. That period was the start of the Street's push to build technology analyst teams in the Silicon Valley region. Analyst power and status surged. Their compensation soared as the decade progressed. Technology analysts reigned supreme, especially after the Internet bubble began to inflate. I built a team, held bustling conferences in Miami Beach, published volumes, made my share of TV appearances, and traveled from the Pacific Rim to Italy, Scotland to Australia, to meet with institutional clients. However, as the Internet exhilaration blossomed, my coverage of mundane, profitable, solid computer services stocks was viewed as having missed the boat, not part of the Internet action. Later, after the bubble had burst, institutions flooded back to the safe, low-key, reliable computer services stocks, and my research was back in favor.

Research was respected at the beginning of the decade but discredited by the end. During the '90s Bubble Era, analysts were worshiped like rock stars. Amateur investors, start-up company CEOs, even institutional investors and the press exalted analysts as the new alchemists. But quality, impartial, thoughtful research was degraded by a thousand cuts. After widespread corporate earnings shortfalls, steep stock price declines, and pervasive wrong investment opinions, the damage was done. As the bear market accusations and scandals ensued, analysts were cast as villains. Following the 2000 stock market crunch, people were often aghast when I told them I was a Wall Street analyst. It was as if I were a scoundrel, similar to offenders like Henry Blodget in the dot-com era and rogues like Jack Grubman in the telecom bonanza. Street research began its descent as the new millennium emerged and has continued on a downward spiral ever since.

Analysts Are Young, Are Unseasoned, and Lack Historical Judgment

Since 2000, the number of Wall Street analysts has diminished by more than 50%, and the total is expected to fall by another 30% or more by the end of 2009. Research budgets have been slashed by more than 50% as the main source of funding, commissions, has been cut in half since 2000. The brokerage research model is broken.

Destroyed. Brokerage firms are managing stock coverage by assigning more companies to fewer analysts, or at least cheaper, less-experienced analysts. Compensation has plummeted.

Many high-profile analysts do not have MBA degrees or Chartered Financial Analyst (CFA) designations. The brain drain started in 2000 as analysts fled to hedge funds. In the 1980s and 1990s, smart, ambitious graduate students earned MBAs and headed to Wall Street. Now most of these great minds have gone off to the institutions that perform investing functions such as private equity firms, hedge funds, or venture capital firms. Several have retired. Others have been laid off following the 2008 bear market devastation. Intelligent, creative, insightful analysts are scarce. The brilliant graduates are branching out into more promising fields. Analysts now have little sense of history. Judging corporate executives is a key ingredient in evaluating stocks, and to develop this skill takes 10 or 20 years of observation. Youthful analysts can be misled by rarified access to top executives. They can be hardworking, intelligent, knowledgeable, and good communicators, but there is no substitute for years of seasoning.

The length of time an analyst has covered a stock is key. It takes a seasoned perspective, gained over a long period, to accurately judge a company's prospects. Street insiders respect only veteran analysts covering a sector over an extended period. An analyst needs to see how a firm reacts in bad times, observe its practices in boom times, view management in different situations, and live through industry cycles. Company executives can be caught up in current events and often have minimal long-term perspective. Analysts, like consultants, must bring experienced, time-tested, historical knowledge to bear on any company evaluation. If an analyst has been covering a stock for only two or three years, it is insufficient; ten years is more appropriate. I covered some stocks such as Automatic Data and EDS for more than 30 years. My insight was frequently superior to that of executives who had not participated over the decades in the company's varying conditions.

It is stunning to me how many leading Wall Street analysts have had less than ten years' experience on the Street. The three-year bear market from 2000 to 2002 and plummeting compensation pushed veterans into retirement, into management, or to the buyside. In 2008, the horrid bear market, the massive brokerage firm red ink, and the investment bank failures and mergers closed the lid on the Street research coffin even tighter. Now research is hollowed out and depleted. Senior analysts have moved on. The average analyst age has tumbled. Without historical perspective, Street analysts are subject to repeating the poor judgments made in the 1990s. Analyst recollection of the '90s Bubble Era excesses are dim, not to mention the 18 consecutive years from 1966 to 1982 when the Dow Jones Average stagnated. In the 2008–2009 bear market, analysts were caught with Buy ratings on stocks that collapsed into oblivion. It was highly embarrassing. Bad judgment and faulty recommendations were widespread. Green analysts have no memory or seasoning from past bear markets.

Buy Ratings Lack Credibility and Are Given Little Credence by Insiders

Most Buy recommendations lack credibility and are of little consequence. Ongoing Buy ratings are often stale. Analysts keep their Buy recommendations too long, enamored by momentum winners. It is tough for us to downgrade an opinion based on excessive valuation alone, even if the stock is grossly overpriced, as was glaringly evident in the 1990s bubble. Analysts need hard facts and events to justify a downgrade. As a result, by the time there is enough evidence such as earnings shortfalls or a drop-off in orders to make a case for a downgrade, it is too late and the share price has already fallen.

The ingrained reluctance to go negative was never as glaring as during the 2008 bear market. The home-building, financial, auto-manufacturing, retail, energy, insurance, and various other sectors had extensive Buy or Neutral opinions all the way down to low single-digit prices. It was a stunning display of bad recommendations. No wonder insiders pay no attention to positive Street opinion ratings.

Wall Street Largely Disregards Market Strategists and Technical Analysis

The main research offered to individual investors is commentary on strategic market direction and the economic outlook. Analysts are commonly coerced into aligning their industry and company outlook with the firm's economic scenario. The only problem is that economists are useless. I cannot tell you how many times the economists at brokerage firms flip-flop their forecasts. Smart analysts totally disregard such predictions lest they be whipsawed in different directions and made to look silly. In early 2004, for example, Street economists virtually all anticipated a monthly gain of 150,000 in employment. The number came out at 1,000, and the stock market nosedived. A *Wall Street Journal* article said it best: "Big staffs, sophisticated models, reams of historical data, and degrees from known schools...and still they forecast about as well as groundhogs."

Market strategists are no better than economists at making money in the market. Their track record is mixed. Strategists are always fascinating and entertaining, and they convey insightful, investing observations and chatter on market direction. But they tend to be big-picture and are as biased as securities analysts. Even more so than analysts, most of these experts run in packs. If they are bearish for too long, their brokerage firms get antsy and push them out the door. This has happened several times. So if their job security is important to them, strategists will not maintain a negative overall market posture for long.

The shining example of excessive optimism is the well-known Goldman Sachs strategist, Abby Joseph Cohen. In December 2007, she forecast that the S&P 500 would be at 1675 at year-end 2008, a 14% gain. She held on to that prediction into March 2008 as the bear market ensued. After the S&P 500 had sunk 13% to 1277, *The Wall Street Journal* disclosed that she had been replaced (it was never publicly announced by the firm) as Goldman's "main forecaster of short-term market moves" by an in-house associate who was forecasting a 6% drop in the S&P 500 for 2008. (This more cautious stance was still way too bullish as the market had dropped 50% by October 2008.) And the story mentioned that "she now agrees with Mr. Kostin's forecast." Curious way to hear about her belated, silent change of view.

Research strategists rarely tell the analyst when they decide to label any of his stocks attractive or gloomy—and if we wait a month, their view changes. Moreover, strategists are superfluous in attracting investment banking clients. They have now been relegated to a lower status on Wall Street.

Technical analysis is correct only about half the time. Such commentary on historical patterns and market relationships is interesting but of no help in making astute investment decisions. Stock charts of a recent period do sometimes reflect insider trading patterns or material information leaks. An unusual move in a stock price probably indicates something that will shortly be divulged publicly. But past stock price patterns are of little aid in forecasting the future. Technical analysts often create more confusion than clarity. Analysts and most insiders pay no attention to conjectures by these prognosticators.

Smaller Capitalization Stocks Are Neglected

Analysts and institutional investors tend to ignore the massive array of smaller companies that can achieve good growth for decades before maturing or maxing out their market. They focus their attention on large companies and big cap stocks and also heavily favor growth stocks that carry high PE multiple valuations that help make them big cap stocks. Not only Street analysts but also Goliath mutual funds concentrate heavily on the big names. Countless studies reveal the stunning outperformance of small cap value stocks compared to large cap growth stocks since the 1920s. The difference is off the charts. A *Financial Analysts Journal* study showed such small caps outdistanced the big caps by a factor of 100 times from 1926 to the present. Yet Street research analysts and most institutions do not emphasize this attractive segment.

Under-followed stocks on Wall Street generally outperform those that get heavy attention and a multitude of research coverage. The Street tracks big cap stocks to generate more trades. Big caps are where institutional clients are concentrated and investment banking does business. These highly trafficked names are overexploited and well-discovered. A major Street firm assessed some 40 investment strategies it had put forth in 2006. The best one was to invest in the stocks that had the least analyst coverage. According to *Barron's,* the 50 stocks in the S&P 500 followed by the fewest analysts in 2006 had a 24.6% gain versus a 13.6% advance in the entire S&P 500 index.

The greatest recommendation of my entire career was a small cap stock. I was instrumental in the initial public offering of Fiserv in 1986. It provided financial market computer services and compiled an incredibly consistent growth record. The executives were solid and trustworthy Midwesterners. Fiserv was a Buy recommendation almost constantly until I retired and a stellar stock for more than 15 years. Paychex was another small cap name that I identified early. As the biggest player specializing at the low end of the payroll processing market (its average client had 11 employees), it had established a dynamic growth record, impressive profit margins, and a stalwart balance sheet. Competitors could not touch it. The company was able to generate a profit from a one-person payroll client. The chairman and founder was a playful bachelor at the time who, on occasion, took Las Vegas by storm and ran for governor of New York. But he managed the company the old-fashioned way: quantitative targets, a narrow specialization, cash generation, and organic growth. I staked my reputation on the stock with a Strong Buy. It performed fantastically. I rode this horse for years, and it is now a big cap. These are examples of how good small cap stocks can perform well for decades.

Deletion of Coverage Can Be an Ominous Indicator

Dropping stock coverage is often subtle—the Street downplays the move—but it is telling. Analysts rarely walk away from following a winning company that has a promising outlook. Dropping coverage is a graceful method of avoiding an unpleasant downgrade. I remember an experience I had with HBO & Co., a languishing, troubled company in healthcare computer services. It hired an impressive, smooth, new hotshot CEO to commence a turnaround. After monitoring the progress for a couple years, I finally added it to coverage with a Buy rating. The business was heavily software-based, and quarterly bookings drove the numbers. There was only modest visibility but terrific momentum as the company expanded its sales force, moved into adjunct markets, and made acquisitions. Quarterly earnings were sparkling.

Then I began to develop a sense of uneasiness. Acquisitions blurred the operating results. The company's size made it a challenge to sustain the high growth that executives were forecasting and investors anticipated. Competitors' results were lackluster. Its earnings growth and profit margins were vastly superior to those of its counterparts in the business. As WorldCom would demonstrate a few years later, this contrast can be a telltale sign. Software orders and related revenue can be variable on a quarterly basis, but HBO's results were smooth as silk, despite minimal recurring revenue to aid stability. It made me suspicious and uncomfortable. I decided to stop following it in the process of reorienting my coverage emphasis. It was a graceful way to avoid the agony of either lowering an opinion or continuing coverage and risk the possibility of the company hitting the wall. Sure enough, later, after HBO was acquired for a huge price of $14 billion, it was discovered that numerous sales were fictitious and fraudulent. Four members of top management pleaded guilty in criminal cases, and the chairman was indicted. This was the best negative call I never had to make.

A Glaring Lack of Coverage Might Indicate Skepticism

When all the analysts tracking a certain sector follow a stock or a sub-grouping and one analyst avoids that coverage, it probably connotes doubt. Take note. Analysts take some heat when the shares of a stock that all the others cover are soaring and it appears he has missed the boat by not following or advocating it.

It is nerve-racking to appear to be an ostrich. In the 1990s, I did not follow the market toward the growth of Internet eBusiness consulting firms. The sector was Internet-based, demand was off the charts, and the expansion was meteoric. It was "the new thing." Some of the stocks hit triple figures. A certain sentiment emerged on the Street that I was a dinosaur. Other analysts recommending these names focused on revenue growth, new client additions, and futuristic trends since the companies bled red ink and had essentially no profit potential for the foreseeable future. The analysts had little historic perspective on prior bull market excesses, technology boom-busts, or obscenely overvalued investments.

I had been on Wall Street during a euphoric period in the early 1970s and, as a history follower, had read books such as *Extraordinary Popular Delusions and the Madness of Crowds* and Kindleberger's *Manias, Panics, and Crashes.* I had a seasoned perspective. These Internet-based companies were dazzling, curious, and exciting, but as investments they were incredibly speculative, with nothing but red ink. All the eBusiness consulting stocks subsequently disappeared into a massive abyss. Most of the analysts promoting the eBusiness stocks were fairly junior, and almost all soon disappeared from the business. I rode out the debacle unscathed—and later pundits quipped that I had come back into fashion.

Insiders Attempt to Leap Ahead of Upgrades

The best investment opportunity is not what an analyst is currently recommending. That is yesterday's news and is already fully reflected in the stock price. The stock has probably been a Buy for a while, and other analysts are likely pushing it, too. Insiders seek the stock that carries a Neutral or Hold opinion but may imminently be upgraded to Buy. An analyst might be leaning more positively toward a particular stock long before upgrading it to a Buy. The first indication is a change in the rating from Underperform or Sell to a Neutral or Hold. Sometimes the less-negative leaning might be detected in the research commentary.

Analysts are looking for early signs of recovery. Any such positive signals and the evolution will begin toward a more favorable view. At an early stage with scant evidence, it is premature for an analyst to shift the formal rating. But we always have inclinations, feelings that there is potential, so we monitor developments. There is little downside to maintaining a Neutral opinion if steady improvement does not unfold. If there is headway for a few months, the seeds are sown for an upgrade to Buy. When a Street recommendation shifts from Sell to

Neutral or Hold, it is a good buying opportunity, before the opinion moves up to Buy. You might say in that case, "Neutral means Buy."

Institutional Investor Poll Rankings Warp Research

The stature, influence, impact, reputation, and compensation of Wall Street analysts are heavily determined by their annual ranking on the *Institutional Investor* magazine All-Star Team poll results each October. Analysts are compelled to amass *Institutional Investor (II)* votes during the spring each year when the poll is being conducted among the client base of institutional investors. Angling for *II* votes supplants objective, quality research, investor service, stock picking, and most other research goals. *II* rankings transcend virtually all other research objectives. The compensation for analysts landing in the top three positions in their category is essentially akin to that of professional sports all-stars. An *II* magazine analyst compensation survey indicated that the mean total comp of a "ranked" analyst in 2006 was $1.4 million, compared to $590,000 for other senior analysts—irresistible incentive to make the team. Year-end evaluation is influenced to this measure. It corrupts research, taints the process, and skews analyst efforts.

Analysts often embark on unusual, high-profile endeavors to attract the attention of mutual funds, banks, and other such institutional voters. A dramatic opinion upgrade is one way analysts curry favor with major holders or attract notice from potentially interested investors. But do not be drawn in. Street insiders discount any flamboyant opinion upgrades from April to June. It is just electioneering. Such recommendation changes need to be put in perspective. They are not necessarily erroneous, but the catalyst behind the action is questionable and the timing is suspicious.

In contrast, rating downgrades are avoided like the plague during this period. Analysts do not want to provoke the ire of institutional holders by attacking a stock during this critical voting stretch. They postpone such unpleasant actions until the polls are closed. Be prepared for a mini-flurry of catch-up downgrades during late June or in August. July is earnings reporting time, and it is awkward and risky to lower an opinion just ahead of results, when an analyst might appear to have inside information or might be immediately embarrassed. To avoid this peril, analysts ease rating reductions under the rug during the August vacation month, hoping to go unnoticed.

It is insane to think that a professional industry trade magazine's annual research rankings are a central driving factor for almost all analysts, but career advancement and year-end bonuses are critically weighted by placement in this poll. These standings generate widespread publicity and are noticed by the chairman and all other management in the firm. The entire investment industry, the press, and even the public exalt "All-Star" team members. High-profile All-Star team status is determined heavily by analyst marketing and communications as opposed to the quality and accuracy of the research. It is similar to how the movie studios advertise and lobby early each year for Academy Award nominations. Analysts do the same thing to enhance their *Institutional Investor* standings. It is all about marketing.

Owing to this *II* voting in late spring, January to May is a period of marketing frenzy. Brokerage investor conferences are almost all conducted during this span. Most analysts jam in several executive road shows to meet with institutional clients during these months. Analyst marketing trips around the country are double or even triple the amount done in the fall. Industry studies, dramatic opinion changes (usually favorable), and other such special research endeavors are embarked upon. Phone calls to heavyweight, influential institutional clients skyrocket. All of this is drummed up and delivered in an artificially concentrated period.

Major Buyside Institutions Have Access to Selective Information

Big institutions have closed-door, exclusive access to corporate executives. Even smaller money-management firms and hedge funds seek such entree. Brokerage analysts, their research now less differentiated, achieve impact by arranging these meetings, like a concierge, for their top clients. Brokerages even judge their analyst performance partly based on their capability here. Brokerage in-house entities have been established to plan such meetings, field trips, tours, and engagements. According to Greenwich Associates, institutions indicate that some 26% of research commission fees are for "direct access to company management." The giant buyside institutions and sellside analysts are teaming up to book executive visits to the exclusion of small investors.

When Street sellside analysts accompany executives on a road show, they are usually excluded from some of these sessions. One-on-one confabs with management at analysts' conferences are closed. Only the biggest-paying institutional clients gain this exclusive access. This extremely unbalanced degree of access is conducive to inside tidbits, shadings, and extensive communication through body language. Such gatherings are not Webcast to all outside investors, or even broadcast on an open telephone conference call. Executives tend to communicate special insight to their most dominant institutional stockholders.

At the same time, big holders have inordinate influence over executives, whose hearts pound at the thought of a 5% owner possibly dumping its position. A block of stock puts an institutional holder almost on par with a board member in terms of executive exposure and information flow. In comparison, Street analyst entree to executives is tantamount to that of the company's nighttime janitor.

They also have advantageous social contact with executives. There are abundant opportunities at conferences, in meetings, on the golf course, or over drinks for portfolio managers and even buyside analysts to glean key information from corporate executives. As a sellside analyst I, too, occasionally played this game, at places like the Los Angeles Country Club and the Turnberry golf resort in Scotland. It gave me an awareness superior to that gained in any formal encounters. Individual investors are not normally privy to these functions and once again are treated unfairly.

Hedge Funds Distort Research and the Stock Market

At the outset of 2008, there were more than 10,000 hedge funds controlling more than $2 trillion in assets. The top 1,000 hedge funds by assets are detailed in *Barron's* each week. Some two-thirds of all hedge funds are unregistered with the Securities Exchange Commission (SEC). The owners and managers of these entities, unlike mutual funds, keep for themselves some 20% of the annual investment gains. Because of this extraordinary compensation, hedge funds took on the handle "hedge hogs." They tend to be extremely aggressive. (During the 2008 bear market collapse in stocks and subprime loans, they became known as "hedge dogs.") They became powerful during the years of folly in the 1990s, adding a new dynamic to the market. Formerly unregulated, they soared into prominence, their capital gains surged off the charts, and their assets bulged. Curiously, hedge funds do not hedge. They are not neutral. Instead they take *unhedged* positions with the intention of generating major gains. And they did in the 1990s.

Universities, state pension funds, unions, and corporations earmarked a portion of their investments and piled into these speculative, high-performance hedge funds. The gains were too enticing to ignore, despite the risks. When the bear market took hold in 2008 and these highly leveraged hedge funds started to incur big losses, the aforementioned institutions in the public trust lost billions.

Hedge funds make the playing field totally unfair. Brokers, money managers, mutual funds—almost all sides—must conform to SEC regulations. Not the hedgies, despite the new registration requirement. Their investment holdings do not have to be reported. There is little to prevent them from spreading false rumors, giving out misinformation, and making spurious attacks. Hedge funds can essentially manipulate stocks to their own advantage. Such investment groups can selectively or serially dribble out misinformation or half-truths. There is no requirement to disclose any deceptive story to outsiders all at the same time. Brokerage firms, mutual funds, even corporate executives are constrained from such methods, but not hedge funds.

Because they are trading-oriented, hedge funds generate enormous commissions for brokerage firms. Many hedgies, assertive by nature, feel no hesitation in flexing their muscles. They can push analysts and brokerage firms in inappropriate directions to unnaturally stimulate their funds' stock performance. Street firms tolerate such behavior. It is all about money.

Analysts are compelled to be cooperative in meeting their demands, realizing the importance of these monster commission-generating traders to their own brokerage firm. Hedge funds sometimes coerce the Street into endorsing their positions, addressing and promulgating their stances, and occasionally trying to alter research views. They can use the Street as a tool, passing self-serving stories about stocks that are then taken literally by salespeople and traders. Analysts must then react. If they vehemently disagree, they generate the ire of these lucrative clients. The stories sometimes have an air of believability, just enough to get the ear of analysts and investors. For the most part, though, such talk is just hedge fund propaganda to stimulate the price of trading positions.

Corporate Executives Corrupt Street Research Opinions

Inexperienced analysts often fall prey to the cheering and puffery of corporate executives, easily interpreted as confidence. Executives tend to take a Panglossian view of their outlook and try to suck analysts into this boosterism. Microsoft is a notable exception, and so was another stock I covered, Paychex. Its founder and chairman, Tom Golisano, pointedly referenced, during analyst conference calls, his trepidation amid all the ecstasy of the late-'90s Bubble Era that his smaller, loyal shareholders and employees would eventually get hurt when his stock valuation returned back to earth. He was correct. But such an attitude is rare, and executives are seldom as forthright.

It is difficult to regulate against corporate executives' tendency to over promote their stock. This behavior started in earnest during the 1990s euphoria. Executive efforts to drive their stock prices ever higher, like running up a one-sided football score, pushed analysts into a similarly biased role. Executives dangled investment banking business as a carrot for bullish investment ratings.

An eBusiness Internet consulting company that I covered tried to appeal to my most basic desire. My investment opinion was lukewarm, actually skeptical, on this glorified Web page design firm. I did not trust management, and the stock was wildly overvalued like all the other Internet names. The CEO sought to have me fall in line

with all the exalted, biased, bullish investment opinions on his company. To curry my favor, knowing I was an avid golfer, he offered me
the ultimate carrot: "Would you like to play at Augusta?" That is the
quintessential Nirvana for anyone who plays the game. It is the home
of the Masters, a "major" PGA tour event. The enticement was
tempting, but I boldly responded no. The thought of such an obvious
inducement made me feel like barfing. Besides, I had already kissed
the hallowed grounds of Augusta on two occasions; the photo of me
standing on Amen Corner was already proudly displayed on my office
wall.

Corporate executive efforts to influence their stock continues
apace. In conference calls, managements spend 19 minutes accentu-
ating the positives and 1 minute or no time at all on the negative
issues, before opening the floor to Q & A. Some 99% of corporate
press releases pertain to favorable news; the infrequent negative
announcements are brief and hedged. TV interviews and analyst
meetings are forums to push the bullish scenario. The spate of mostly
bad news and stock-price free fall in the 2008 bear market presented
a serious challenge to the corporate spin masters. Blame was cast on
outside influences. Survivability was emphasized. "Favorable" long-
term prospects were highlighted.

Most companies hold an annual one- or two-day analyst and institutional investor conference at their headquarters. The time they
waste frustrating us with promotional marketing bull drives us nuts.
The positives are accentuated because the press is in attendance and
the sessions are sometimes broadcast to the public. It is a PR show.
Analysts have to attend, fearing we might miss some nuggets or
inflections, but original, tangible, insightful content is miniscule. Any
really useful information is extracted primarily from informal chats
with executives during coffee breaks.

Executives play favorites with analysts. And analysts are often too
close to the management of the companies they cover. Executives'
control over analysts is subtle, but effective. They give preferential
treatment to analysts with bullish recommendations on the stock.
This relationship inhibits objective research.

Sometime after the Internet bubble burst, an enthusiastic analyst
was dismissed from his job after the National Association of Securities

Dealers (NASD), the Street's regulatory body, charged he had issued misleading research reports and was too close to the management of a technology company he covered. In that tech company's legal proceedings, there was testimony that it spent $20,783 to investigate the analyst's fiancée, just as a favor. The same analyst bestowed a case of 1995 Chateau Margaux on the CEO costing $4,547, an unseemly gesture, returned in kind with a $2,208 case of champagne. According to *The Wall Street Journal,* the analyst referred to himself in an e-mail as a "LOYAL (company) EMPLOYEE." The NASD charged him with publishing reports on the firm that lacked any mention of his actual reservations. It fined the analyst $225,000 and suspended him for a year from the industry for providing "misleading and skewed research." This is an extreme case, but it illustrates the far-reaching influence of corporate executives on Street research.

Unfortunately, corporate executives can punish analysts for negative opinions. A negative opinion creates an adverse reaction within the corporate ranks and the natural tendency is to retaliate. Our access to executives can be limited. Phone calls will not be returned or will be relegated to a low-level investor relations person. A bearish analyst is shunned when requesting a meeting, a form of being cut off. Another subtle penalty meted out by executives for any analyst recommendation lacking an upbeat tone is relegation to the end of the line in the Q & A batting order on conference calls. Analysts always want to be early, if not first, to prove their clout to others listening in on the call.

In conversations with institutional investors, CEOs might lambaste analysts, disparaging them in order to discredit their unfavorable stock opinion. At the same time perfectly legal perks and favors, such as access, speaking at conferences, and road shows are still provided to analysts carrying positive opinions, which, according to studies, reduces the likelihood of a downgrade. By the early 1990s, having been on Wall Street for more than two decades, I had established a credible record, as the leading analyst in computer services and software. The gregarious, glib, intense CEO (I tagged him as the Rhett Butler of the computer services industry) of a company on which I carried a reserved opinion stridently castigated my analytical abilities all over the Street. His ad hominem attack was heard by numerous institutional holders of the stock who filtered it back to me. He hoped they would pressure me to upgrade my recommendation. It diminished my respect for his team forever, even though I later begrudgingly took a more upbeat stance on the stock.

Analysts must maintain friendly, collegial relationships with executives of the companies they cover to obtain a prompt and continuous flow of information. If we are cut off by executives, our research content is affected. We need them, and they need us. We must preserve our management sources, but a friendly association often has the deleterious effect of biasing our investment opinions.

Corporations still tie their selection of an investment banking firm to research coverage and analyst opinions. It is amazing that executives continue to quietly seek favorable analyst coverage as a prerequisite to doing banking business with that brokerage firm. At a brokerage firm's pharmaceutical and biotechnology conference in early 2004, *The New York Times* reported a notable example of such a stance. In reaction to the analyst's required statement of his firm's investment banking intentions, the president of a biotech company was quoted as declaring with asperity, "The likelihood of an investment banking relationship is pretty close to zero until they upgrade their rating." The analyst's rating on the stock at the time was Neutral.

There are a few companies that are more evenhanded, but such enlightened behavior is abnormal. I remember when the president of Automatic Data Processing, Frank Lautenberg, currently in his fourth term as U.S. Senator from New Jersey, wrote me a letter after I had downgraded my opinion on his stock. He communicated a magnanimous attitude of understanding and promised to continue giving me open-door access. That instilled in me a feeling that I just could not wait for the time when I could appropriately upgrade it again. But that equitable approach is rare today.

All these inherent factors distort the investment process. Street insiders are totally aware of these influences, and their investment decisions are not skewed by these detrimental practices. Investors should not be naive regarding how the Street, institutional investors, and corporate executives distort research.

3 —————————————————

Strategies in Quest of the
Ideal Investment

Whenever I mention my professional background to people for the first time, they almost always react by asking me for investment advice. In 2008, these queries pertained mostly to what to do after losing 40% of their capital. The expectation is that, as an insider, I can prescribe a nostrum that will put them back on a sure track to stock market riches. After I've tried to change the subject, my normal response is to first inquire as to their goals, requirements, and financial situation. And the reply I usually hear goes something like, "Well, my broker has put me in a bunch of stocks and mutual funds, and I have lost money in…." Individual investors sure need help, especially in preserving capital and avoiding risk, and it is not coming from Wall Street. Casual investors seem to believe that what they obtain from their brokers or Wall Street is reasonable investment advice—a big mistake. This chapter lays out strategies and guidance so that you can make your own investment decisions, which, combined with an understanding of how the Street operates, should provide you with the tools to make smarter investment decisions.

My time-tested, rational, conservative investment strategies should serve as a basic investment foundation. I also lay out best stock market transaction practices. My last book, *Shakeout,* published in 1984, offered 15 axioms "to protect the investor from the snares and pitfalls lurking behind every corner." Most are timeless: It never rains bad news, it pours; the first drop in profits is never the last; when insiders sell, you should too; beware of stock price fixation; the bigger their (corporate executives) egos, the harder they fall; turnarounds do not work. If you read it in the morning paper, it is too late; when management says things are bad, assume that they are terrible; if you do not understand a company's business, management might not either; and new digs are a bad sign. This chapter is an updated, vastly expanded version—strategies and practices that I believe are elemental for any investor.

A 2001 study at the University of California, Davis, by Barber and Odean, found that women's portfolios outperformed men's because females were more patient and did their research. They traded less frequently and based investment decisions on factors unrelated to just the numbers. The study said women "typically look beyond the shiniest, newest biotechno gadget and focus instead on…products they can't live without, and on consumer goods they buy in their day-to-day lives." I recommend a similar approach. Investors need to do some homework. Pay attention. Invest carefully. Be conservative. And take a long-term approach.

Selecting the Best Company to Invest In

The first step in the process is the quest for the perfect company. How to examine companies as prospective stock candidates is discussed in detail in Chapter 5, "Evaluating Companies as Investment Candidates." As a starter, here are a few simple characteristics to look for that are key to any quality investment.

Find Unique, Focused Companies Leading a New or Niche Market

The ideal company is unique: a leader in an emerging market or technology, dominant in an attractive niche sector, or somehow set apart from the rest of the industry. The distinctiveness might be in the strategy it takes within an established market. Look for focus and expertise that is unusual, or a structural characteristic that allows robust, dependable profit generation. This is the "story" aspect: why is the company dissimilar to peer group competitors. Avoid the me-too, second- or third-largest players in a sector unless they are taking an atypical tack that makes them unique. Assess this element of singularity first when considering an equity investment.

Look for Specialized, Simple Businesses

Firms *specializing* in a singular product area, market, or approach—such as Automatic Data Processing, Southwest Airlines, Whole Foods, or Activision—always outrun the generalists. Specialists have notable advantages over bigger, broader lumbering giants. They are more nimble, aggressive, and focused. As in a PGA tour golf tournament on Sunday, it is easier to come from behind than defensively protect a lead. Invest in *simple* businesses that are readily understandable. Complex areas such as high-tech and biotech necessitate extreme expertise to judge the merits or appraise the outlook. Emulate the Warren Buffett style.

Seek Double-Digit Growth or Robust Cash Generation

The ultimate indicator of steady expansion is *revenue,* not profits. Growth companies should be achieving double-digit revenue gains on a consistent basis with no evidence of such funny stuff as unbilled revenue or unusual, unsustainably large upfront contract deals. Seek *real* growth that is repeatable going forward. But beware of excessive growth. Expansion rates of over 25% cannot be maintained over an extended period, and the stock probably fully reflects the current exorbitant pace in the form of a high price/earnings multiple. Companies can readily manipulate earnings by cost cutting, accounting treatment, reserves, restructuring, stock buybacks, and any number of measures. Profit improvement can be achieved with mirrors for quite a while. Revenue is the true test. There are myriad cases—IBM is one—where profits expanded for years with little revenue growth. This indicates maturity in the business. There should be evidence of vibrant growth prospects. Favorable cash flow is always important. Negative cash flow is a red flag. If you are investing for dividend yield returns, then positive cash flow is imperative.

Pursue Healthy, Stable, or Expanding Profit Margins

This is another measure of corporate vigor. It is not the absolute level of operating margins or pre-tax profit margins (that varies by industry); it is the overall pattern of profit margins during the past few years that counts. I prefer profit margins at the higher end of the peer group norm, indicating either good management or a unique business approach. More important, margins must be steady, with no pattern of erosion or slippage. Some improvement is the ideal. Evaluate margins over the past ten years, and absolute earnings expansion over the past five to ten years, especially through weak economic periods. The combination of revenue growth plus profit margin expansion is a powerful favorable earnings impetus. Be leery of companies where profit margins are so far superior to those of any other industry competitors that there might be no more room to widen—that is, where margins might be maxed out and possibly at risk.

Insist on a Robust Balance Sheet and Quality Finances

Companies with high levels of debt are risky. I prefer no long-term debt and minimal short-term debt. The debt-to-capitalization ratio should be under 20%. Other balance sheet items should also be superior, with accounts receivable turnover under 90 days, no unbilled revenue, and nothing complex or out of alignment. Read the footnotes to understand the rationale behind such things as deferred revenue, capitalized software, depreciation/amortization, and capital spending. On the quarterly conference call, listen to find out whether such balance sheet items disturb the analysts; see whether they raise caution flags. The simpler the better; multiple pages of extensive footnotes in quarterly and annual reports or SEC filings are an ominous sign.

Look for All-Around Quality in Executives, Customers, Board Members, and Partners

Seek and stick with quality companies. The first step is to consider the company they keep. Are their customers blue-chip entities? Is there an ongoing, year-after-year relationship with major clients? The best accounting firms, commercial bankers, investment bankers, securities analysts, board members, law firms, and joint venture partners should be associated with any firm you are considering as an investment. Excellence also pertains to executives, employees, products, and services, even to the major institutional investor holders of the stock. What is the background of management? Where was their past experience; did they work at winning companies? High-class companies understate earnings by an average of 5%, whereas low-caliber firms overstate their profits by 10% to 15%. Looking at companies is like assessing a new home, automobile, job, or spouse: You want quality to the greatest degree possible.

Avoid Arrogant, Overconfident Management

Corporate executives who have an egotistical and arrogant attitude make for a high-risk investment. They usually have a blind side and are set up for a fall. Overconfidence is a killer. Look for management who are humble, understated, conservative, and who have a sense of humor. It is fine for them to be aggressive, enthusiastic, with a belief in their mission. But I like to see humility of the sort embodied by Harry S. Truman during the 1944 Democratic Convention. He was informed by President Roosevelt—who because of ill health the world knew was unlikely to serve out his next term—that he would be the vice-presidential candidate. His reply was, "Oh, shit!" Not that I want corporate executives to banter abundant expletives, but I prefer executives with an unassuming nature.

Prefer Smaller Companies Over Giants

Small and mid-sized firms are more suitable to be specialists; they are able to stay focused and manageable. Small companies are capable of changing directions quickly to more swiftly attack the competition. New thrusts and strategies still have an impact. It is easier for good management to be creative and original, to make a small-sized company distinctive. Companies under $1 to $2 billion in revenue can sustain vigorous growth and attract better employees. They are sizable enough to have financial strength and stability but are still on the make, seeking to achieve industry leadership. Such companies have less Street research coverage, and are less widely owned by institutions, so their stocks might not be excessively exploited or over-bought.

Avoid Weird Stock Structures or Sweetheart Management Setups

Avoid companies that have two classes of stock: one for the founder carrying all the voting power, and another for outsiders with little effective governing powers. Google is a case in point, with dual-class voting stocks, one for the founders/management and the other for public shareholders. This obviates management's accountability to shareholders. Phantom shares are similarly suspect, wherein stockholders do not own the assets but only a right to dividends. Sometimes classes of stock are created as an anti-takeover device, to artificially protect management. Look for other vested interest management deals that indicate parochial behavior, such as close friends or pliable supporters on the board. Sometimes such information is available from chat rooms and Internet sites discussing a particular company. Be leery of stock appreciation rights, reissuance of stock options at lower levels after a stock price nosedives, and other lucrative, sweetheart management arrangements. Backdating of stock options is essentially a corrupt practice and speaks volumes about management principles. I abhor the disproportionately high management compensation so prevalent these days. Be careful of managements that have too many perks, such as preferred parking spots, company drivers, corporate aircraft, sumptuous headquarters, sports arena courtesy suites, or names on stadiums and ballparks (Enron Field comes to mind).

Investment Strategies Must Start with Capital Preservation

Here are some key investment strategies—simple and straightforward, and some that might seem surprising. I present them in approximate order of importance. Think quality rather than quantity. It is not how many stocks you own, but rather how good your holdings are. Keep it simple. The key variables that determine stock market returns are dividend yield, earnings growth, and the stock's price-to-earnings (PE) ratio. Be wary of complex company financial statements. When investing in a stock, first evaluate the downside risk and how much you might lose, before considering the appreciation potential. As an individual investor, you have the flexibility to use these suggestions and take advantage of your position outside the constraints on institutional portfolio managers.

Preserving Capital Is the First Priority

Protection of capital is paramount, an investment objective far ahead of gains and returns. If you doubt me, just ask anyone who watched their nest egg evaporate when the 1990s bubble burst, or who watched it dive 40% to 50%, along with their home equity, amid the 2008 bear market meltdown. The magnitude of gains is almost irrelevant compared to the preservation of your investment pool. After a 50% drop in a stock, it requires a 100% rise in the price to get back to even. It is of less consequence if a stock rises 10% or 50%, but it is a major disaster if it declines 30%. So always be conservative, and think in terms of downside potential and risk. Take modest losses, say 10% to 20%, before they become a serious debacle, a drop of more than 25%. Avoid the psychological aversion to admit to a loss. You are a hero, or actually a wealthy person, if you just retain your investment capital and perhaps achieve 5% to 10% appreciation annually for 30 years. Maintain low expectations. Do not assume audacious future returns because that will distract you from your foremost objective of preserving capital. A *Financial Analysts Journal* article by Asness summarizes my feelings precisely: "In true Hippocratic fashion, Do No Harm!"

Be cognizant that highly improbable "Black Swan" events having extreme impact occur from time to time. As pointed out in *Black Swan,* by Nassim Taleb, unpredictable occurrences are a part of the investing landscape, such as the day the market crashed 22.5% in 1987, the 9/11 terrorist attacks, Hurricane Katrina, or the demise of Bear Stearns and Lehman Brothers. Many times they are short-lived shocks that should not disrupt a long-term investment strategy. But occasionally, as in the case of the Lehman Brothers bust, such an event sets off a more long-lasting stock market shift that is cause for alteration in investment strategy in order to protect capital.

The point here is *don't lose.* That is the secret of superior investing. Charles D. Ellis makes the point, in another *Financial Analysts Journal* article, that "large losses are forever—in investing, teenage driving, and fidelity...and are almost always caused by trying to get too much by taking too much risk." He discusses the excitement of "the big score," which causes the investor to put too much emphasis on offense, with little regard to defense. Laurence D. Fink, CEO of BlackRock, quips that "the pain of losing money is far greater than the glory of making money."

Another mutual fund, the T. Rowe Capital Appreciation Fund, also illustrates the point. As of 2007, it had achieved a gain every single year of its existence, 16 years in a row. That included the three years when the market declined, 2000–2002. It did not attempt to maximize its upside but rather minimized the downside to protect its capital. The attitude expressed by its fund managers, according to an article in the *Wall Street Journal,* was "How much can we lose if we're wrong?" You can always be wrong about the market. Ben Stein emphasized in his *New York Times* column that "from 1926 to 2007, the S&P 500 index fell three out of every ten years." His quip relating to preserving capital is "Cash does not crash."

The greatest impediment to proper investing is underestimating risk. There are no excessive returns without commensurate risk. Even professionals fall prey to the appeal of high returns—Citigroup, Bear Stearns, Lehman Brothers, junk bonds, Long Term Capital Management, the Internet bubble, and now subprime loans and collateralized debt obligations (CDOs). Unwarranted risk is trying to pick up $100 bills in front of a steamroller. Instead, settle for $5 bills on the lawn. Wall Street pays almost no attention to risk. Brokerage firms and research analysts rarely indicate the worst-case downside risk in a stock, only the upside price objective. Amid a bear market in the first half of 2008, during the crisis of confidence while the financial sector was being decimated, a major Street firm advised investors to purchase growth stocks, emerging market stocks, and international stocks, and to diversify. There was little reference to cash or how to avoid losing money in its outlook report. Investors are already taking enough risk by owning common stocks and even more so by holding only a few names. A conservative approach is always warranted.

Do not get trapped in a state of denial if bear market circumstances exist and the evidence is glaring. The most challenging aspect of readying an investment portfolio for a major stock market falloff can be in recognizing the ominous conditions and deteriorating stock market. The investing element is more straightforward; that is, determine the appropriate, expendable stock positions that can be sold to generate cash. An important goal is to establish a pile of cash, or a liquid equivalent such as a true money market fund, to hold on to if the rest of the market tanks. Bear markets are deceptive, behaving in a manner that disguises the downward drift. Each time there is a precipitous drop, it is followed by a modest recovery. Beginning in November 2008, following a more than 50% collapse, there was a better than 20% recovery through year-end, a typical pattern. Bear markets move in phases, and in the end, everyone gets hurt.

Invest in Themes and Rising Industry Sectors

The way to take long rides on stellar performers is to be early in an industry sector that is breaking out for decisive, sustainable reasons. Identify an area where business prospects are shifting positive or where circumstances should be improving over the next year or so. Real estate and REITs were superb as interest rates dropped in 2003–2004 and as real estate prices climbed in 2005; the energy sector—oil and gas—took off in 2004–2007 because of war and shortages, an economic upswing, Chinese demand, and world political uncertainty; precious metals and commodities were a robust area in 2005–2007; and in 2008–2009 amid the world economic debacle, various financial disasters, and a failing dollar, gold gained momentum. Technology was the target of overinvestment for more than a decade; it was overcapitalized, with too many venture capital firms shoving billions at the sector during the same period. Energy was undercapitalized; amazingly, there was too little investment capital. Then the opposite occurred as oil reached $147 per barrel. Real estate became overcapitalized, with REITs and other investors having plowed in zillions there.

Stick with sectors that are still underinvested and underexploited. It is not too late to invest in stocks in a sector that is already starting to accelerate; there is typically a long ramp. Figure out the emerging new theme. But be cautious of trends or fads. Sometimes they might be narrower, more mature, or already fully exploited by investors by the time you recognize them, say, Starbucks, JetBlue, and eBay. Look for broad themes rather than trendy ideas. Pay attention, read, observe, and think ahead.

A particularly easy method by which to participate in an industry sector is through exchange traded funds (ETFs). There are many such funds now representing everything from ownership of the S&P 500 to short positions in the S&P to financial stocks to gold. They are a concentrated, representative participation in the segment, holding a fixed number of stocks. In the case of commodities, they own the actual material, such as crude oil or gold. They are actively traded, are listed on the major exchanges, have low fees, and are simple. You can own a specific, narrow grouping within the market without buying five or ten individual stocks on your own. If you like the health/biotech industry as a theme, you can buy that ETF, or one for the insurance sector, tech, oil, silver, precious metals, Japanese stocks, short-term U.S. Treasuries, utilities, telecom, natural resources, European stocks, the emerging market, or even the entire international market excluding the U.S. There are even ETFs that short emerging market stocks, others that focus on ignored stocks with little or no analyst coverage, and ETFs that hold stocks reflecting favorable corporate insider buying and Wall Street analyst upgrades.

Be aware that if the ETF owns the actual commodity, so do you. Gains are taxed as collectibles, at a maximum of 28%, rather than at a 15% long-term capital gains tax if the ETF comprises stocks. Occasionally there are year-end capital gains distributions. Another caveat is that investors might start to think they are consistently proficient in choosing the right sector at the right time (sector timing), and this can become a form of trading. Do not get into a cycle of flipping ETFs every few months. They should be viewed as investment vehicles. And there are no dividends. So do not go crazy.

Hold Only a Modest Number of Stocks and Choose Familiar Companies

Own no more than five or ten different stocks. Holding too many means being ignorant about your investments. A casual friend sitting next to me at a black-tie dinner who fancied himself an avid investor boasted that he held 300 different equities! After gagging on my salmon, I inquired whether he was a portfolio manager of the huge

Magellan Fund, which probably does not hold anywhere near as many positions.

A few dozen stocks degrade performance toward that of the overall market averages. You might as well own a mutual fund. There is no way to stay abreast of more than a half dozen names. Peter Lynch refers to owning too many stocks as "de-worse-ification." A survey by the Universities of Michigan and Illinois found that investors with only a handful of names outperformed more diversified portfolios. Investors holding numerous stocks slightly lagged behind the markets. It has to do with knowledge, familiarity, and information. Local firms are even better; an investor is likely to have more thorough understanding of these businesses. And according to the survey, smaller stocks, those that are less well known, outperform the S&P 500 index in these concentrated portfolios. A plethora of stocks hardly reduces risk. An array of so-called "alternative investments" offers little protection in a falling market. World financial markets are so interlinked nowadays that diversification is not what it used to be. Investors can adequately diminish risk by broadening within the five or ten stocks, representing different industries or sectors.

Value Stocks Reduce Risk and Outperform

Not only do stocks that have low-PE multiples carry less risk, but studies have proven that over long periods they also outperform growth stocks, even during bull markets. I prefer stocks that carry lower PE multiples than the norm of companies in their sector. This provides more opportunities for multiple expansion and tends to reduce volatility. There is less downside when bad news surfaces. If there is even a slight disappointment, high-PE multiple stocks will be slammed by a double whammy—an earnings estimate reduction and major multiple contraction.

Growth stocks underperform value stocks because Wall Street tends to project the current earnings growth rate on into the future. If expectations are high, so is the valuation. Value stocks carry lower expectations and thus better prospects for a positive surprise. The stellar stocks, over time, have always started out with reasonable valuations. Even fabulous companies with brilliant prospects can be poor investments if the entry price is too high. John B. Neff, who was a renowned manager of value mutual funds at the Vanguard Group for 31 years, said it all in a CFA Institute Financial Analysts Seminar in mid-2006: "Having a low PE is the primary principle."

Growth stocks almost always reflect lofty PE ratios, and usually they are popular fad stocks. Graham and Dodd's book, *Security Analysis,* first published in the 1930s, stressed value investing as its key concept. It is still valid today. Many decades ago, Dodd made the comment to a youthful Wall Street student, "Always remember the Horace quotation—there is no substitute for value, and popularity has little to do with it." Each year a Bloomberg columnist identifies the ten U.S. stocks with the lowest PEs out of all those over $500 million in market cap. For several years in a row, they far outperformed the S&P 500. That major brokerage, the one whose best strategy in 2006 proved to be the under-followed stocks, found its second-best out of 20 investment strategies that year was to hold stocks that had low-PE multiples. Various other studies have also shown that high-PE multiple stocks yield low returns to investors compared to low-PE stocks.

Dividend Yield Is Important

During the 1990s bubble years, dividends were neglected; companies paying them were considered dodo birds. Then after the Internet bubble burst, and the 2000–2002 bear market ensued, yield came back into vogue. From 1926 to 2006, the total stock market return averaged close to 11% annually, and *41%* of this, or 4.4% of the gain each year, stemmed from dividends, according to the *Motley Fool* Income Investor. From 1999 to 2008, the stock market declined some 40%, but dividends, when reinvested, offset almost the entire drop. Astonishingly, dividend paying stocks outperform nonpayers, even in bull markets. The *Motley Fool* observed that from 1980 to 2005, while the S&P 500 surged from around 100 to 1250, dividend stocks outgained nondividend equities by more than 2.6 percentage points a year, much of the difference stemming from superior stock price performance.

A safe dividend provides some downside protection during a setback. A $20 stock that pays an $0.80 dividend (a 4% yield) is unlikely to plummet to $8 (which would be a 10% yield) unless the firm is about to slash the dividend payout. The downside is more likely to be $10 to $15, that is, a 5% to 8% yield. Dividends might play an even more important role in the future if the market gains ease to 5% to 8%, or worse. Jeremy Siegel, a professor at Wharton, illustrates the importance of dividends with a striking example: From 1950 to 2003, IBM's revenues, earnings, and dividends climbed faster than those of ExxonMobil. The oil company paid a healthy dividend during the entire span, while IBM started its payout much later and at a lower level. Equal investments in both stocks in 1950 with all dividends reinvested through 2003 would have resulted in a 24% better total return from Exxon.

Studies like the one by Robert D. Arnott, editor of the *Financial Analysts Journal,* show a direct positive correlation between dividend payout ratios and earnings growth. The higher the payout, the faster the earnings pace. This startling relationship probably indicates that managements paying out higher dividends have confidence in bright future earnings growth prospects. Dividend yield is a key indicator of financial stability, good cash flow, and quality earnings. Dividends reduce excess cash on hand, forcing executives to be careful and make wise decisions in picking new investment projects. There is no reason for companies not to pay out 50% of their profits. But many managements are afraid that investors might misinterpret this as a sign of maturity and an inability to reinvest in the growth of the business. Instead they use cash to repurchase shares and this often drags down returns.

Hold Stocks Long-Term

Own stocks for at least one year, preferably for several years. The best performance is invariably with stocks that prove to be winners over five to ten years. Perfect timing in entry price and capturing the top price tick on the sale is virtually impossible, especially on a trading basis over the short-term. Such factors are minimized if you are investing rather than trading. Investing also implies lower capital gains taxes and fewer commissions. This is a long-distance race requiring self-discipline and patience. A long-range perspective will help avoid unwarranted reactions to sudden stock market moves. How many times have you heard "you never lose money taking a profit"? Wrong. You pay a commission and full taxes on a short-term gain. And if the shares continue to climb for the next five years, the opportunity cost will be staggering.

There have been numerous studies proving that a long-range buy-and-hold strategy reduces risk. According to Burton G. Malkiel, Professor of Economics at Princeton University and author of the classic text *A Random Walk Down Wall Street,* in any given one-year or five-year period, the market return historically has ranged from a 25% to 50% gain to a decline of 25%. But in virtually any 15-year span, the annual market return has always been ahead by some 5% to 20%. A study by Ilia Dichev, a professor at the University of Michigan, detailed in *The American Economic Review,* reveals a 10% average return for investors who bought and held listed securities from 1926 to 2002. For traders, the return was 8.6%. And for buying-and-holding NASDAQ stocks from 1973 to 2002, the average annual return was 9.6% versus 4.3% for the typical trader.

There is a curious correlation between the kind of people who drive fast and those who trade frequently, as found in another study by professors at UCLA and the Helsinki School of Economics. The study found that people who rack up speeding tickets are likely to be actively trading stocks rather than holding them long-term. Both behaviors are dangerous. They suggest a tendency toward thrill-seeking. Long-term investing is just too boring for these people. But the results of the study indicated that trading did not produce superior results, especially given the attendant transaction costs. Do not seek excitement or entertainment from trading. Be serious and invest.

During most of my career, I made client marketing treks to Europe on a regular 18-month basis. On these trips to meet with institutions, I observed an attitude that can be valuable to you as an individual investor. European institutional investors allocate a portion of their portfolios to U.S. stocks, and they bring a refreshingly more rational investment philosophy compared with the U.S. trading mentality. The distance, the time difference (NYSE trading begins at 2:30 p.m. in Paris), less contact with U.S. company executives and analysts, and a tendency to be more patient than Americans might be the reasons. European investors are not as absorbed by quarterly portfolio performance. I found that Europeans tended to *invest* in U.S. stocks over the *long-term*. U.S. investors should take a hint from Europe. Be an investor, not a trader.

Trading Is Entertaining but, Like Gambling, Usually Fruitless

Short-term trading is highly challenging even for veterans on broker-age trading floors, who are in instant contact on all rumors, opinion shifts, news, and other influences that have an immediate impact on stock prices. If you think you are smart enough to achieve consistent gains by furious buying and selling, you are probably also telling your friends you always win at the tables in Vegas. Trading is also linked to male testosterone, and as most youthful guys learn, it can also lead to irrational risk taking. Studies show that young men with elevated testosterone levels are more apt to take greater financial gambles. Cambridge University research reports that "money and women trigger the same brain area in men."

A relatively tiny portion of your portfolio should be earmarked for trading, maybe 5% to 10% maximum, if you need such thrills and spills in your life. Maybe after you lose that 5% of your assets, you will be cured of the addiction. And do not think holding stocks for a few months is not trading. Trying to make money by buying and selling stocks during a several-month span is a fool's game. Be an investor—trading is hazardous.

Wall Street is caught up in a short-term tyranny. So are CNBC and other media sources. They constantly promote quick-paced, in-and-out trading. This generates transactions and commissions for brokers and guarantees an ongoing audience for the media. Jim Cramer, the star of *Mad Money*, is the ultimate example of media-induced trading frenzy. He shouts out several new ideas on a daily basis. The only problem is that his "recommendations underperform the market by most measures," as analyzed by *Barron's*. Street recommendations are almost never aimed at more than a one-year time frame. The average length of time New York Stock Exchange stocks were held in 2006 was under seven months, according to Sanford Bernstein. Compare this to a 12-month average back in 1999, the height of the day-trading era. You need to avoid getting caught up in the sizzle or gambling aspect of trading. It is a losing game. You can outperform the Street by steering clear of that frenzy. That is their game. Play your game.

Prefer NYSE-Listed Stocks over NASDAQ Shares

Almost all the names in a portfolio should be New York Stock Exchange companies. The listing requirements of the NYSE are more rigorous than NASDAQ and provide an improved measure of quality and stability. The pool of NYSE listings carries stocks with lower PEs and better dividends. NYSE stocks are more actively traded and get more attention from the press. Only a tiny portion of a personal portfolio, no more than 10%, should be devoted to aggressive, speculative equities, more prevalent on the NASDAQ.

Tread Lightly with International Companies

U.S. companies entail less risk for investors and are easier to follow than international firms. Foreign entities have different accounting methods and securities regulations; they are subject to foreign currency fluctuations and myriad other factors that complicate the picture. If a Japanese stock rises 25% in yen value but the currency declines 25% relative to the U.S. dollar, an American investor breaks even, with no gain in dollar terms. If a European stock rises 20%, but the dollar climbs by 20%, the gain is offset. During 2006–2007, the trendy theme pushed by the Street was to invest in international and emerging markets. The rationale was that such stocks were "alternative" investments, not correlated with U.S. stocks, and in high-growth economies with stronger currencies. U.S. investors poured a quarter-trillion dollars into these types of mutual funds. In 2008, non-U.S.-developed market funds tanked 45% and emerging market funds sank 55%, according to *The New York Times*.

Even if the shares are listed on the NYSE or have ADRs (American depository receipts) traded in the U.S., it is still a dice roll. Forget about trying to scrutinize the financial statements of an Indian or Brazilian company. Satyam in India is a case in point. The books were cooked, and it turns out that the financials were unreliable. Studies prove that securities analysts are more informed and give more accurate earnings forecasts on local companies in their own country, compared to the foreign stocks that they cover. It is no different for investors. Focus on domestic companies which are far easier to understand. The only exception might be Canadian equities, though there still could be foreign-currency perils.

If you insist on owning an international company, be sure that it is listed on the NYSE, it follows FASB accounting rules, management speaks in English on conference calls, and Wall Street publishes reports and earnings estimates—in other words, invest only in a company that you can readily analyze and track. Maybe you think that Chinese or European stocks will be a robust investment area, or perhaps that the U.S. dollar looks weak and you want to benefit from stronger foreign currencies. A lower-risk method of participating in international markets is by investing in an ETF composed of international stocks.

Turnarounds Almost Never Work

Say a company crashes, revenue and earnings nosedive, new competitors come along trashing the old guard, and finally the board replaces management with a promising new team. Then all of a sudden the outlook is bright, pregnant with renewal prospects. It is a mirage. Do not fall for it. Restructuring, divestitures, write-offs, new directions, fresh strategies, and different management are a temporary game. Stocks can rise on the illusion of a turnaround. But often companies are merely milking the operation for cash flow to return to investors, usually in the form of stock buybacks, a financial means to inflate earnings per share. But real revenue growth and sustained improvement in operating earnings rarely happen in such a situation. Lowering the cost structure, lessening the debt burden, and financial reengineering boost profits only momentarily. Real orders, contracts, demand, and growth are almost impossible to reestablish after a company has run off the railroad tracks. The IBM story over the past 10 to 15 years has involved negligible internal revenue growth, but rather foreign currency gains, acquisitions and divestitures, write-offs, and stock repurchases. A turnaround is a trading opportunity at best, but almost never a good long-term investment. See the section "Turnarounds Rarely Work Out" in Chapter 5.

Do Not Try to Catch a Falling Safe

You might think a stock is cheap after its price has been sliced to a fraction of its former high. It is not. The stock almost always continues to descend. Remember how Internet dot.com wonders that hit triple figures seemed cheap when they got to $10? Most fell to $1 or zero. The first bad news is never the last. In spring 2007, the subprime mortgage lending firms were imploding. A *New York Times* story referred to a Bear Stearns analyst who upgraded one such company, whose stock had been axed in three weeks by 50% to about $15. The familiar refrain was that downside risk was limited at that point. A couple of weeks later, the shares were selling for less than $1. In 2008, Citigroup seemed to be a bargain after diving to $20, then to $10, but by early 2009 it headed on down to below $3. Down from its $42 high, GE looked like an "offer you could not refuse" at $26 in mid-2008, but it just kept fading to $20 in October and then $13 in November. Do not position yourself under a falling safe and think you can catch it. You will get flattened.

Avoid Initial Public Offerings (IPOs)

Obtaining shares of an IPO is a fool's game. As an individual investor, you will never be allocated any shares in a hot new offering. Brokerage firms direct the best deals almost exclusively to their biggest-paying clients, the institutions. Only the new issues that cannot attract enough institutional interest are made available in size to individual retail clients. And those are precisely the stocks you do not need to own. A broker called me in 2007 indicating the availability of a private equity fund offering, just as that sector was hitting a brick wall amid the subprime-induced credit crunch. Funny, I did not get any Google during its IPO deal in 2004. Even if you are able to wrangle a few shares of an attractive IPO, the initial pricing is usually no bargain.

Buying shares a few days after a company becomes publicly traded is even worse than getting in on the IPO. The hype and support are at their peak. Investment banking firms ballyhoo the story before the offering. Then there is artificial propping of the price for a period after the offering, and, invariably, 30 days later the analyst comes out with a positive investment rating. After that the euphoria starts to subside. Six months after the issuance, the management lockup period expires, and they become eligible to sell their insider shares, adding an overhang pressure. At this stage, gravity sets in and the shares have to sink or swim without contrived support. The bottom line is that the track record of IPOs is lackluster; they underperform the market.

Mutual Funds Are No Panacea; the Cost of Safety Is Boring Mediocrity

Avoid mutual funds. Most of them underperform the market. From 1983 to 2003, the S&P 500 return averaged 13.0% annually, well above the 10.3% average return from equity mutual funds. Mutual funds offered no safe haven in the 2008 bear market. The average loss for all domestic equity funds was 36.7% that year, according to Morningstar, similar to the stock market record. In fact, more than 60% of all mutual funds lagged the S&P 500. Large value funds were down 38%, large growth −41.5%, foreign large value −43%, and foreign large blend −44%. The sizable Legg Mason Value Trust sank 55%. It had compiled a stellar record from 1991 to 2005; then its results reversed, and it lagged the market the next three years in a row. Mutual fund investors invariably chase past performance.

The bigger the size of the fund, the more difficult it is to outperform the overall market. Some mutual funds have upfront or exit fees, all have management fees, and there are also tax considerations. Active turnover in a fund can generate material tax liabilities for the holder. The average mutual fund expense ratio is now 1.6%, in excess of the commission you pay on a stock transaction. By comparison, index funds have expense ratios of 0.2%.

Mutual funds hold stocks an average of 11 months and are therefore short-term traders. They have high portfolio turnover, 80% to 100% annually, and are necessarily aggressive due to quarterly performance measurements. They play heavy offense and little defense. Individuals can act differently and avoid such speculative behavior. Funds tend to rent a stock; you can own a stock. Manage your own personal mutual fund of five to ten stocks. This number will give you enough concentration in individual securities that each holding can make a meaningful impact. At the same time, you avoid having all your eggs in one basket. And it provides the exhilaration of putting your own stamp on your own portfolio. Unlike big-time mutual fund portfolio managers who are burdened with constraints, individuals who manage their own portfolio have the potential to outperform the market.

My reservations about mutual funds are in concert with Louis Lowenstein in his book *How Mutual Funds Are Betraying Your Trust.* Fund managers are heavily compensated based on the amount of assets in their fund. For the most part managers are paid regardless of the fund performance in any given year. Many funds pay the 600,000 retail brokers at U.S. investment houses to promote their particular mutual funds. It is all about marketing. Almost 90% of the money that flows into mutual funds stems from brokerage firms. Investors are not getting objective advice from their broker on which mutual fund to invest in. Lowenstein points to the brokerage Edward Jones, which collected $172 million in fees in 2005 from seven preferred mutual fund groups.

Mutual funds are okay if you choose to completely outsource your investments, but if you were planning to do that you probably would not be reading this book. Sure, balance, a wide assortment of securities, and professional management at mutual funds all lend a measure of protection. But mutual fund investors were stunned in 2008 when they saw their 401(k) assets drop by 30% to 40%. (These retirement funds took on a new identity after that: "201(k)'s.") Most investors would do no worse on their own. The price of this supposed safety is boring mediocrity. If you just want to be a stock market participant, go with index funds or ETFs that track precisely a given stock market or industry sector and charge minimal fees.

Disregard Brokerage Recommended or Emphasis Lists

These "preferred stock recommendation" lists published by most brokerage firms state the obvious. As discussed in Chapter 1, "Decoding Wall Street's Well-Kept Secrets," they perform no differently than all the other Buy recommendations at that investment bank. The names are already in favor, and the stocks are up in price and no longer represent a good value. They are broadly held and well discovered. It is too late. As described earlier, brokerage approval committees are like lemmings. If the stock is depressed and has lagged, it will not be added to the list because it appears wimpy on the charts. If it is a good story and the share price has shown nice progress, it is easy for them to shove it onto their best idea index. To an individual investor, the stocks on these lists should continue to be held if already owned, but they are certainly not original, insightful new investment proposals. After a stock is on the list, there is only one way to go—and that is eventually off the list, often on a whim, which propels the stock price lower.

Pragmatic Investing Practices and Techniques

After you have a grasp of overall investment strategies, there are some pragmatic investing practices that I recommend. These are the mechanics that should help optimize results and prevent emotional reactions that can cause an investor to make the wrong transaction decision. Think of it like football. After a winning game plan has been established, each individual play must be executed. It is important to have good technique.

Do Not Be in Denial; Move On

When a stock holding has cratered and the prospects for the company have turned bleak, do not get trapped in a state of denial. Take the loss and move on. Holding on despite continuing price erosion just compounds the first mistake. Investors sometimes hold the naive attitude, "I can't afford such a big loss. I'll just hold on to it." Bad move. Your investment capital can always be better engaged in a more promising stock.

When You've Decided, Take Action

After researching, analyzing, and considering, and finally determining an investment choice, pull the trigger. Do not sit around and hesitate. Make the move. And do not quibble over pennies per share in price. Limit orders are appropriate when the stock is not actively traded. But do not try to low-ball a purchase price or be too greedy on a sell. Implementation is more critical on the sale. Do not try to be too cute and waste time on the exit. Your order might not get completed. Trust your conclusion. Have confidence in your decision. There is nothing more exasperating than making the correct investment decision and not benefiting because you have procrastinated or messed up the simple process of concluding the transaction.

Flag Your Purchase Date; Focus on the One-Year Mark

Note the date when a stock investment passes the one-year holding period, which is when the reduced 15% federal long-term capital gains tax rate kicks in. After a stock has been owned for a year, it is easier to take a long-term view and ascertain whether your original investment thesis is proving to be correct. Early in my career, I was embarrassed a few times when I—stupidly—pulled the trigger on a sale a mere week or two before the holding period went long-term; that is, just before the one-year mark. I should never have sacrificed the bargain 15% tax rate. The corollary to this advice is to avoid allowing tax considerations to overrule or heavily influence basic investment decisions. Your objective should be sound long-term investing, not juggling year-end tax liabilities. The amount sacrificed in making the wrong investment call dwarfs the pittance of savings in taxes. Sure, sometimes it might be worth waiting a week or two to gain a tax advantage, if the circumstances allow. But usually it is a risky maneuver. When you've decided, take action.

Short-Term Trading Positions Should Be Contracted

Once in a while, there might be a rare short-term trading opportunity, say when a stock has plummeted on an overreaction to negative news and a "dead cat bounce" or rebound is expected, or when favorable news seems imminent or you anticipate a forthcoming negative event. If it is a *trade,* stick to the short-term plan, and eliminate the position within a limited time frame regardless of whether the idea was a winner or a nonevent. Do not let the stock sit around and clutter up your portfolio with only a modest gain. If it is a trading position, do not be pacified or lulled beyond a short couple months' span.

Avoid Selling the Day of a Dramatic Downgrade

Most of the damage to a stock has already has been done within an hour or so after a summary drop in an investment opinion is issued by a brokerage analyst. Do not get caught up in the emotional rush to the door. There is invariably a bounce back the next day, or within a week or so. Hold your fire for a better selling opportunity after the dust settles. And you probably should not sell anyway. Do not do what Wall Street says. The same goes for a striking opinion upgrade. Wait a day or two for the excitement to abate and the stock to back off. And this holds true for stocks that are added to or deleted from brokerage recommended lists. Delay any transaction until the initial commotion wanes.

Do Not Buy or Sell in Reaction to Press Articles or Media Information

By the time information appears in newspapers, magazines, on TV, or anywhere in the general media, it has already impacted the stock price. The story probably raced around Wall Street the day before or even weeks prior. The tendency of the investor when such a piece appears is to be too emotional, irrational, and reactive. Wait a couple of days for things to settle down. Make a more dispassionate decision after you have had time to look at all the factors. There is an old saw about investing that bears repeating: "Buy on rumor, sell on news." I mention it because most individual investors do the opposite. They buy on news. Press stories should be used to gain in-depth background information and a more thorough understanding of a company and its prospects. The media can give you insight on sectors, trends, markets, areas, and long-term stock investment ideas that might be good food for thought, but stories that appear on stocks are already common knowledge to most Wall Street insiders.

It is good to be aware of what others are thinking—for example, that a company might go bankrupt or that new bookings are slipping in a certain industry. Brilliant investors weave a web of information, a quilt-work that might lead to an investment insight. Just do not think you have happened upon unique, early insight stemming from any particular story in the media. Do not think it is actionable. When the story is on a magazine cover, it has been analyzed and researched by the author for a while. It is not news. A *Financial Analysts Journal* study by professors Arnot, Earl Jr., and North at the University of Richmond showed that favorable cover articles occurred after a period of positive results, and that the opposite was true for negative cover stories. In fact, when these cover stories were published, the news was about to reverse, according to the findings. Even *Barron's,* a publication that I devour each week, must be utilized properly. It is hardly infallible. After four years of having the stocks it highlighted in positive stories outpace the market, the 122 companies that it favorably discussed in 2007 declined in price by an average 2.3%. Two-thirds of those underperformed the S&P 500. In 2008, the 108 stocks it featured in favorable stories swooned 29%.

Pay Attention to Contrary Evidence

After you have made an investment commitment, there is a tendency to pay special attention to favorable support that bolsters your decision. Human nature pushes you to disregard any contrary, negative input that could prove you wrong. The trap is to fall in love with your viewpoint, always seeking evidence to fortify your position. Investors must be brutally objective, skeptical, and questioning. Even if you are correct initially, things change over time and circumstances might necessitate rethinking the original stance at some juncture. Keep an open mind. Constantly probe for negative developments. John Bogle, founder of The Vanguard Group and a brilliant investor, suggests, "Instead of looking for corroboration of our views and ideas, as we tend to do, we should be looking for the opposite—the observation that would prove us wrong." Be wary by nature. Similarly, if you have avoided a stock because of a gloomy view, there might be a point where it is appropriate to take a more positive attitude.

Periodically Clean Up Your Portfolio and Rethink Your Strategy

The best occasions to review your investments are at year-end or during vacations. Disciplined reassessment and review is especially critical in December to make year-end investment changes that have tax implications. Rethink your overall strategy or themes and shake off any emotional paralysis that has locked you into certain stock positions. A market analyst I respect, Ray DeVoe, Jr., terms this "liberation from the prison of past decisions." Some stocks might have attained too heavy a weighting for your peace of mind. However, I disagree with most "experts" who advise periodic rebalancing by trimming back oversized positions. The biggest winners, which become the outsize positions in your portfolio, are probably the last thing you should contemplate selling. Hold a higher weighting in your best investments rather than just a normal position. If you believe that the prospect remains favorable for one of your most sizable stock positions, buy more, if anything, rather than cutting it back.

Other stocks you own might have lagged for so long that it is time to give up. What is your comfort level with each individual stock in your portfolio? Maybe your theme is stale. Are there newly emerging trends to begin investing in? There are tax considerations when taking gains; maybe there are losers to be used as an offset. A reluctance to sell stocks that have not worked out—that is, to admit past mistakes—is normal. But by not selling your losers and moving on, you commit another mistake. Accept your failures, step up to the plate, and dump your junk so that you can start afresh. It hurts only for a bit, and then you feel liberated.

A relaxing change of venue, such as a beach resort, where you are not inundated by everyday distractions, is a perfect place to ponder your holdings. Take your monthly brokerage statement and mull it over at the pool with your piña colada. Do this a couple of times a year. The more rum punches, the better my investment strategies...well, kind of. One footnote here: If you have been away and out of touch with the stock market, financial news, and price changes in your holdings, do not pull the trigger on any portfolio transactions on your first day back. First get up to speed and familiarize yourself with the investment news you missed.

Be Alert to the January Effect

Yes, investors, there is a January effect. That is, as January goes, so goes the whole year. There does not seem to be any logical or broadly accepted reason. So do not try to analyze it. As found by professors Cooper, McConnell, and Outchinnikov and laid out in the *CFA Digest*, if the market is up in January, the average gain is 14.8% over the remaining 11 months. When the stock market drops in the first month of the year, the average return for the year, as tracked by CXO Advisory Group from 1940 to 2006, is about break-even. S&P claims that in 60 of the past 80 years, January has given an accurate prognosis of the market direction for the entire year. To take it to an extreme, the market trend in the first week of January is a telling indicator of the direction for the whole month. Watch January closely for clues to the year ahead.

Exchange Ideas with Informed Associates

Seek out like-minded investors, not traders, who have a degree of investment maturity, experience, and knowledge. Exchange opinions and views with these associates about the market, industry trends, investment ideas, and other stock-related insight. Do not accept their commentary blindly, though; use it as a source to further investigate and research. Ponder the information, the qualifications and reliability of the purveyor, and any vested interest of the proponent. Take advantage of your professional contacts, such as a friend of a friend who is a member of management. Get ideas from golfing partners and old high-school buddies. But always balance such input. The best fertilization comes from ongoing relationships in which there is consistent contact, not one-shot run-ins.

Beware of Amateurs Recommending Their Stocks; They Love Reinforcement

You will rarely get an objective stock idea from friends or acquaintances who are rank amateur investors. Friends can be a highly subjective research source, so be skeptical. They are in love with the stocks they own and are partial. If you take their recommendations, it reinforces their picks, makes them feel better, and gives them a sense of power or influence. This is dangerous. It is personal. They feel their portfolio selections are justified when others play copycat. Always research any ideas before acting.

Read The Wall Street Journal, *Be Aware, and Stay Abreast of Trends*

Peruse *The Wall Street Journal* or *The Financial Times, The New York Times* business section, *Barron's, Forbes, Fortune,* and other such financial publications for background knowledge. Keep up with current investment strategies, changes and shifts, sector trends and ideas, and the bigger picture. TV investment programs, such as Bloomberg, CNBC, or Lou Dobbs, are good for gaining perspective on equities, bonds, real estate, treasuries, commodities, options, annuities, and all types of investments. The same goes for a plethora of Internet sites. But do not get too bogged down in details or specific investment recommendations.

Do Not Put Too Much Weight on Quarterly Earnings Press Releases

When a company's quarterly earnings appear on the newswire, do not expect to learn much. Quarterly reports are of relatively little value, mostly puff pieces or watered-down commentary. The numbers are far from the real truth of what is occurring in the business. Reported results are superficial. Street analysts figure out the real meaning within a few minutes; they hop on their firms' squawk boxes, and the substance of the report is immediately reflected in the stock price. Interpret the results by looking at the stock price. Do not feel you must instantly jump on the press release. Scan it leisurely later. To ascertain a more complete picture of a company's quarter and its current outlook, tune in on the conference call.

Listen to Corporate Quarterly Earnings Conference Calls

Conference calls are publicized ahead of time on the company's website and can be dialed into; or the Webcast can be viewed via the Internet. The replay is usually available for a few days or even up to a month after the live broadcast. Pay attention to the management tone; discern whether they sound trustworthy. Become familiar with the business operations. Are the executives humble, focused, detailed, and objective? Or are they are full of hype and BS? Are the Wall Street analysts' questions negatively couched or neutral? This is as close to an inside look as you will ever get. It is a fabulous one-hour investment of time. After you've listened to a few of these, you will get a sense of whether the executives make you uneasy. It is far better than reading boring, unoriginal, tedious research reports and filings. It is the difference between reading a biography and sitting down to chat in-depth with the actual person. Conference calls are examined further in Chapter 7, "How Street Analysts Really Operate."

Avoid Investing Ahead of Executive Briefings and Analyst Meetings

Annual all-day analyst meetings at headquarters or major New York briefing sessions for Street analysts invariably propel the stock price downward that day or the next morning. Even if the news is positive, most likely the shares have already run up in anticipation of favorable management comments. It is the same situation when executives do a roadshow and meet with several institutions one-on-one. The stock climbs weeks before such events and then begins to wane almost from the start of the first meeting. There is rarely anything stunningly favorable announced at these sessions to drive the share price materially higher. Instead, there usually is a letdown, nothing that bullish, no occasion to raise earnings estimates or growth prospects, rarely enough to top the already upbeat expectation. Sometimes new negative elements or surprisingly cautious remarks surface and create a downdraft in the shares. Do not purchase a stock just before a meeting with the anticipation that it might be a positive catalyst. In most cases it has the opposite effect.

Use Stop-Loss Orders Judiciously to Protect Big Gains

Sharp stock price appreciation in one of your holdings, especially in a brief 6- to 12-month interval, is valuable. Your temptation will be to safeguard the profit. But investments also need to be long-term, leaving room for fluctuation. If you utilize a stop-loss order after achieving a hefty gain, hopefully long-term, leave ample room on the downside, perhaps 30% below the current price. A stock that moves quickly from $15 to $50 can be protected with a stop-loss at $35. Never give up a huge profit, as so many of the naive amateur "investors" did after the 1990s bubble burst and again in the 2008 bear market. Gigantic losses must be prevented. But use stop-loss orders sparingly.

Establish your own mental stop-loss levels to keep control. Have two selling price levels in mind to prevent major losses. The first trigger price should represent a 20% loss, and the fail-safe protection mechanism to eliminate a disaster is a point that is 30% to 35% down from the purchase level. If your holding plunges by 20% to 30% or more, something was amiss—the timing, the market, maybe even the company's fundamentals. Take the loss, analyze what went wrong, and start anew. Some of my best transactions have been of this nature—losers for sure—but I evaded a calamity.

Hedge Fund Positions Are a Source of Credible Investment Ideas

You will occasionally come across, in the media, the names of stocks held by a hedge fund. You know that these are credible names because the hedge fund managers have a direct personal stake. The partners are paid directly based on annual portfolio appreciation. Their bottom line is stock performance, so there are no conflicting influences or biases as in brokerage firms. In contrast, mutual fund managers are often rewarded based on the asset size of their fund or capital inflow to their funds. And mutual fund performance is evaluated on a basis relative to market and sector indexes. Hedge funds make money only if their portfolios rise in value on an absolute basis. So the partners' personal compensation is on the line. Their stock selections are impartial. Yes, hedge funds often attempt to manipulate the stocks after a position is established—a hidden agenda to promote their long positions—but they are true to their objectives.

Incidental Professional Stock Recommendations Are Problematic

If you run into a Street insider on an airplane or at a social function, be wary of any stock ideas you might obtain. The same goes for company executives or other professionals who have some insight given their industry position. You are certainly not the first person who was apprised of this investment scoop. Their recommendation might be a valid investment suggestion currently, but it can go stale in the future as situations change. Such an acquaintance is probably not going to be there to advise you in the future. If their opinion reverses, or the scenario alters materially a year from now, you might never hear about it until it is too late. Even if you attempt to stay abreast of the story because you own the stock, you will not have the insight your contact had. Individuals can benefit from a stellar idea from a professional initially, but they end up losing money later if the stock collapses when the outlook reverses. The investor almost never is in a position to receive a timely heads-up on the downside.

Technology Stocks Are a Huge Risk and a Maturing Industry

Most investors view high-tech stocks as exciting, high-growth, wave-of-the-future names where they might hit the jackpot. Images of Intel, Microsoft, Cisco, Amazon.com, and Google dance in their imaginations. Be supremely cautious. Tech is a maturing business. There is essentially no revenue growth at many of the established stalwarts. Smaller emerging companies are chased by institutions to excessive stock price levels. Product demand can shift quickly; quarterly order rate bookings can disappoint in a heartbeat. It is impossible to predict what will happen all the time. Fad stocks boom and bust in a hurry—electric cars, solar energy, cell phones, handheld devices. Competition in these sectors is ferocious. Disruptive leapfrog developments undercut existing products and businesses. Markets get penetrated fast. There is ease of entry given all the venture capital money that was tossed at the industry, amid a dizzying amount of new venture investment pools formed over the past few decades.

Technology stock prices move up on product cycle factors, on positive earnings surprises, and during autumn—when hope for the new year surfaces. But these are fleeting. The sector is over-covered by Wall Street analysts, and their opinions keep shifting, adding to volatility. The stocks are almost always overpriced. My friend Ray DeVoe says it best: "Technology companies make lousy growth stocks...you pay a high price for excitement and entertainment." If you owned any of the major high-tech names in the Dow Jones Average from the market peak in 2000 to the end of 2008, you know what

I mean. They were some of the worst performers among the 30 stocks, declining as much as 80% (Intel) over that span. Vaunted Microsoft slumped by 63%. High-tech seems so enticing, scintillating; it is the avatar of the past few decades, as railroads were in the 1800s and automobiles were in the first half of the 20th century. But tech might be closer to the end of its era than the beginning. These stocks should be viewed as short-term trading vehicles.

Give Stock to Your Kids

The lessons to be learned by children in owning stocks are priceless. When my kids owned stocks and achieved some gains, they immediately became capitalists. It does not take kids long before they start asking questions about which stocks to own, the reality of gains and losses, dividends, investing, business, and capital accumulation or savings. Youngsters can glean financial training for life when they actually feel the gravity of owning stocks. I let mine help choose the theme and even make mistakes in picking stocks. My son loved model trains and real railroads, so I bought him a few shares of Union Pacific. The education far outweighed any losses. I gave them my alternatives or suggestions but allowed a wide berth for them to make the call. It is even fun to have a competition: my stocks versus theirs. I once talked to my daughter's fifth-grade class about stocks by giving them the annual reports of The Gap and The Limited. My kids are long since out of college, but we still do this investing thing My daughter is a zingy, liberal, creative screenwriter and now restaurant chef, but she still loves capital gains.

These guidelines are directives based on my observations from over 32 years on the Street and more than 45 years of stock market investing. Tailor my investment principles and procedures to suit your personal profile: your age, work status, financial position, investment objectives, risk tolerance, and temperament. Your blueprint might not be the same as mine, depending on your own circumstances. But you need to establish a direction and some order in your investing process. I find that most investors tend to flounder haphazardly, buffeted around by the Street like a boat adrift. What is missing is a good discipline. My recommended principles, strategies, and practices will provide this necessary investment regimen.

4

Investment Strategies to Survive in a Bear Market

Wall Street is not going to tell you it is a bear market, even if the indexes have fallen by 20% or 50% from the high, as in 2008 and again in 2009, the most severe market nosedives since 1931. It is a serious bear market when stocks have dropped by 25% over a six- to nine-month period. Brokerage firms want to keep investors in the stock market. Preserving your capital is not their concern. Like the media, the Street wants your attention day-to-day, so it will sugarcoat the situation, and keep coming up with new stock recommendations to keep you involved. Be wary of the Street's eternal optimism. This chapter will make suggestions for weathering a severe market falloff.

Read a book on the history of bear markets and the Great Depression to get a frame of reference. Most investors are not familiar with bear markets, so they remain in a state of denial far too long. The critical consideration is what you believe is in store for a stock going forward. Bear markets in midstream can still drag your stock holdings lower by at least another 15% to 30%. Do not hang around for the entire blood bath. Stand aside and take another look in about a year.

At first the damage to your investment portfolio in a bear market might seem as devastating as a sports injury, a divorce, flunking out of college, or losing your job. But the potential exists to overcome the setback and still flourish in the future. The huge 401(k), IRA, and retirement pension fund losses in 2008 will necessitate changes in long-term retirement planning and lifestyles. For most investors this is an unfortunate result of poor risk management in the face of a major bear market. You should be ready to draw a line in the sand, when your financial pain is material, perhaps after losing 20% to 25% in your investments. Get into an investment-survival mode during a bear market to ensure investing capacity in more stable periods.

Take a stand and react to a bear market before it is too late so that your investment portfolio will not be damaged irretrievably. This includes reducing stock holdings and giving up some dividend income. It might be advantageous to lower your living expenses for a while to help preserve investment capital. My wife's Uncle Max is a terrific illustration of how an individual investor should react in a bear market. He is retired and not dependent on portfolio income for living expenses. His stocks melted down through the summer of 2008, but he became convinced of the severity of the market malaise when it dropped more than 500 points one day in mid-September. He sold his entire portfolio and went into cash. Max protected his capital from the subsequent 31% stock market descent two months later. He went skiing in Deer Valley this year with a certain sense of serenity.

A Bear Market Is a Contraction of At Least 20%

Most investors define bear markets by a falloff in the stock market averages of at least 20%. There have been 11 such market drops since 1945—the average drop being 37% over a year-and-a-half period. The worst of these was the 1973–1974 plunge of 48% that lasted for almost two years. At the nadir of a bear market, the list of stocks hitting 52-week lows is lengthy, while zero stocks are hitting their highs. There have been four bear markets since 1973, and in each occurrence, as *Barron's* observes, the S&P 500 index fell another 9% to 35%, after the initial 20% drop. Rallies of more than 5% occur frequently during bear markets. There were a dozen of these upswings during the 2000–2002 downdraft.

Bear markets can be deceptive, behaving in a manner that disguises the downward drift. Each time a precipitous drop occurs, it is followed by a modest recovery. It is two steps down and one step up—giving a sense of hope and keeping you confused. Interim recoveries of sometimes up to 20%, such as the one that occurred from November 2008 to early January 2009, tend to entice investors and distract them from taking the proper capital-preservation defensive measures. I wish I had been familiar with this aspect of bear markets in 1971 when I first arrived on Wall Street. The first stock I owned was Ramada Inns, 100 shares purchased for $35 a share. At the end of the 1973–1974 market collapse, the stock was trading at $5 a share, even though the company was still in business. It was a bear market lesson—stocks go lower and stay there longer than you expect. Typically, investors are later paranoid about owning stocks that led the prior bull market. Earlier this decade there was an anathema regarding Internet and technology stocks, damaged badly during 2000–2002. This time it might be financials that were crushed in 2007–2009.

Long-Term Bear Markets Can Last Decades

Take a look at the history of long-term bear markets to gain a sense of where the stock market might be currently. From September 1929 to April 1942, the Dow Jones dropped by an average of over 10% annually. At the end of the 12 and a half year span, it was off 72% in total. From just 1937 to 1942, stocks dropped by 60%. Amid the 1930s market contraction, there were interim rallies of 20% to 30%, but they were not sustained. The Dow Jones did not regain the peak of September 1929 until late 1954, more than 25 years later. The Great Depression presumably represents the extreme case of bear markets, but the 2008–2009 economic debacle was the worst the stock market has seen in any period since that time.

The next secular bear period lasted from early 1966 to mid-1982. It was a long malaise, with the annual decline averaging 1.5%. Long bear markets are grinding and lead investors to despair. The gloom is widespread. Prognosticators, the media, the general consensus all become universally cautious. At the bottom of the bear market in 1982, *BusinessWeek* ran a cover story on "The Death of Equities." I started my job on Wall Street during these years and remember the various interim two-year drops ranging from 27% to 48% interspersed with upsurges that fooled investors into thinking the bear market was over. Those years produced deep recessions, massive inflation, high oil prices, countless brokerage firm failures, a home price dive, government stimulus packages.... Does any of this sound familiar?

One can make the argument that the 2008 bear market actually commenced in 2000. The S&P 500 reached 1527 in March 2000 and plummeted 50% during the ensuing two years (a bear market within the longer-term bear market). The subsequent five-year "bull market," which gained back the entire previous drop, should be put in the context of the nine-year span, during which the S&P 500 had capitulated by more than 40% overall by early 2009. Entering 2009, the stock market was equal to where it was in mid-1997. There has been a lost decade. Investors purchasing stocks from 1997 to 2000 or from 2003 to 2007 are well underwater. The last mega bull market ran 18 years, 1982–2000, despite a brief 101-day 34.5% bear market disruption (which included a 22.5% dive on Black Monday, October 19, 1987). So mega bear markets can endure for a decade or two. The current secular market down-draft hits its nine-year anniversary in spring 2009 and could conceivably continue several more years. Investors must think long-term and realize that the stock market moves in decade-long cycles. Even the shorter bull and bear markets, within these longer cycles, last for years, not months.

The Macroeconomic Picture Is a Key Influence on the Market

Stock movement is usually a good indicator of the outlook for economic and corporate profit. The market reacts to telling indicators and key influences on earnings such as consumer spending, capital spending, credit availability, interest rates, and inflation. This is why the stock market starts rising six months ahead of an economic upturn. Stock price valuation, that is, PE multiples, is another major variable affected by a number of economic factors—consumer confidence, interest rates, GDP growth, to name a few. Market PE multiples shrink during a bear market, sometimes to as low as 10x, from the long-term norm of 16x.

Bear markets are stoked by uncertainty. In 2008–2009, consumer spending was falling while savings rates moved higher. Credit contraction, home prices, excessive federal government borrowing, and unemployment are difficult trends to forecast. It is unknown how fast, how far, and how long these trends will endure. The depth and duration of the recession that commenced in 2008 is indefinite, causing doubt and skepticism. When the prospect for the economy is dire and is expected to translate into drastically lower corporate earnings, diminished cash flow, and curtailed dividends, the overall stock market moves lower in anticipation.

The scariest aspect of the 2008–2009 scenario was that no one really knows the extent or duration of the financial and economic devastation. This is typical of major bear markets. Jeremy Grantham, chairman of GMO, said in *Barron's:* "I hope that someone else gets it, because I don't. And I have no idea, really, how this will work out. All I can conclude, by instinct and by reading the history books, is that it will be longer, harder and more complicated than we expect." He is one of the few professionals who are telling the truth.

In 2008–2009, the economic crisis revolved around debt. An outsize leverage pyramid was created by the banks and investment firms with debt instruments such as collateralized debt obligations (CDOs), home mortgages, consumer credit card debt, and corporate debt. Brokerage firms in the 1970s were not allowed to have more than 10:1 debt-to-equity ratios. By early this decade investment banks were leveraged out more than 30:1. Fannie Mae at the time it was taken over by the federal government was leveraged at close to 50:1. No wonder that after the crash began, Fannie Mae and other firms such as Bear Stearns, Lehman Brothers, and even Merrill Lynch could not recover. The only two major survivors, Morgan Stanley and Goldman Sachs, converted into regulated banks.

De-leveraging is a necessary readjustment that puts a damper on the economy and corporate profits. This process is proving to be painful for companies and consumers. A vast portion of the prosperity of the 1990s and continuing all the way until late 2007 was achieved with financial engineering between financial and investment institutions, and by consumer spending of home equity, credit-card bingeing, corporate-share repurchases, and private equity corporate takeovers utilizing debt. Such actions were enabled by the credit bubble. In mid-2005, condominiums and houses were being traded by consumers like Internet stocks were in the late 1990s. The contraction phase of most bubbles is normally a function of the prior period of inflation. The de-leveraging process that commenced in 2008–2009 might prove to be a damper for years.

Bear markets are often started by a burst bubble. The Roaring '20s was a legendary era of euphoria. That bubble popped in the historic October 1929 crash. Japan experienced its bubble in the 1980s, as stock PE multiples topped well above 100x. The land underneath the Imperial Palace in downtown Tokyo was valued higher than all the real estate in California. The Nikkei average reached almost 39,000. That bubble burst in the 1990s and Japanese stocks dropped almost 80%.

In the past decade, there were multiple bubbles around the world—technology and Internet stocks, the Chinese and emerging markets, debt leverage, consumer spending, home prices, oil, and commodities—the list goes on. The bursting has led to stunning financial institution failures, rising unemployment, plummeting corporate profits, millions of home foreclosures, and a gargantuan federal bailout with drastic economic stimulus measures. Commercial real estate and credit card debt were bubbles notably deflating in 2009. Trust may have been the ultimate bubble that burst—trust in Wall Street, financial institutions, corporate executives, and government. Bubbles that burst stay burst for a long time. Efforts to reinflate them are usually futile. The magnitude of federal financial assistance is leading to deficits in the $1 to $2 trillion range. And this is creating additional concerns about inflation, a weakening dollar, and other unforeseen consequences.

Excesses necessitate difficult adjustments. When a stock goes ex-dividend—the day when it is too late to be eligible to receive an upcoming dividend—the stock price is adjusted lower by the amount of the dividend. Similarly, in broader stock market terms, the bear market that commenced in 2008 pushed stock prices lower to sell ex-leverage or ex-financial engineering. Federal government actions amid bear markets are, for the most part, directed at stimulating the economy. During 2008–2009, there were questions as to whether federal actions to support the economy would set the stage for a normal recovery or cause new problems. *The Forgotten Man,* by Amity Shlaes, investigates the extent to which Roosevelt's policies in the 1930s might have exacerbated the Great Depression. Government actions can temporarily lift stock prices, but if no material economic upturn results quickly, they only add to investor frustration and drive prices down again. Amid deep bear markets, reforms and regulations directed at Wall Street are often adopted, such as prohibiting the short selling of bank stocks or fuller disclosure by hedge funds. But they certainly do not serve to boost the stock market or stimulate stock prices.

Wall Street Is Blinded by Optimism

Wall Street is even less help to you as an individual investor in a bear market than during bullish times. Investment banks are sales organizations, not investment advisory firms. Besides, as we saw in 2007–2008, their record of managing their own risk has proven to be pathetic. Brokerage-firm investment advice rings hollow and lacks credibility in light of its own risk-management record. Wall Street fortunes and the stock market are interlinked. The market never does well when investment firms are reporting red ink, mergers, extensive layoffs, and plummeting bonuses.

The poor Street performance in forecasting earnings in normal times is even less reliable during economic downturns. Analyst earnings estimates lag behind reality, and trail downward only after companies report their quarterly earnings and lower their guidance. Even amid a deep recession, estimates almost always reflect pie-eyed optimism and anticipated improvement in the next year.

Stock recommendations are similarly worse during a bear market. Sell opinions are scant, late, and of little help. Timely advice to Sell, move into cash, and preserve capital never emanates from Wall Street. Only after it was glaringly evident that Lehman Brothers was about to capitulate in September 2008, and the stock had cratered to around $7 from over $80 the prior year, did the three biggest firms on the Street finally get around to downgrading their ratings. Likewise, a couple of brokerages did not downgrade recommendations on General Motors to Sell until late 2008 when the GM stock price had already eroded from over $40 in the prior year to well down into single figures. One of these firms had a Buy rating on GM until it had withered to $24, when it shifted its rating to Hold. Citigroup moved its opinion on GM to Hold in May 2008 after the shares had fallen to under $18. It finally threw in the towel and moved to a Sell when the stock fell below $8. It was as if these firms forecast that the Titanic would sink only after observing its bow end jutting straight up into the air. Thank you very little. It did not take rocket science to see that the auto industry would tank after oil prices skyrocketed, consumer spending on discretionary items stopped, and the economy started collapsing.

During bear markets Wall Street optimists concentrate on bottom-fishing, recommending stocks that have fallen far enough to appear as good values. This is tantamount to encouraging investors to catch a falling safe, as described in the preceding chapter. A full-page ad by a leading brokerage firm, nine months into the 2008 bear market, hailed: "Our analysts are bullish on companies in…healthcare, consumer staples, and on companies creating innovative technologies in energy and agriculture." Its Chief Economist was featured in the ad saying, "The U.S. manufacturing sector is on its best competitive footing internationally in 30 years." In February 2009, 16 months into the bear market, its ad flashed: "Defensive investing does not mean staying out of the markets. Look for conservative opportunities." And it teased investors with, "The markets will see less volatility in 2009. When volatility goes down, the markets do tend to rally." Even in one of the worst bear markets since the 1930s, the Street wants investors to purchase stocks, rather than protect capital.

Historical Bear-Market Stock Valuations Give Perspective

Wall Street makes a case for buying stocks throughout bear markets. Like an automobile dealer hyping a bargain price to make an immediate sale, the Street fails to mention that the price will likely be lower in the future. Price-earnings multiples are key in valuing stocks. Put a bear market in proper perspective by looking at the long-term picture. For over a hundred years, the average ten-year PE ratio (stock prices divided by mean annual S&P 500 earnings during the prior ten years) has been 16x, as reported by David Leonhardt in *The New York Times*. In roaring bull markets, such as those of the 1920s, 1960s, and 1990s, it broke out above 20x. In late 2007, it reached 27x. Ominously, every time PEs surged above 20x there followed a sharp decline and at least a decade of subpar returns. In bear markets, such as those of the 1930s and 1970s, the average PE ranged below 10x. In 1932, the average PE swooned to 6x and in 1982 it was just 7x. The ten-year average PE was 16x at the outset of 2009. Until this long-term average PE ratio reaches the 10x level, it is a stretch to make a case that the stock market is undervalued.

Another way to assess shorter-duration bear markets is to use trailing five-year annual average S&P 500 earnings. There were four euphoric market periods during the past hundred years when this PE multiple topped 25x, most recently during 2004–2007. In six bear markets during the past century, this PE multiple fell to between 4x and 8x. In early 2009 the five-year PE multiple stood at 17x. During 2008–2009, corporate earnings eroded materially. Both the five- and the ten-year trailing corporate-earnings averages were sliding. Wall Street, in its never-ending attempt to entice you into stocks, tends to discount current depressed corporate profits and highlight potential "normalized" future earnings. Given the feckless Street earnings forecasts, be wary of such reasoning.

Investment Strategies to Survive
in a Bear Market

Initially, investors normally face a bear market by going into a state of denial. When stocks have collapsed far enough or long enough, denial is replaced with bullheadedness. Stubbornly, investors hold on to a position already underwater, thinking that if they wait long enough it will eventually recover. This is ostrich-like behavior. Think of how long the wait might be. RCA stock purchased in 1928 would have taken 40 years to reach break-even. It might take a decade or a lot longer for stocks such as Citigroup, Intel, Microsoft, and GE to reach their formerly lofty levels.

Take time off during a bear market. To preserve your capital, stand back and reduce or eliminate your exposure to stocks for a while. Take a year off from stock market investing. *You cannot be a long-term investor if you lose a major portion of your capital in the short-term.* After nine months, it is time to get real. The Street thinks in terms of days or months, certainly not in years or decades. Base your investment strategy on the long-term outlook. Pull out and wait. Saving money is the new making money. Collect some interest and maybe some secure dividends. Sleep at night. You will not miss a thing except some painful losses.

Face a bear market squarely. You cannot afford to have your holdings vastly diminished or washed out. Missing capital gains opportunities in a stock market rebound will be nowhere near as painful as heavy losses. Avoiding whopping losses is the secret of superior investing. Get beared-up, bear-market resistant, or at least bear-market retardant. Avoid all stocks if possible. Assess the downside risk of every investment in your portfolio and assume that the overall market might tank another 20% or maybe even 40%. Determine which of your stock positions are expendable and can be sold to establish a cash position. Think in terms of a pile of cash or a liquid money market fund amounting to, say, 25% to 33% of your holdings. Be aware that your brokerage firm will not invest your cash in a money market fund unless you ask it to. Brokerages prefer that your cash sit in their own bank, where you will earn virtually no interest.

Market timing critics disagree with the approach of exiting the market during bad times. They claim the bulk of stock market gains occurs in a few massive breakout sessions. I argue that the same is true for most market declines: They are usually concentrated in just a handful of trading days. Although you might miss some big up sessions or mid-bear market bounces, you will be better off in aggregate by avoiding the sharpest down days.

Take the attitude that it does not matter what your stock or investment has done up until now—it does not matter whether it is still ahead from where you purchased it or underwater. This change matters only with regard to taxes when you sell. When I recommend selling a stock that has plummeted far below the purchase price, people often retort: "I can't do that; I'll lose too much money." They think the loss is not real until they sell, that it exists only on paper. I reply, "What if it falls by another 30% over the next 12 months? Would it not be a good idea to sell now to avoid further losses?" Consider what is in store for the stock going forward. The only aspect you can control is today's investment decision. You cannot alter previous mistakes.

Do not listen to the Street. It makes no commissions if you are on the sidelines. Brokerage firms constantly try to entice you into the market by recommending that you try to catch a falling safe or "bottom-fish." It is more risky to get back in too early than to miss the first portion of the recovery. There will be ample time to wade back into a gathering bull market. Alan Abelson at *Barron's* notes, "It's the second mouse that gets the cheese."

If you're not altogether out of the market, at least eliminate growth stocks or any equity carrying a hefty PE ratio. Be sure that your stocks are dividend payers, with reliable earnings streams, and that they are value priced with modest PEs. High-yield value stocks do not crack as badly as high PE multiple growth stocks. Bonds and fixed income are always important anchors. Holding a short position or two as a hedge makes sense. A good method to address a bear market is to own an exchange traded fund that shorts the market. Given the perilous and gloomy economic times, gold, in the form of an ETF, might also be an appropriate investment.

It is never too late to be prepared. Conserve, protect, hoard. For those holdings that are genuinely long-term, dividend-paying value stocks, be prepared to suffer some pain and anxiety if you plan to ride out the bear market. You are on your own in such times. Brokers, street analysts, and the media will never help you protect your capital. In bear markets it is all about return *of* your investment, not return *on* investment. There will be ample time in the future to readjust your portfolio for a rising market. Do not lose more money during another down leg. Let the insiders, the "experts," thrash around and lose money by trading during a bear market. The government will not bail you out as it is doing for financial institutions and other megacorporations. It is all about managing risk. Stay abreast. Be realistic. And behave in a prudent manner.

5

Evaluating Companies as Investment Candidates

Evaluating companies as investment candidates should be a fairly straightforward activity. You do not have to be a rocket scientist. Be perspicacious. Get a feel for the character and profile of the corporation and its business operations. Keep your antenna tuned. Opportunities to pick up information and impressions of a company arise all the time. Start with the positives. There are several ideal corporate attributes that indicate probable future achievement: uniqueness, focus, strong leadership, healthy finances, blue-chip customers, conservative accounting, and consistency. There is no such thing as the perfect company that demonstrates all these attributes. But the more of these attributes in a company, the more likely that it will be a favorable investment. In judging the future outlook, you must also assess the negatives, the flaws and defects: Companies can overreach, create diseconomies of scale, neglect current clients, over-centralize, and attempt hopeless turnarounds. In many cases, these signs should discourage you from making an investment.

In the review process, be attentive to any opportunity to gather intelligence on a company. I remember the time I was jamming a pillow behind my back to get comfortable in a business-class seat on a

flight from Phoenix to Philadelphia when I overheard the noisy badi-
nage among several pals-ey executives pertaining to hospital and
medical system topics. I spotted the letters SMS on one of their carry-
on bags. It dawned on me that they probably worked at Shared Medical Systems, located in the suburbs of Philly. That was a stock I
covered. Following SMS was frustrating, because there was little
executive access and scant disclosures. As the chatty, collegial SMS
executive group onboard tossed down libations, I realized that they
were the top sales producers returning from the annual chairman's
club revelry. I clammed up, grabbed a piece of scrap paper, and men-
tally amplified my virtual hearing aid volume.

Over the next couple hours, I learned about that company's problem contracts, new hospital client prospects, financial constraints,
product and service issues, sales techniques being used to deceive
management, derogatory views of top executives, and other highly
intriguing revelations. I cast myself as a computer systems consultant
with barely even a passing academic interest in order to ask a few
questions. I was exceptionally familiar with the company, so I pur-
posely couched my inquiries in general, bland terms to avoid raising
any suspicions. And my note taking was undercover. Corporate executives in situations outside the office tend to have loose lips. Analysts
never miss a chance to jabber with them in these conditions, to discover what is really happening. My fortunate coincidence with SMS
added vastly to my understanding of the company.

Specialists Do It Better

The best companies have a narrow market concentration. In seeking
investment candidates, look for companies that have created their
market and retain a leading edge. If the company is the second or
third entrant in the market, be cautious unless it is the leader of a
particular, confined segment. The company should be focused on
a definable niche. Uniqueness can be in the customer base, selling
approach, manufacturing, timing to market, or some other aspect.
But you should be able to identify how it is different or special.

I love companies that are disciplined, that avoid veering off on
market tangents. Diana Shipping is a Greek firm with oceangoing

vessels transporting dry bulk commodities. When asked on its quarterly conference call why it did not do swaps of its ships and other financial transactions to enhance its results, management replied that they were a shipping company and were going to act like it. That is staying focused. When I started covering Concord EFS, it was only the fourth-largest credit card processor, but it was dominant in the emerging use of debit cards in supermarkets and gas stations. This gave it a unique edge, so it effectively gained share from the leader, First Data. The same could be said for Paychex in its payroll niche.

No matter how flourishing the market, avoid "also-rans." Look for firms that are front-runners in their space, even if it is a narrow sector. Size is not an issue—I prefer small companies—but a company must be either the biggest player in its niche or demonstrably out in front of the competition. It should display leadership or a controlling market position. If it is a broad market, then only a far-reaching company will have the most sizable share. Smaller companies can dominate minor or emerging sectors. Although Automatic Data Processing dominates the payroll-services market, Paychex is still a great company because it caters to businesses with fewer than 15 employees. So although it ranks third in size in payroll processing, it is focused on the low end of the market and has a distinct position there.

The challenge for small specialists is in transforming and evolving as they outgrow their initial niches. They often attempt to break into adjunct markets already led by other participants rather than finding more original, virgin areas to pursue. Always be alert to when a company is outgrowing its sector. It might need to broaden and thus it risks becoming less specialized. This is exactly what happened with Starbucks as it expanded to become a giant company. *The Wall Street Journal* described its predicament as follows: "In its zeal to hit an expansion target of 40,000 locations globally, the company made poor selections for new sites, distracted itself with forays into movies and music, cluttered stores with too much merchandise and lost its focus on coffee."

Companies that are tightly focused are more effective competitors than generalists. Those that broaden out into a wide-ranging market might have economic power and scale but begin to lack flexibility, so it is more difficult for them to compete against narrowly aimed firms. It is like an 18-wheeler versus a sports car—the semi has heft, but it is not as fast and agile. Affiliated Computer Services could not go head-to-head against EDS or Accenture in data-center outsourcing and consulting. So it staked out the more specialized area of business process, paper-intensive, back-office outsourcing, a different area and an original, emerging market where it could be the primary player. IBM and others have now piled into this new area, but Affiliated, as a specialist, is in the forefront. Big generalists are usually lumbering and mature. Leave them to the mediocre mutual funds. You can do better.

Look for Stability and Consistency

A company with recurring revenue can sustain its growth more predictably. It is easier to maintain a healthy growth pace if customers do not need to be replaced by new clients in the future. The computer services firms that I tracked had long-term contracts, so they could rely on guaranteed revenue in the current quarter and year ahead. Hardware and software companies have to book new business each quarter to generate revenue, making it difficult to predict revenue even one quarter ahead. By contrast, oil-pipeline companies generate revenue continuously from all their users. Sizable new business prospects, repeat orders or contracts from existing customers, new market penetration, and accelerating demand for new products or services all lend a measure of predictability. Avoid having to hold your breath each quarter, hoping a company's orders were robust enough to achieve expected earnings. Stability and clarity are important to eliminate the roller coaster volatility in earnings and growth, a nightmare for investors.

Companies that generate reasonably consistent revenue and earnings growth are usually well managed, in a healthy market, and have a stalwart competitive position. Management should take a long-term view, run the company as if it were private, sow seeds for the future, and not get caught up in the short-term quarterly reporting game. I want dependable performance but not a perfect clothesline, which would be highly suspect. There should be truthful reporting, similar to Warren Buffett's style. He says, "We won't smooth our quarterly or annual results: If earnings figures are lumpy when they reach headquarters, they will be lumpy when they reach you." It is not the absolute level of profits or the actual growth rate that is so important. Rather, it is the sustainability and dependability of the company's growth that count.

Examining the past record is important in evaluating a company's financial achievement during good and bad times. Although a certain degree of steadiness is a key measure, be suspect of perfection; it is usually faked. An impeccable straight-line earnings record suggests that inappropriate actions have overly massaged and distorted revenues and profits. It makes me nervous. Such even quarterly numbers do not reveal the real health of the business underneath the covers. Business patterns and trends are never perfectly smooth. The reality is that business is volatile. Companies have ample room to fudge, pad, or shave the numbers; to a degree this is fine, but the results should reflect true business conditions. I trust growth records that fluctuate modestly, showing modest gains of, say, around 10% in difficult periods and an expansion of over 20% in a favorable environment. Any wider variation than this means cyclicality—that is, the business has big ups and downs depending on the economy. Business is not always perfectly smooth-flowing. It varies. Reported results reflect such deviations if they are credible. Only manipulation produces perfectly smooth numbers.

Sales growth is the core engine, and without it, earnings gains cannot be maintained over a long period. I like to see a solid double-digit revenue expansion pace, but nothing too excessive that would make it a challenge for management to maintain control and pose a difficult comparison the following year. Profit margins before taxes should also be double digits—high enough to reveal robust profitability but not so lofty as to be maxed out and unsustainable. Gradually rising margins are the ideal, adding operating leverage to obtain even faster earnings improvement. The tax rate should be full, over 30%. Any advance in profits that results from reduced taxes is superficial. The income statement needs to be clean, void of special gains, such as recent write-down reserves being flowed back through or other non-operational contributions.

Operating cash flow is similarly critical. This is net income plus depreciation/amortization minus capital expenditures and dividends. The level should be positive. Review the other less-important line items in the cash flow statement if they are material. Healthy companies should be generating cash. They cannot be outgrowing their internal financing capability. Income statements and cash flow accounting should be straightforward and conservative.

Earnings Quality and Conservative Accounting Are Paramount

Talk about a controversial topic these days: Accounting treatment has been the culprit behind countless corporate debacles during the past few years. If financial statements have too many footnotes, your antenna should rise. Pro forma earnings demand extreme scrutiny. Income statements with too many "exceptional" items, subject to pro forma adjustment, are suspect. Inspect footnotes for commitments and contingencies. Earnings should be pure with no so-called one-time factors. Look at operating earnings to understand what is really occurring. Is the company disclosing a far higher level of profits in its shareholder statements than it is reporting to the IRS for taxes? Despite the now more restrictive guidelines, there is still room for a measure of upfront revenue recognition and underrecording of current costs. Contracts can be booked in varying manners. Be sure revenue is being recognized conservatively. Percentage-of-completion accounting is hairy and wide open to abuse. Some companies try to portray steadier progress by deferring revenue, recording unbilled revenue, and using flaky receivable terms.

Big upfront reserves, established when an acquisition is being made, sometimes give companies a slush fund with which to manage future earnings. Off-balance sheet financing is a handy way to hide true indebtedness or liability levels. Read the footnotes here, too; add the debt back in. Examine the fine print for accounting mischief—inventory valuation, pension-fund accounting, deferred taxes, and reserves. The issuance of options, in reality a future liability, also gives me pause. Use of options should be modest. They can dilute the future earnings stream. If you see any of this stuff, deeper probing is mandatory.

Misleading pro forma, adjusted smoothing of earnings results, is the key manner in which corporate executives alter reality. Adjusted, normalized, reconfigured, or perfunctory earnings give me pause. Pro forma is great fiction in a perfect world. It is the way management delivers expected results for investors despite innumerable crosscurrents and setbacks. Any train-wrecked company can show beautiful numbers with misleading pro forma earnings. One-time hits and write-offs have become so commonplace that they need to be factored into PE multiples and stock-price valuations. Despite the current requirement to report GAAP earnings, most companies are also emphasizing the window-dressed, suspect pro forma number to virtually eliminate evidence of negative (sometimes even positive) impacts. Earnings restatements are also a red flag. They are a way of rewriting history and carry accounting implications. In 2005, there were around 1,200 such restatements.

The Google IPO offering statement indicated its intention to reflect current reality in its interim earnings reports, which was a refreshingly honest approach. Google's IPO Owner's Manual for potential IPO investors claimed that "outside pressures too often tempt companies to sacrifice long-term opportunities to meet quarterly expectations. Sometimes this pressure has caused companies to manipulate financial results in order to 'make their quarter.'" It went on to say, "We are not able to predict our business within a narrow range for each quarter. A management team distracted by a series of short-term targets is as pointless as a dieter stepping on a scale every half hour."

Google does not give earnings forecast guidance. The company's strategy is to continue concentrating on the long term even if this focus has short-term financial impacts. Google's founders stated in the prospectus that they "would remain risk takers, willing to place bets that had only a 10% chance of earning a billion dollars over a long period of time." The bottom line is that Google was trying to avoid the insane, artificial ironing out of all the legitimate, normal kinks in quarterly results that most companies manipulate to pretend perfection.

Executives play down the negatives and accentuate the more upbeat factors with many other subtle techniques. Explanations of key financial items are usually buried in latent filings. Such detail is normally disclosed in lengthy, boring, belated SEC 10-Q and 10-K reports published sometimes a month or two after the reporting date.

The negative results are lost and forgotten by that time. Simple, balanced, truthful elucidation of important financial items on the balance sheet and cash flow statements are rarely placed in earnings releases, to the detriment of investor understanding. Such clarifications should be required especially of numbers that have altered materially since the preceding reporting period. I once covered a company whose financials became increasingly skewed. The extent of the damage and the true cause—a massive contract that was out of control, running awry—was not fully revealed for a couple years. It was material. It should have been disclosed on a timely basis.

A Healthy, Solid Balance Sheet Is a Must

A balance sheet should demonstrate both strength and the flexibility to finance future activities. There should be nothing flaky or out of whack. Start by looking at cash; a hefty level is key. Then observe debt—preferably there is none, but at most, debt should not total more than 20% of capitalization. This is the debt-to-capitalization ratio, debt as measured against the total of debt and stockholders' equity. As much as 50% might be acceptable, depending on the type of business. Servicing too much debt with burdensome interest payments puts pressure on earnings. Accounts receivable should be under tight control, 60 to 90 days sales outstanding at a maximum, and they should not be on the rise in recent periods. Inventory levels should be under similar control. Next scan for unusual items that could be warning flags, such as unbilled revenue, deferred costs, bulky accounts payable, and different classes of common stock. If any of these factors exists, they must be thoroughly assessed and clearly understood.

Pay Attention to the Dark Side

Assuming that a company shows stable and consistent growth and clean finances, you also need to assess the dark side, which is usually more obscure, more subtle. Positive attributes are easier to identify because corporate executives and their steroid-driven marketing and PR departments work overtime to publicize the positives. And favorably biased Wall Street research also constantly emphasizes the upbeat aspects. Having reviewed hundreds of companies, I have observed that certain corporate defects crop up repeatedly, decade after decade, as companies come and go. When these faults pop up in my appraisal process, they make me guarded. They are usually not obvious, and management always cloaks them in a favorable light, rendering them more benign on the surface. Investors should be wary of companies displaying such imperfections.

Generalists Do It Worse

This is the corollary to "specialists do it better." In this era of specialization, narrow focus, and niches, companies lose an advantage as they expand and broaden their product line, services, and market. Size often leads to being a generalist, which renders a company susceptible to emerging niche players grabbing market share and exploiting new areas. Generalist giants fight a defensive battle, protecting their established market and client base. They are fearful of destroying the existing product or service, and rendering it obsolete, so they become stodgy, setting themselves up to be toppled as markets and technologies change. They become boring. They lose their cutting edge, and their creative, risk-taking personnel depart. They can hang on for a long time, giving the appearance of dominant leadership stability, but single-concentration competitors will eventually push the generalist into oblivion. Specialists lead new market waves. Almost all new markets and developments are pioneered by up-and-coming firms aimed in a single direction. Eventually, these winners also get oversized, become generalists, and lose out in the next major market-inflection point. If a long explanation is necessary to describe a firm's business, it is a generalist. Assume that its prospects are lackluster.

My experience in covering the technology industry for over three decades is that when firms become huge, they stagnate, begin making decisions by committee, become inhibited by consensus, lose touch, and constantly plan or strategize rather than execute and act. They just run out of steam. It is difficult to attract creative, excited employees to a massive bureaucracy. Good workers leave and only the laggards hang around. Such supertankers take too long to turn in new directions, are usually late in shifting with markets, and are easy targets.

Bigness connotes dinosaurs (unless the company is narrowly focused), with only a few exceptions such as General Electric and Wal-Mart. But even GE can grow only at the rate of the economy. General Motors stood still as Toyota blew by it like Hurricane Katrina. Toyota is big but focused. By keeping a narrow concentration, Whole Foods is making established supermarket chains look like lumbering giants. Size is a constraint to growth and carries with it diseconomies of scale. Most big companies are cumbersome; they are just waiting to become extinct. We analysts are always told of the advantages of size: market share, market power, and dominance. In reality, it is quite the opposite. Smaller firms have better cost controls, are more flexible, and tend to be more niched. They lead the new developments and market changes. And smaller companies with more dynamic growth attract the best personnel. Investors should not be led astray by companies that claim their mammoth size is a favorable attribute. Corporate bulk is usually a negative.

Centralized Control Can Get Out of Control Overnight

Be wary of domineering, heavy-handed, overly controlling top management. It fosters wimpy yes-man executives outside the corner office. Although it is fine for particularly small companies to have a heavily centralized management structure, most firms sizable enough to be publicly held stocks should be fairly decentralized. Companies and markets quickly outgrow a concentrated top management's ability to make all the choices. An ivory tower group loses touch with lower levels. Companies run into problems shifting from an initial core top management decision-making setup to entrusting others to run operations and steer in opportunistic new directions. This transition is almost impossible when the founder is still present. Founders rarely yield control until it is too late.

Centralized control is smooth and effective, lulling investors into thinking it is good management, until overnight material problems hit like a flash flood. The executives at the top, thinking only they were qualified to micromanage most aspects of the company, find that they were unaware of massive underlying issues or threats until they finally become manifest. Centralized control appears to work fine to outsiders until it does not anymore. It is like a dictatorship, which seems more polished and practical than a messy democracy. Things can collapse quickly when the top is strong while the supporting structure is weak.

A Dramatic Acquisition in Troubled Times Is Diversionary

Sometimes executives, realizing that the company is in trouble—lethargic, losing market share, mature, growth diminished, and earnings outlook murky—attempt an inappropriate leapfrog: They make a dramatic, major acquisition to mask the condition. This is a sure warning that the company is running out of gas. It is a bridge too far. The purpose of a monster acquisition is to toss financials and operating income statements into complexity, obscure current operating numbers, and set up a *strategic* story for the future. The company can then promise enhanced results stemming from the stunning deal. Profit improvement via *synergism* and duplicate cost elimination is always a year or more away, but investors are told to be patient. By making a titanic, splashy merger, executives can forestall the need to demonstrate immediate earnings and cover up an imminent earnings shortfall. Such a measure is overreaching. It is a disguise.

The Daimler takeover of Chrysler in 1998 is a good illustration of what can happen when executives attempt a gigantic pole-vault act to offset doldrums in the rest of the business. Daimler was struggling, so it laid out $36 billion for the deteriorating U.S. also-ran. Nine years later, Daimler coughed up another half-billion to get a private-equity firm to take it away. In the end, it was a mere $37 billion mistake. Sprint's stock caved from around $75 in late 1999 to the low or mid-20s in 2005, when it made a frenzied effort to acquire Nextel. At the end of 2007, it made a $29.7 billion write-down of the entire Nextel market capitalization, eliminated the dividend, and took on some $20 billion in debt. The shares sank to under $6.

Carly Fiorina's frantic turnaround efforts at Hewlett-Packard also fit this mold. In 2002, she acquired Compaq, a flagging PC producer. Compaq's poor financials and eroding market share made it a fading player looking to be bailed out. Fiorina caught flack from several quarters, including the Hewlett Foundation, and she barely obtained enough shareholder votes. It made little sense, doubling up in a lousy business. She was proven definitively wrong a couple years later. In *Fortune Magazine*'s article on the failure of the Compaq deal, Warren Buffet explained: "When a management with a reputation for brilliance tackles a business with a reputation for bad economics, it is usually the reputation of the business that remains intact."

In 2008, as major banks were failing, some of the biggest made similar diversionary acquisitions. JPMorgan grabbed the collapsing Bear Stearns and Washington Mutual. Bank of America purchased Countrywide Financial, which was reeling from the subprime mortgage debacle, and at the close of the year it also swallowed Merrill Lynch. It did not take long for these desperate measures to haunt BofA. The company bit off more than it could chew and by early 2009 sought tens of billions more in government bailout capital as its stock crashed to below $4.

In the 1980s, AT&T committed a similar blunder. The idea was to vault into the computer industry to compliment its telecom services. A regulated long-distance carrier in the competitive high-tech industry? I realized the extent of the farce at a conference when I heard an AT&T in-house techie describe the search process. Their extensive evaluation listed 11 computer company possibilities from best to worst fit. NCR was last on the list. But the chairman decided otherwise and launched an unfriendly takeover of NCR. AT&T ended up way overpaying, the graft-on was a failure, AT&T's chairman was replaced, and NCR was later written down and spun off at a huge loss. A debacle. Predictable. Just another attempt to dig out of trouble through diversion.

Sometimes the deflection tactic is not an acquisition. It could be a dazzling move into a radically new market, as when a consumer PC software firm launches into the corporate market. Or the leap might be a striking shift in the business model, such as a computer services company deciding to sell software. Spectacular actions are often convenient cover-ups for near-term financial underperformance.

Executives refer to the transition costs as temporary. Analysts and investors are directed to cool their heels and await the big payoff, which rarely comes. Those naive enough to hang on for the glorious outcome end up being disappointed.

Managements and boards love acquisitions because the larger the company, the more important they feel; they obtain more clout and more pay. Most of the time, they justify expansion with fallacious reasons such as synergy or economies of scale. The bigger the better is the byword. But sizable companies making an acquisition to get even bigger is a death knell. Instead, they should be divesting and downsizing to become more streamlined.

Customer Base Should Be Hardy and Vigorous

The best companies have other thriving, vigorous companies as clients; those companies themselves are expanding, have good profitability and money to spend. Lucrative industries such as energy or pharmaceuticals are preferable clients to struggling sectors such as banking and retail. Commercial markets yield higher profit margins and faster growth than government or heavily regulated industries. If it is a consumer business, the end market should be abundant and flush.

I always ascertain the quality of a company's client base. Are their major contracts with customers teetering on the verge of bankruptcy? Is there heavy dependency on a few sizable clients that are floundering? Or is the customer base composed of firms like GE, Coca-Cola, Merck, or Citicorp?

An element that executives usually overemphasize in the pursuit of business is new clients. Pursuing and landing new contracts is exciting for corporate leaders, but sometimes this is accompanied by neglect of existing clients. Executing on existing contracts and satisfying current clients is the heart and soul of building a flourishing business, getting referrals and add-ons, raising profits as contracts mature, and building follow-on revenue. But it is not sexy and gets little internal corporate kudos. The high-profile acclaim goes to salespersons and teams bringing in new deals, especially megasized contracts or big Fortune 100 names as customers. Stocks trade higher on sizzling press releases proclaiming impressive new clients and contracts. Management declares the new business as a building block for future growth. The problem is that once obtained, the clients might be taken for granted, underserved, and shuffled over to managers who were not part of the initial selling.

Analysts normally check customer satisfaction when initiating coverage of a company, but tend not to follow up later. This component is critical. Client dissatisfaction can spread quietly and be overlooked for a long time. When it eventually surfaces, it can bring a company to its knees, like General Motors and Ford. I remember one time in the mid-1980s, IBM stressed its major theme as "the year of the customer." At its massive four-day user conference that year, the chairman failed to make a speech or even show up to schmooze with customers. It told me everything. The subsequent new chairman brought in from the outside immediately paid genuine attention to the current client base. New deals are cool and can be catalysts. Investors can get wowed by new sales, but it is more difficult to determine the quality of existing-client caretaking. Tending to current clients is real work. Companies that execute these operational aspects might appear dull but they are solid and enduring.

Beware of Established, Entrenched Companies That Stand Pat

Managements want to book new business all right, but rarely are they willing to take the risk of developing new products and services that leapfrog and render obsolete their current market offering. A common corporate mind-set is to protect the base, and avoid impacting existing business or obsolescing current client installations. When successful, companies become defensive and are afraid of change. This is often the case when founders stick around or when firms have reached spectacular heights with their initial focused business thrust. Companies should be making changes and doing creative new things, never standing still even though the current business might be robust.

The natural tendency is to stand pat, make minor adjustments and improvements, and protect the base. Xerox, with its copiers in the 1970s, was a classic example. Digital Equipment in minicomputers was another case. EDS suffered by sticking with its core expertise, data-center outsourcing, as that sector matured. Meanwhile, upstart competitors led the charge into business back-office process outsourcing. The supermarket chains missed the shift to healthier food. Detroit automakers overlooked the trend toward hybrid cars. Companies often miss market inflection points. It is difficult for entrenched enterprises to admit that there is a market or technological shift occurring that might imperil their existing business. They take a cautious posture and, like an NFL football team protecting a late lead, play prevent defense, giving up ten yards per play waiting for the clock to expire. It usually means prevent victory.

Turnarounds Rarely Work Out

When a company has lost its edge and deteriorated, and earnings shortfalls have begun to ensue, the board's normal response is to replace management. The new team champions a turnaround, typically entailing financial restructuring, cost cutting, downsizing, divestitures, and a new strategy. Usually new managements storm into troubled companies, hire fresh executive teams, promise massive change, take jarring write-offs and reserves, and slash costs, often with improved investor communications. All the excitement around transformation gets heavy press and analyst attention. These seemingly bold actions are alluring to investors. Unfortunately, the company never really transitions into a flourishing leadership role again.

Carly Fiorina's efforts to overhaul Hewlett-Packard failed, especially after she jammed the mega-acquisition of Compaq. The board did not think her efforts were panning out and she was summarily replaced. The old, original AT&T, as its business degenerated, employed a number of new CEOs to embark on turnarounds, and finally was itself acquired. Xerox has struggled with a half dozen efforts to transition and reenergize itself over the past 25 years.

By early 2005, EDS, after years of little progress in its turnaround and another year of struggle ahead, was in desperate need to find a carrot to dangle at its analyst meeting. So it promised some boxcar bookings down the road. It flashed $23 billion in anticipated orders for 2007, hoping analysts would forget the dismal 2004 new contract total of under $15 billion, not to mention the maturing industry, overseas competition, and all the other adverse influences. The year 2007 was far enough out to avoid scrutiny for a long time. It is tough enough to predict next quarter, let alone three years in the future. Outlandish, distant promises amid ongoing setbacks are a clear signal that the foreseeable turnaround outlook is poor. Under two turnaround regimes, EDS never did regain its prominence, and it sold out to Hewlett-Packard in 2008.

Turnaround promises always entail investors waiting a couple years or longer. Most of the time the best case is when new management shores up the finances, declares victory, and merges the company. Sinking ships do not resurface as forward-attack-position aircraft carriers. Do not expect a dramatic metamorphosis or reinvigorated growth from any of these changes. Turnarounds never manifest such results.

Opulence and Luxuriousness Are Alarm Bells

As an investor, always be on guard for companies that display unnecessary extravagances. Investors should be turned off by companies that have exceptionally luxurious offices: deep-pile carpeting, antiques, artwork, and plush furniture. If it is too extravagant, it suggests that executives are in it mostly for themselves. When companies create a vast new headquarters campus, they are surely setting up for a fall. The given rationale is always employee proximity, or even economics. In reality, it is just an upgrade on the lavishness scale. This is sometimes conspicuous in the annual report.

I first learned to shy away from companies that build lavish new home-office facilities with Xerox in the 1970s. The chairman and early founder, Peter McCullough, proudly paraded a big analyst group, on a full tour of the new building in Stamford, Connecticut, highlighting the rich parquet floors, the employees' gym, and the assorted uses of marble, brass, and mahogany. We walked around stupefied. Although the new headquarters might not have been a direct cause of Xerox's struggling business, this display of superficial financial prosperity turned out to be a good warning sign of the company's checkered record over subsequent decades.

Other signs of splendor might be a fleet of executive automobiles, an excessive number and use of corporate airplanes, corporate country club memberships, stadium suites, the corporate name on stadiums, first-class flights, rooms at Four Seasons hotels, designer suits, exclusive executive dining rooms, pricey client and employee outings, and even extravagant locations of analyst meetings. It makes me suspicious when the annual analyst briefing session is held at a posh resort or country club location.

Corporate offices and management style should ideally by similar to those of John Chambers, the CEO of Cisco, an egalitarian with a humble approach. He has no corner office; he has a 12-by-12-foot space in the center of the floor with no view. The outside window offices are for lower-level employees; management is located in the middle. This atmosphere indicates to employees that they are important, and it fosters good communication. Conference tables are round to emphasize equality rather than a hierarchy. Chambers' desk has a laminate top, chairs have plastic arms; his modest West Virginian background comes through. Some contrast to the more than $1 million John Thain, the CEO of Merrill Lynch, paid to have his office redecorated before the firm sold out to Bank of America. Cisco has no reserved parking spaces and no special executive office pecking order.

Be Cautious of Excessive Hype and Promotion

Some companies have massive marketing machines, churning out press releases daily on the most inconsequential, immaterial matters. The investor relations contact might as well be from a publicity firm, has only meager information on the company's operations or outlook, and blithely offers generic commentary to investors. We analysts come away from a meeting or conversation as though we have just had bad Chinese food, still feeling empty. This kind of marketing, press, and advertising is a smoke screen. Take note of glossy, overly fancy, expensive annual reports, and too much glamour. Instead look for understated content and meaningful discussion. Companies with depth do not need excessive boosterism. A plethora of announcements makes analysts and investors tune out, so when there really is an important message, it is diminished. When I see executives making too many public showings, press interviews, and media appearances, I wonder who is minding the store. It also makes me question their intentions. Are they managing the company or the stock? Is management attempting to manipulate a favorable perception, fearing that outsiders will realize the truth? Companies with hyperactive publicity campaigns lack substance.

A former director of investor relations at Tyco International during the days of Dennis Kozlowski's errant personal spending binge testified in court to this promotional conduct. He claimed his investor relations unit was pushed into becoming "the marketing department for the company's stock." Knowing that "the function of investor relations is to provide true and accurate information," Tyco's approach with analysts and investors was instead "to highlight and accentuate the positives and mitigate the negatives."

Be suspicious of executives who are vague or ambivalent. There was an analyst meeting in which the chairman of a beleaguered company said, "Growth is both our challenge and our biggest goal." He went on to blurt out, "By cutting overhead, we can grow our business." This style of communication strains credibility and generates distrust. Cost reduction aids profitability but it requires new orders and sales to attain revenue expansion.

Companies can further distort the picture by presenting slanted and spun earnings results. Typical press releases pertaining to a stunning earnings drop might carry a headline like "Revenues Climb x%, New Contract Prospects Encouraging." There will be no reference in a caption to the massively disappointing plunge in profits or the reason behind the tanking. If the news is negative, it should be portrayed that way and fully detailed. Executives commonly pull the wool over the eyes of the investing public with cagey, manipulative releases. Press announcements seldom detail the uncertainties and risks when announcing positive news, such as a new contract. Adequate time is never given to challenges and issues during formal conference calls and briefing sessions. An almost-universal practice is to willingly discuss positive news in detail, but avoid drilling into disappointing setbacks. Another ploy is late-day conference calls to spell out bad news; the hope is that Wall Street will have already gone home and that press coverage will be limited due to nearing deadlines. By contrast the buoyant news is described ad nauseam during prime-time calls.

Stock Buybacks and Dilutive Stock Options Are a Turnoff

Stock repurchase plans—when a company buys back its shares in the open market—are a patently pathetic action to artificially boost earnings and the stock price. Executives rarely announce such deals when business is ripping, the outlook is brilliant, and the stock is running. Buybacks usually occur when profits have stalled or the stock price has languished. This type of financial maneuvering is not the same as real growth or genuine fundamental progress such as market share gains.

According to Standard & Poor's, there were $589 billion in stock repurchases during 2007, more than double the $246 billion that corporations paid out in cash dividends. From the fourth quarter of 2004 through 2007, the S&P 500 companies did $1.4 trillion in buybacks, compared to less than $1.6 trillion in capital expenditures and just $721 billion in dividends. This is cockeyed. And these firms certainly regretted their depletion of capital after the bear market was in full force during 2008.

An S&P study, discussed in *Barron's*, points out that buybacks are usually a waste of money. Less than 25% of the 423 S&P 500 firms that repurchased shares from 2006 to mid-2007 had their stocks outperform the index by the end of September 2007. That is, 76% would have been better off doing nothing. One-third of these companies paid a buyback price that was materially higher than the stock price in autumn of 2007, let alone during the bear market of 2008, incurring a serious loss in book value. Furthermore, S&P found that the companies executing the biggest stock repurchases experienced the worst stock performance. Up until the 2008 bear market, companies were even borrowing, issuing debt, and leveraging the balance sheet to repurchase stock. It was shortsighted, and it made me suspicious.

Home Depot, its business affected by the nosedive in the housing market, is a case in point. It issued debt and launched a whopping repurchase of 25% of its shares in June 2007 at a price in the $37-to-$39 range. The stock was under $20 by late 2008. Several home builders now wish they had retained all the cash that they blew on share repurchases over the past couple years. Likewise, Sallie Mae (SLM Corporation) behaved absurdly using derivatives-equity forward contracts to buy back its shares. This was fine when the stock was rising, but it was a debacle when the shares slid. It was a multi-billion-dollar mistake. Citigroup bought back $7 billion in stock in 2006 at an average price of almost $50 a share. By 2008, in need of capital, it lined up for tens of billions in federal bailout money. The stock was below $2 by early 2009. Guess it overpaid.

General Electric repurchased $29 billion of its stock from 2005 to mid-2008 at an average of $36 per share. In October 2008, it needed to sell some 12 million new shares for over $22 each to raise capital, and four months later the price fell below $10. Lehman Brothers was buying back its stock in the first half of 2008, before collapsing in September due to lack of capital. *The Wall Street Journal* called the action "a move akin to giving away the fire extinguisher even as your house begins to fill with smoke." In 2007, Macy's bought its stock back at around $39; its shares were below $10 by fall 2008. Sears purchased 22 million shares in 2007 at an average of $135. It cracked below $30 by November 2008. You get the idea. Be cautious when companies are borrowing, selling assets, and buying back their shares. To quote *Barron's*, "Most stock-repurchase programs are like diets: In the short-term, they raise hope, but they usually do not produce lasting benefits." Moreover, they indicate executive panic and are probably stopgaps following a corporate disappointment and/or a flagging stock price.

Another negative indication is the practice of issuing dilutive stock options, rights to employees and management to purchase shares in the future at the price fixed on the grant date. There is a quantifiable dilution to potential earnings per share when millions of stock options are issued. Shareholders need to be more aware of this impact. A mandate that the full effect on earnings be calculated and reported advances the goal of reporting legitimate, genuine results. It puts a damper on this lucrative freebie that, until recently, had been entirely at the shareholders' expense. When a stock price plummets and options are underwater, corporate executives and employees dodge a personal loss by the reissuance of new options at a lower price. Too bad stockholders cannot redo their purchase price after the drop. I probably do not even need to mention the proliferation of basically illegal backdating of stock options—another ploy to enrich executives at the expense of investors.

Stock option policies are overly liberal because of the past "freebie" accounting treatment. Broadcom is just one of the many examples of heavy option issuance. Though incurring almost $1 billion in red ink in 2003 and negative retained earnings of almost $7 billion at the end of that year, it proposed an option plan in early 2004 equivalent to 12% of its enterprise value, diluting current shareholders by almost 4%. And it had previously reissued lower-priced options after the initial ones plummeted underwater in 2001 and again in 2003.

Brocade Communications was another poster child for excessive distribution of options. Its stock came public in 1999 at $4.75 per share; by October 2000 it had reached $133, and it now trades in the single figures again. In early 2005, it restated its results for the prior six years—every year it was public—to correct errors in its option accounting. It turned out that its 2004 net loss was $32 million instead of the $2 million it originally announced. In mid-2007, the former CEO of Brocade was brought to trial by federal prosecutors for defrauding shareholders through illegal stock options timing practices and he was sentenced to prison for 21 months and fined $15 million. The Federal District judge in the above backdating case stated, "This offense is about honesty...Repeatedly, over a three-year period, he [the CEO] was lying."

There are myriad other examples. Hewlett-Packard's shareholders voted in favor of expensing all options in 2004, but management did not listen and continued their impact in financial reports until accounting regulations changed in 2007. Countrywide Financial, in late 2007, after its share price collapsed from $45 early in the year to a low of $12, extended its option expirations for senior executives by a year or two. I'll bet public shareholders wish they could get an extension like that. Google similarly repriced its stock options in early 2009 as the bear market put 85% of its employees options underwater. Funny how managements desire to limit the downside but not the upside, all at the shareholders' expense. In late 2007, UnitedHealth Group's former CEO assented to paying back to the company more than $600 million in stock options after a backdating scandal was exposed. Other officers had to relinquish $300 million in the face of a justice department criminal investigation. Bloomberg News quoted a Street analyst's reaction: "We now can attach a dollar value to hubris." UnitedHealth stands out among more than 200 disclosures of companies doing similar stock option backdating; half of these companies had to restate prior financial results during 2006–2007. Some 90 executives and directors have lost their positions and more than 400 legal suits have been filed stemming from backdating. Be wary of companies that partake in flagrant self-serving actions.

I favor Berkshire Hathaway's approach. It has never issued stock options. Warren Buffett, its high-profile leader, has been a proponent of expensing options. He also believes that when options are exercised, executives should not be allowed to sell the shares for a reasonably long period. In 2007, Microsoft started the march toward eliminating issuance of options. Beginning in the spring of 2006, the Financial Accounting Standards Board began requiring options granted by corporations to be fully expensed on the earnings statement. Such grants shrinked quickly. Gee, what a surprise. Yes, stock prices might, to a degree, already discount potential future stock option dilution if a company is particularly generous or stingy in its option issuance. But such an argument reminds me of when companies completed a huge purchase acquisition, adding enormous revenues and earnings along with massive amortization expenses. I heard the argument so often that we analysts and investors should overlook the amortization cost impacting reported earnings and concentrate on operating earnings, including all the earnings contributed by the acquired entity. Corporate executives wanted it both ways. I sense the same desire in management efforts to treat options as though they are free.

As an investor, you should always be a skeptic and search for a company's vulnerability. It is easy to spot the brilliance, the excellence of a corporation. Wall Street, company executives, and even the press spout superlatives constantly. The flaws are hidden, and there are many interested parties who have a major stake in keeping them covered up. So the challenge is to identify the concealed shortcomings that might be a deal-breaker for an investor.

6

Executive Traits Are a Revealing Investment Gauge

A critical part of the investment appraisal and company evaluation process is gauging management effectiveness, character, and values. Surprisingly, the Street often disregards these quality differences among the companies it covers. In crucial moments, when events panic investors and stocks nosedive, executives are usually temporarily incommunicado. In such circumstances, investors need to know whether management can be trusted. This also holds true over the long term. Who would you rather invest in, trustworthy executives or cagey executives? You need to get a handle on executive values in companies where you have an investment.

On occasion I have had the opportunity to size up executives during a round of golf. I have gained more insight observing and schmoozing over 18 holes than I could ever have obtained in a meeting. Once, a struggling high-end payroll processor preannounced a disappointing earnings shortfall the day before my annual investor conference started in Miami. The stock tanked, and the executives were blistered by investors at their sessions. Then it happened again the next year. Because he was from the Midwest and it was January, the CEO stuck around after the conference for a game of golf with me on the Blue Monster at the Doral, where my confab was centered. I assigned the portfolio manager from the biggest mutual-fund holder of the stock to our foursome. He brutalized the unfortunate executive for two-and-a-half hours with caustic jabs. After nine holes, I started to switch the CEO's clubs from my cart onto that investor's buggy. The CEO stopped me cold, beseeching, "Don't do this to me; my round's already ruined!" That showed me he had humility and a good-natured genuineness; he was a good guy I could trust.

Wall Street analysts deal with such an array of corporate executives that when we confront a new one, we usually recognize some past style or type. We can almost predict a company's future by recalling previous experiences with similar management at other firms. Investors, too, can sometimes spot certain significant traits and behaviors in their pursuit of potential investment opportunities and in staying abreast of their current holdings.

There are various recurring styles—some are constructive and others are detrimental. Many times executives are not lying; they are just uninformed, naive, or overly optimistic. They can be eternal lowballers, always in a hype mode, taciturn, or shrewd storytellers. Executives make common mistakes when problems surface. Investors need to identify good executive traits and undesirable ones.

Listen to Executives on Conference Calls

Individual investors do not have the access to executives that is available to many Street insiders. Just about the only way to get firsthand exposure to management is by listening in on quarterly conference calls. You can hear the executives' prepared remarks and their answers to questions live by Webcast or telephone. These calls are scheduled a week or two in advance of earnings results and are publicly announced in a company press release. If you need more details, such as telephone access numbers, call investor relations at the company. A replay is normally available for another week or so after the call. The sessions are available to everyone in a listen-only mode, but only Street analysts and institutional investors can ask the executives direct questions.

A conference call is worth a thousand reports. This is where you will get some feel for the company's management style and character. It is like observing a press conference. Judge the level of confidence and conviction, arrogance or humbleness, candor, and conservativeness. Take note of the executive's temper. Sometimes they sound hesitant or unconvincing. Listen carefully to how management answers questions from analysts who often act like piranhas. Beyond just observing a management's character, these calls are exceedingly valuable in gaining insight on a company's business, current trends, and outlook. They are more useful than research reports in discovering countervailing analyst attitudes, and the Street's concerns and uncertainties.

Read between the lines to determine the real message. And pay attention to other more subtle aspects of these calls. You can glean as much from the nuances in delivery as from the actual remarks. Take note of the executive's tone and length of commentary. Prepared remarks can drone on for 45 minutes, leaving only a brief 15-minute segment for Q & A. Such temporizing might indicate a coverup to dodge penetrating questions and cross-examinations. Get an overall impression. Is the picture clear and favorable, or clouded and uncertain? These calls provide the closest look you will ever get at a company.

The Visionary Leader or Founder Who Adapts

A company leader willing to adapt is rare and relatively easy to spot. These individuals define each corporate era. Analysts feel honored when they have the privilege of knowing such leaders and experiencing firsthand the emergence of these exceptional companies. Bill Gates of Microsoft, Robert Noyce at Intel, Ross Perot from EDS, and possibly Larry Ellison with Oracle are such exemplars with whom I had personal contact over the course of my career. You can add to the list Warren Buffett, Jack Welch, Steve Jobs, John Chambers, and executives at companies such as FedEx and Wal-Mart. Bill Hewlett was another example. I will never forget the twice-a-year New York analyst meetings held by Hewlett-Packard in the 1970s. Hewlett, who founded HP in a garage with David Packard, would preside over the meeting for over four hours, straight-talking from the heart. He did not shy away from concerns or negative aspects. It was a thorough working session, with no nonsense. He had credibility.

What distinguishes these founders or leaders is that they transform and adapt as their fledgling start-ups become dominant worldwide juggernauts. Sometimes this causes them to take their giant firms in reinvigorating new directions. Bill Gates has taken Microsoft from PC operating systems to PC applications to business software, on into the Internet, and now into games and entertainment. He just keeps transforming and broadening with the markets. Visionaries identify a new market, create it, lead it, and shift their company's direction as the old sector matures. Such leaders set high standards of performance and their associates rise to that level. They drive continuous improvement; they listen and seek to understand and empathize with the end customer. These are charismatic leaders, colorful, outspoken, driven, creative, aggressive, fearless, and self-confident.

Listening to such executives is enthralling. When I questioned Bill Gates during coffee breaks at meetings, he would rock back and forth, mulling questions over in his mind several seconds, and then articulate brilliant, balanced answers. The more unassuming and genuine the executive, like Gates and Noyce, the more convincing their comments are. Still you must also avoid being ensorcelled, blindly believing these executives' spiels without critical assessment. This is a challenge for analysts and investors who can fall into hero worship. When a leader is arrogant, with an attitude, analysts have a more natural and healthy skepticism.

Sometimes Founders Are Boom-Bust

Boom-bust leaders, though inspired, inventive creators of dynamic, winning companies, overstay their time. As markets shift and the company matures, the one-time pioneer is stuck in the original business. The early vision that drove the firm to great heights crests, but this mastermind is blind, defending the established business instead of going in new directions. Business history is littered with examples. Some I dealt with as an analyst were Peter McCullough at Xerox, Scott McNealy of Sun Microsystems, Ken Olsen of Digital Equipment,

Charles Wang at Computer Associates, William Norris of Control Data, and Jim Sprague with National Semiconductor.

The challenge for investors is to recognize, in the boom period, founder executives who might eventually end up in this category. Watch emerging companies with innovative approaches that could pose a threat to established market leaders. Boom-bust founders pooh-pooh competitive warnings, are overly defensive and entrenched in the existing strategy, and are unwilling to cannibalize the current business in order to stay on the leading edge. Founders seldom change, but markets and technologies always move on. Ken Olsen at Digital, in reaction to the emergence of the personal computer in the early 1980s, stridently pronounced that his firm would not participate in that business—"the PC was only a toy!" He developed only "serious" computers. It is ironic that after his company crumbled, it was absorbed by Compaq, an early pioneer in PCs. The future becomes history, and these companies remain fixated on their early dominant lead. They will not acknowledge that their original product or service is becoming mature or obsolete. After founders preside over their own bust, they are replaced by turnaround executives, usually to no avail.

Founders Cannot Perform Magic Twice

Be cautious of founders who have created one winner, and then move on to launch another start-up in a different area. You might assume that they can build a second big winner given their reputation of achievement the first time. But remember that an initial breakthrough requires a confluence of the right market circumstances. It is not possible to bring together all the same catalysts perfectly for an encore. Serendipity cannot be planned or re-created. Analysts and investors are often fooled by a founder's reputation and thus seduced into believing that lightning can strike twice.

This was impressed on me back in the 1980s when Gene Amdahl, who was instrumental in creating generations of mainframe computers at IBM, launched a stellar start-up company, called Amdahl, to develop IBM knockoff computers for a drastically cheaper price. Following this achievement, he attempted to repeat the triumph with a new company called Trilogy Systems. No computer technology ever surfaced from its laboratory, and it quickly faded into oblivion. There can sometimes be modest achievement with a second go-round, but never expect to see the first pinnacle matched. Be cautious when these founders' egos lead them to try repeating the magic.

Founder returnees are a variation of this theme, and likewise rarely manage to pull off a turnaround after a company has floundered. Following the start-up, initial financing, and early explosive growth phase, a different set of management skills is required. Most of the time, when a prodigal son is brought back to reignite the business, it proves ineffective.

During 2007, Yahoo! was reeling and brought back its co-founder Jerry Yang. He walked away from an acquisition offer by Microsoft for $33 per share, turnaround efforts faltered, the shares had sunk to below $10 by late 2008, and he was replaced by Carol Bartz in early 2009. Michael Dell returned to the CEO position at Dell in February 2007 and could not recover the former glory. The stock fell from $23 on his homecoming day to below $8 two years later. Starbucks hoped in 2008 that the return of its founders could recapture the good times.

The Classic Operator, Realist, and No-Nonsense Driver

The realist is another favorable executive style. These types are typically chief operating officers. Sometimes they are chairmen who succeed founders and approach management as operators rather than magnetic, imaginative leaders. They are tough, organized, detailed, quick-studies, decision makers, serious, hardworking, and unafraid to confront other senior executives. Steve Ballmer of Microsoft, and in the past Lou Gerstner of IBM, Ray Lane of Oracle, and Josh Weston of Automatic Data Processing, are such figures. When Weston was head of ADP, he ran a tight ship. I remember when I was meeting with other executives at the headquarters, he requested to see me for five minutes. As I marched into his office, he explained that his question would take one minute, I would have two minutes to respond, and that would leave two minutes for me to have one counter question and a reply. As I exited, a glimpse at my watch indicated I had been there for exactly five minutes. Weston and his executives had computer mainframe printout paper sliced into smaller pieces and stapled as scratchpads to save money, and they would write responses in longhand directly onto incoming letters and memos and send them back to save time and paper. That is how he ran the business.

These executives are informed on every aspect of their company. But they have little patience for analysts and investors because their intense focus is on operating the firm. The chairman of Fiserv once impressed me by knowing the name of every worker down on his loading dock. A member of EDS upper management picked up errant used paper towels on the men's-room floor and placed them in the waste disposal. That is meticulous, rigorous attention to detail. Generally, these are inside managers who make few outside public appearances. They can knock heads together, make things happen internally, build organization, oversee, scrutinize, drive midcourse corrections, budget, track, and direct business operations. They are not much fun and have a short attention span, suffering no fools, but investors have little fear of a company faltering when such an executive is in charge.

Worrywarts Disguise Success Under a False Veil of Fear

The worrywart is a rare breed who is highly competent, confident, even strident. Only a winning company constantly downplays its success. These executives emphasize all the clouds and threats: competition, low pricing, new product uncertainties, industry changes, and unpredictable customer preferences. They also minimize earnings growth prospects and low-ball their forecasts. The top executives of Microsoft are the poster boys of this style. At analyst meetings, they never fail to punctuate every presentation with the negative aspects, even though they are typically peripheral and often a stretch. Their earnings predictions each year are always conservative. We analysts become inured to this manner of reporting and give these cautious warnings little heed. IBM executives in the 1970s and 1980s halcyon years acted in a similar mode. Maybe when a company is so dominant and successful, it feels compelled to play down its fortune, embarrassed by the level of achievement, as big oil companies do today. Investors need to realize that when management is overly conservative, it is normally a reassuring sign.

Good Ol' Boys Are Charming While Deflecting Scrutiny

Be chary of charm. Certain executives can be particularly enchanting. Most analysts and institutional investors are unaccustomed to this demeanor and are easily swayed. Such sweet-talkers have a good sense of humor and are entertaining. They are fun to be with for golf, wine, football, and other events, but this is their way of selling. Analysts and investors need to remain objective. Good ol' boys do not appreciate intense scrutiny or skepticism. They usually dodge penetrating questions with a funny story or a humorous quip. Their attitude is "trust me." Although these executives want to appear to be your friend, in actuality they are not.

A cool, powerful, macho, tobacco-chewing CEO of an Atlanta-based firm once offered me a beer when I entered his office for a routine one-on-one analyst meeting. He was my best friend when my investment opinion was bullish, but trash-talked me to investors when I had a more cautious stance. It is easy to be seduced at first. This behavior is attractive and can breed initial trust. But watch out— it is dangerous. Investors can be taken in by nice guys who are just trying to curry favor with Wall Street.

Watch Out for Techie Geeks Who Know Their Stuff

Beware of persuasive talk by technology nerds, who are usually founders of their companies. You will find them in biotech, pharmaceuticals, and other business sectors based on science. Their knowledge of tech products, software, and systems is deep, so they are compelling when discussing the technology. Such executives confuse the issues with tech talk that is complex, way over your heads. Analysts and investors rarely know the right questions to ask. If executives cannot present their product complexities in an understandable fashion, watch out. Follow the Warren Buffett principle: Investors should not be involved with companies they cannot grasp. Geeky CEOs can intimidate investors into accepting their auspicious explanations. These executives brag about their company's leading-edge expertise and attempt to snow investors with technical terms and commentary. Geeks are confident, but are so narrowly focused that they miss broader issues, challenges, trends, and competitive shifts. Either avoid this type of company or gauge prospects broadly, not relying on the nerdy executive pitch.

Turnaround Artists Are Chasing Windmills

Be suspect of any executive who arrives with a turnaround plan. These executives are impressive, eloquent spokesmen, professional, and all-business; seem a breath of fresh air; and appear as a savior with a plan. They are engaging, normally quite convincing, providing leadership in a time of company turmoil. Executives parachuted in to salvage failing companies are subject to publicity and heavy Wall Street scrutiny, so they are desperate to produce steady, quantifiable progress. Expectations are high; analysts and investors are eternally optimistic. But change artists often have little to work with, because the company being resuscitated is usually a basket case. Michael Blumenthal (once U.S. Treasury Secretary) at Burroughs, Richard Brown at EDS, and Carly Fiorina at Hewlett-Packard are a few notable turnaround artists that I have encountered. Their efforts were for the most part failures.

These types are presented as rescuers who have arrived just in time. It is tempting to buy into their enthusiasm and confidence. Financial restructuring is usually their game, and that is easy. Cost cutting and stock buybacks are always the strategy. But such measures only buy time. The best these executives achieve is to streamline operations and tee the company up for sale. The problem is that in their zeal to prove to the world that they are the redeemer, they begin to believe that they can actually revitalize the firm, an unrealistic stance. They are ordinarily not interested in selling off the company quickly. The emphasis is on proving their turnaround artistry. In due course, the turnaround fails, and there are no willing acquirers to be found who are ready to pay big bucks.

Promotional Hypesters Lack Substance

Hypesters usually have a sales background and are experts in marketing. They mistakenly believe that the essence of their job description is selling. We analysts sit at meetings listening to their exciting presentations full of pizazz. After 45 minutes, we look at our yellow notepads and find no jottings—nothing material has been uttered, just piffle. Frequently, they make off-putting remarks such as denigrating the competition. A little hype goes a long way in covering up for lack of substance in a company. These executives treat analysts and investors like customers and the press, always pitching a positive spin, ever seeking an affirmative response, and sometimes resorting to promotive legerdemain. The curious thing is they believe in their own blarney. Their press releases are stuffed with adjectives such as leading, enhanced, unique, significant, integrated, powerful, innovative, advanced, high-performance, and sophisticated. They use such lingo as mission-critical, strategic focus, go-forward plan, proactive, goal-oriented, and a lot of other commendatory buzzwords.

This management type is evangelistic. They never stop trying to convert. Larry Ellison at Oracle has this tendency. The chairman of Burroughs back in the 1970s was a scintillating salesman. From his mouth the outlook was always bullish, trends were continuously promising, the company could do no wrong. We could not ask any penetrating questions. He took them as an insult and returned to pushing his agenda. The company later skidded off the track and crashed. Most prominent leaders of the '90s Internet Bubble Era fit this mold, proselytizing their eBusiness as a profitless new market pursuit, claiming it an inflection point and a transformation. Some of these were established titans who came from major corporations. They should have known better than to jump onto the Internet bandwagon. These zealots were convincing, charismatic, and cool, but their promises almost all came to naught. Investors should be on the lookout for convincing salesmen whose story is hollow.

Exciting, Fast-Buck Smoothies Will Break Your Heart

This type of chairman or CEO is smooth as silk, the perfect host for a dinner party. He is enchanting, captivating, and engaging; has a gift for gab; speaks with the confidence of an airline pilot; and is a good storyteller using colorful humor to punctuate points. Like the pilot in a storm, he always seems to have things under control. At least he gives off that impression. This demeanor can mislead naive analysts or investors. Business is never that steady or secure.

Slick, glib executives are good onstage and relish an audience. They regale customers, employees, industry groups, the press, and, more dangerously, analysts and investors. Responses to questions are spun in a glowing light, and negative issues are tempered or dismissed. Investors are treated like all other constituencies, cajoled, entertained, pitched, and made to feel good. The sell is subtle but constant. Wall Street is treated as just another type of client in the marketing effort. This executive is overconfident, arrogant, with a certain condescending attitude toward analysts, although these characteristics might be well concealed by their deportment. So when business turns sour and results tank, it is a shock that there was never any indication of developing issues beforehand. Investors need to be highly suspect of this polish because it is impossible to get an objective or informative view from this executive.

Quick-Hit Executives End Up in Quick Defeat

Breakneck opportunists typically show up on the scene with no industry background related to that of the current business. They sense a fleeting chance to get rich, so they start up or acquire entities to obtain a stake, and foist themselves off as new wave executives in an emerging niche. Since they have little or no past history in the current sector, there is no record to review. The executives use this to their advantage by claiming to be an original. Their actions are aimed at immediate results, big contracts, notable high-profile hires, acquisitions, upfront deals—anything that will push the stock price higher.

Watch their conduct for indications of their intentions. Their remarks are always measured, businesslike, and rational. But there is an underlying element of ambition, hurry-up, reaching, and opportunism. Their comments carry an undertone of bragging. They demean the competition and their managements.

In front of investors, these executives have a stridency, an attitude, and an arrogance. It is easy to get swept up in the exhilaration of a fresh face leading a novel business with designs of making it big quickly. Growth forecasts that are exceedingly high are probably unsustainable. This executive is often a winner initially, which leads analysts and investors to jump aboard the moon shot. But the success does not last long. This kind of management does not build for the long run—it is like a zephyr—so the underpinnings soon crumble. Attempting a surge strategy ends in a defeat. It is impossible to manage and control hypergrowth for long.

Ostriches May Be Stable but Trail the Field

Ostriches have a low-profile, diffident, defensive, parochial, old-line management style. These executives do things the old-fashioned way; they are slow to move in new directions. They are probably Luddites and do not use email or carry around laptops. Management picks up on new trends late and is skeptical of anything different, suspect of emerging forms of competition, and satisfied with the status quo. They are like government bureaucracy, lacking enthusiasm, creativity, flair, or originality. Although they are not susceptible to the mistakes of cutting-edge pioneers or aggressive, ambitious industry front-runners, their style eventually leaves companies in a laggard industry position. Their rationale is that they are conservative, current-client focused, stable, low-risk, with robust finances. Although there is some benefit to this approach, especially in a downturn or a slow period, this behavior can also result in lower profit margins and slower growth than those of the competitors. The dull management demeanor produces a similarly bland corporate character: that of a straggler.

When analysts or investors meet with these executives, they are put to sleep. Analyst meetings and conference calls are boring affairs. These executives avoid the media. Their stocks have low PE multiple valuations. Investors are never allowed any high expectations. Wall Street makes the mistake here of either being overly skeptical of these companies or wishfully thinking that there will be a breakout. But generally the lackluster middle road is the accurate outlook.

Liars, Deceivers, and Manipulators Always Lurk

Despite the rage of regulators, legal pressures, governmental oversight, and '90s Bubble Era fallout, executives who mislead investors are ever lurking. Sometimes misleading is intentional, but it can also occur under the nose of a naive CEO, who perhaps chooses not to question how his top executives achieve their numbers. These cheaters never dream of being discovered. Some are charismatic, usually highly convincing, and their steady, impressive results can be difficult for analysts and investors to discredit. A flourishing health-care computer services firm I once covered brought in a dynamic, impressive CEO to turn it around. He was a stellar performer for several years. The company became addicted to the immediate, upfront profit stimulus in signing software licenses. It turned out the books were cooked. The perfectly smooth record had been falsified.

Another Internet service and software shooting star had hotshot technology gurus propounding its leading-edge industry expertise. At my conference, they were committed to conducting three breakout sessions but bailed out for the golf course after the first period, leaving investors waiting in an empty room for the second presentation. Two days later, their business scam was unmasked, and the stock crashed to almost nothing. In the end, the con artists who stood up my institutional investors that day might have done them a great favor, since many of these investors then lost faith in the company. A database software firm I once covered had a CEO who sported a gold chain necklace and gave me a certain sleazy feeling. I never trusted him or recommended the stock. He pleaded guilty to securities fraud in 2004, a felony charge of filing false statements with the SEC that inflated revenues, and was sentenced to serve a year in prison. Bernard Madoff's arrest for fraud in his brokerage and investment firms wins the Oscar in 2009. Vigilance and scrutiny to determine the veracity of the income statement is not enough to avoid such crooks. Judging character well takes experience. Who will you trust? Dishonesty looms in many disguises.

Favorable Executive Traits

After you are familiar with certain executive types, there is an array of good traits to look for that indicate management quality. Several reassuring executive characteristics suggest that a company is likely to have promising investment merit. The following are some management attributes to seek out when reviewing investment candidates.

Charisma, Leadership, Courage

Good leaders have a certain charisma that inspires employees and instills confidence in clients. Such executives are effective in moving companies ahead with their power of persuasion. I am impressed when employees have great respect and love for their leader. It demonstrates that these executives have the guts to do the right thing despite criticism, aggravation, and short-term stock impact.

Empowering Other Executives

Effective leaders attract, encourage, and empower other members of management; insecure, power-hungry tyrants do not. Bill Gates trusts Steve Ballmer, and Larry Ellison at Oracle relied on Jeff Henley. The best leaders tolerate independence and strength among executives on their team.

Candor, Access

Executives gain credibility by being forthright and freely discussing negative crosscurrents and challenges. Access is critical; management must be open, available, and responsive to Wall Street and investors, not evasive or secretive.

Humble, Genuine

Company leaders should not be arrogant. Look for a lack of attitude or ego, minimal hype, and modest PR baloney. It seems there is a tendency, for example, for firms in the Midwest to be more genuine. Executives should willingly admit mistakes. No one is perfect or invincible. Rafael Nadal set such a tone in the process of upsetting top-ranked Roger Federer in the 2008 Wimbledon, saying, "I don't feel like the number one. I'm not. I don't like to feel that I'm something when I'm not."

Trust, Quality, Class

Management must be honorable, their comments reliable, their actions straightforward. They should act with class, not be litigious, display no vindictiveness, and do nothing shady or sleazy. Investors need to be able to trust executives to the core.

Hands-On, In Touch

Executives should be aware of what is occurring within the company at all levels and be in contact with the little people, not buffered by multiple tiers of management. Ross Perot was a master at this, always chatting with his lowest-level associates in the elevator and in the cafeteria. John Chambers at Cisco engages all strata of employees.

Outgoing, Aggressive, Confident

I like to see these elements, and yes, they can coexist with humility. Executives should not be shy, inward, or parochial. They should have a certain toughness, assertiveness, and conviction, as long as they are also aware of their vulnerability.

Creative, New Ideas

Leaders should be imaginative, frequently coming up with new strategies, directions, and methods. They need to be flexible, resourceful, inventive, and unafraid to make changes. Transformation can enhance competitiveness.

Old-Fashioned Business Values

Management should be long-term oriented and have a certain discipline. Executives should not practice quick-fix strategies to boost immediate earnings or over-pay for acquisitions to artificially lift results. They should care about low-level employees and small clients. There should be no excessive compensation or sumptuous headquarters, and precious few perks.

Experience, Broad Backgrounds

Executives should have experience in various disciplines, such as manufacturing or operations, and backgrounds in other companies and market sectors. Too many executives have had only sales or financial career paths.

Conservative, Understated

Executives should not mix business with social styling and other over-the-top dress practices. I am bothered by flashy manners, extravagant events or meetings, and anything that substitutes superficial showmanship for substance. I am put off by gold-chain jewelry, monogrammed cuffs, chic designer shoes, or tony fashions.

Hardworking, Dedicated

Management should be as driven and as hardworking as analysts, and arrive before 7:30 a.m. and not depart until after 6 p.m. They should travel on weekends and evenings, and lunch in the office. Their golf game had better be marginal. I knew a chairman who did not do business breakfasts because they were too early. Not a good sign.

Undesirable Executive Behavior

Certain undesirable behaviors raise red flags and should put you on the alert. Such conduct is detrimental and usually indicates a problematic outlook for the company. Investors should be turned off by executives who display these attributes.

Dictator Surrounded by Yes-Men

CEOs or chairmen who are tyrannical dictators, sticking their noses in every detail, encircled by weak, wimpy yes-men, are likely to hit a brick wall. No one is perfect, knows everything, and always makes correct decisions. They chase away real talent and effective leaders. The company outgrows them. Overly domineering autocrats create a vacuum in the management ranks.

Doing Too Much, Lacking Focus

Leaders should not be spread too thin, travel too heavily, or make too many speeches or appearances. They cannot work effectively on the road. Talk and rah-rah boosterism with employees and clients ring hollow; often they are a substitute for the hard work of running the company. Executives need to concentrate on one or two big aspects, not try to do scores of tasks.

Kiddie Corps, New Age Communes, Love-Ins

Certain youthful founders and executives, common in the '90s Internet Bubble Era, are excessively exuberant and spiritual. They revel in community and treat business as a glorified love-in. They refer to each other in cutesy terms: Bobby, Billy, and Johnny. The environment might be creative all right, but the atmosphere is like recess, like playing at business.

Hubris, Ego, Overconfidence

Executives should not be full of themselves. Too much of an attitude is a setup for a fall. Too much ego is blinding. Roger Lowenstein of *The New York Times* said it best: "Hubris is not the worst crime— merely the one that guarantees the surest retribution." In 1998, Long Term Capital Management (LTCM), a hedge fund that will live on in infamy, had, in the words of Ray DeVoe, "an acute case of hubris...[and] formulated a mathematically infallible investment policy. Well, not totally infallible; [only] something that might occur once in about 7,000 years could cause it to fail. LTCM lasted less than ten years, undone by the Russian partial default that blew up the strategy." A superior peacock posture engenders hazardous attitudes, such as believing that a strategy is foolproof, overlooking competition, or not listening to clients. Surprise setbacks are sure to follow.

Hype, Marketing, All Show

Be cautious of executives prominently featured in their own company advertising campaigns. Full-page ads and splashy airport billboards bother me. EDS ran a massive promotion with Super Bowl commercials, justifying the blitz as "air cover for the sales force." When things later floundered, that chairman was replaced. I guess the aerial attack was not enough. Carly Fiorina featured herself in Hewlett-Packard ads and was later dismissed by the board. Beware of over-the-top hype and executive-centered publicity.

Lavish Digs, Perks, Packages

Read the proxy statement and annual-report footnotes for excessive executive pay packages and incentives. Stock-appreciation rights, prodigious options, and $100 million paydays are warnings. Also look for a fleet of corporate aircraft, ski lodges, and opulent headquarters.

Stock Price Fixation

When the daily stock price is displayed at the corporate entrance check-in desk, in the employee cafeteria, and at analyst meetings, it connotes a short-term executive mindset. Executive discussion of stock valuation is repulsive. They are managing the stock price instead of the company. Funny how when the share price is skyrocketing, executives take full credit for their brilliant vision, strategy, and execution and never account for a bull market or a favorable industry sector. For some reason, after the price plummets their stock prattle is muted, and the stock quote is no longer widely displayed around the office.

Private-Life Demeanor, Reputation

I am put off by executives with a line of ex-wives, messy public divorces, marriages to gold diggers, visits to strip clubs, heavy drinking, active outside investment pursuits such as real estate or private businesses, ostentatious McMansions and parties, sports cars, and liberal jet-setting. A study by two professors, as reported in *The Wall Street Journal,* found that "the bigger or pricier a CEO's house, the greater the risk of a lackluster stock performance." The same can be said for excessive golf playing. I can say this because my handicap was always 17. CEOs who are good golfers and have low handicaps, say around 10, are usually playing too often, and probably spending way too much time away from the office. Showy sailboats, cars, planes, second homes, and bombshell women on their arms are bad signs of misplaced priorities. These executives are having too much fun and are not attentive enough to their businesses. Okay, so maybe Wall Street analysts are totally jealous of such lifestyles, especially if executives play too much golf.

Designer Suits, Fingernail Polish, Flamboyant Attire

Beware of executives who are overly coiffed, with fingernail polish, monograms, big rings, and fancy designer suits, who look as though they just walked out of the salon. Too much emphasis on appearance is a turnoff. These types lack substance and genuineness. Other affectations or cutesy personal marks such as male ponytails also bother me. I prefer to see success demonstrated through actions rather than with fancy accouterments.

Trash-Talking, Playing Favorites

Casting aspersions on analysts or competing companies and products is a cover-up for internal corporate inadequacies. Any type of dissing is low-class, and so is the practice of favoring analysts with positive opinions while freezing out those holding negative ratings. When executives criticize a negative research view, it indicates defensiveness. The analyst's insight probably hit too close to home.

Overweight, Overindulging

Fat executives can reveal a certain lack of personal discipline that might translate to a similar absence of corporate control. I like to see executives who are lean and mean, healthy. Obesity can often parallel corporate overhead and indicate a lackadaisical style. I am similarly cautious of heavy smokers, drinkers, and womanizers.

Executive Actions Under Pressure Are Telling

After you have executives pegged, it is helpful to observe their actions in times of crisis, especially when the company is under fire after a serious setback. These are the moments to judge management character; to scrutinize their reactions; to see whether they take a studied, rational, and calm course to rectify the situation. Frequently executives panic, behaving in a deleterious manner that can take various forms, making mistakes that compound their problems. Such moves during troubled periods are like dousing the flames with fuel.

Eternal, Blind Optimists Even in Crisis

Executives are often too close to the firestorm. A stock I covered once, an early leader in the computer industry, announced a shocking business shortfall. The shares fell off a cliff. But the executives acted as if the problems were temporary and things were under control. This attitude of minimal concern was accepted by traders and institutional investors. It was a big mistake. The disaster deepened, and the company collapsed and disappeared. It taught me to step back and assess such business setbacks, use my own industry and company knowledge, and pay scant attention to executive commentary during a crisis. It is easy amid a disaster to be cajoled by management into viewing the situation as not as bad as it appears on the surface. Canards flow freely. Executives can take an insouciant attitude, which is misleading. The problem may easily have more extensive implications than communicated by management because it is too early for them to understand all the ramifications.

In other cases, a setback sends executives into spin control. They become defensive. In such a panic situation when a stock cracks badly, you as an investor can be a better judge of the future outlook than what is being spewed from the suits. Even seasoned analysts often have their own positive bias and vested interest. The individual investor can take a more arms-length view and not get caught up in the turmoil. Trust your own judgment of a panicked company.

Surprising the Street with Bombshell News

Favorable stunners are fine but negative announcements that come out of the blue impact company credibility and cause investors to wonder what else might be wrong. Good executives forthrightly discuss issues, challenges, threats, and other vulnerabilities, giving investors some warning of the possibility.

Assuming It Is a Temporary Setback

Management always wants to believe that the current problem is short-term, no more than one or two quarters in duration. But bad news usually gets worse. Whether the issue is an order rate booking shortfall, a drop in profit, revenue slippage, a contract loss, or an adverse legal/regulatory decision, it can be passed off as temporary or trifling, and corrective measures are tepid.

Blaming External, Uncontrollable Factors

To dodge culpability, management blames outside causes—the economy, credit conditions, war, foreign currency, the government, irrational competitor pricing, or a rival "buying" a contract. Setbacks and disappointing results might also be attributed to non-operational factors such as inferior forecasting, accounting, or reporting systems, rather than lack of competitiveness, weak markets, market-share loss, or other more fundamental failings. Sometimes companies even hold analysts and the press responsible. When Krispy Kreme Doughnuts lowered its earnings guidance and announced an SEC investigation in progress, it attributed slower sales to the low-carb diet craze. Curious that Dunkin' Donuts was not faltering. In 2008, the subprime-mortgage credit crunch was the excuse used for of any and all shortfalls. Even the chocolate company Hershey trotted it out as an explanation. If these executives are trying to fool investors, they are only kidding themselves.

Inaccessible, Turning Insular, Out of Touch

In the eye of a storm, corporate leaders wall themselves off and become inaccessible. Executives might confer but remain out of touch with the outside world. It is calm on the inside while clients, suppliers, employees, and investors are roiled. In late 2007, the CEO of Sallie Mae responded evasively, in an analyst conference call, to investor alarm over its worsening financial condition. In answer to a question about how the company would regain its prior credit rating, he quipped, "You're talking to the wrong guy; I don't know that answer." At the end of the call, he dropped the F-bomb. Hiding from analysts, investors, and the press is a serious mistake. Belligerence, arrogance, and foul language certainly reveal just about all you need to know about a company.

Misplaced Confidence

When a company's stock plummets, the company sometimes takes umbrage; the downturn is taken personally. A sizable stock repurchase program is launched to demonstrate confidence in a recovery. This assurance is usually misplaced, the shares drop further, and the company ends up overpaying. Do not think for a minute that a buyback is a telling indication of executive faith or a sign that the stock is cheap. It is a desperate attempt to feign conviction in a period of duress.

Firing the CFO or Middle Management, Keeping Inept Leaders

The buck stops at the top. But often when companies experience a major reversal or a business disappointment, they fire the chief financial officer as a scapegoat. And lower-level executives responsible for the problem are also terminated. Upper management should similarly be dismissed if a company is taking serious steps and not just shuffling the deck chairs. Higher-level executives are rarely held accountable. The cancer spreads because of denial or lack of enlightened direction at the top.

Frenzied Leaps, Strange Maneuvers

Companies in crisis can act frantically, making last-ditch attempts to bail out of trouble, doing such things as mega-acquisitions. This diverts analyst and investor attention, casts a complicated, "strategic" new element into the mix, and buys time. They grab a gigantic contract at any price or give liberal payment terms to steal business—anything to boost immediate sales. Dramatic splashes in times of trouble never work.

Financial Schemes to Aid Earnings

Profits are temporarily boosted by stock buybacks, asset sales, capital gains on securities, write-offs, negative cash-flow deals, and other balance sheet–related tactics. Stock repurchase plans are mere financial reengineering. They aid earnings and the stock price temporarily but are a poor substitute for real growth. Financial transactions are tricks to offset or obscure the operating problem. They merely underscore management despair, avoid addressing the predicament, and fail to provide resolutions.

Insisting That Stock Overreaction Is Unwarranted

When stocks drop violently, management's first reaction is to insist that the price should not be so low. In speaking to investors, executives address the stock price rather than the operating dilemma, criticizing Wall Street for overreacting. Stock prices are normally a good indicator of the outlook and can be a better signal than many executives are willing to admit.

Appraising management is essential to determining a company's prospects. After all, these are the folks who will make or break your investment. You are relying on them to do the right thing, so you need to be a good judge of executive aptitude. Certain recurrent personality types and management styles can be readily identified. Other times, you need to look more thoroughly for what makes executives tick. Character is vital. In judging a company, you must gauge management first and foremost. Carefully ponder the quality and effectiveness of a corporation's executive leaders before deciding to invest in the company's stock.

7

How Street Analysts Really Operate

Wall Street research took root in 1934 with the publication of the seminal investment text *Security Analysis,* by Graham and Dodd, a detailed guide to fundamental, conservative, long-term value investing. Today, Street research entails quilting together information and observations from myriad sources, and then drawing conclusions regarding the future outlook and potential for a stock. As an individual investor, you might on occasion find yourself in a situation in which you can conduct research like an analyst, maybe casually sitting next to an executive on a plane flight or at a social function. You certainly can tune into conference calls and read research reports and published company financials. If you emulate effective analyst research methods, you will be able to make your own investment judgments.

Back in the day, before analysts became so overwelmed and distracted by the demands of marketing and client contact, they actually did some decent, unbiased research. Recognizing how Street research has evolved and transformed will aid you in using today's Street research effectively and doing research yourself.

When Research Was Really Research

Research in the 1970s was thoughtful, substantive, unbiased, and long-term. Investors should conduct their research in this manner, even though analysts and the Street can no longer operate this way. The 1970s was an era before desktop PCs. When I started, electronic calculators did not exist. Slide rules were the tool of the trade. At our boutique firm, we had one stock price quote machine for the entire research department and a single Dow Jones newswire service constantly printing out long reams of paper. There were no company conference calls. We often learned of quarterly earnings results by spotting them in the next day's newspaper. Analysts had to call the CFO to ascertain any company numbers beyond reported revenue, net income, and earnings per share. There were no voicemails, fax machines, cell phones, pagers, or Blackberries. After company meetings or at airports, we would run for the payphones and use our AT&T calling cards. Travel agents wrote out by hand or typed airline tickets. There were no frequent-flyer mileage programs. It was the Dark Ages.

Things moved slower, distractions were fewer, market volatility was modest. The only stock market TV program was the 30-minute Friday night *Wall Street Week* with Lou Rukeyser. Analysts had time to do real research. Because analysis was less quantitative, with no earnings models or spreadsheets, we tended to look more often at business fundamentals and the bigger picture. My research reports had earnings model forecasts of a sort, but they were broken down annually rather than quarterly, and featured only five line items: revenue, profit margin, tax rate, share count, and earnings per share. Now that is simplicity. Reporters called infrequently, mainly from *The Wall Street Journal*. Television was not interested in analysts. Dialing clients took time, but because there was no voicemail and most calls resulted in busy signals, there were relatively few actual direct conversations per day. We just had more time to do pure research.

It was also a time of few research conflicts. All the early quality-level research was done by a few dozen boutique research-only firms like mine, Spencer Trask. One year in the early 1970s, it was ranked as the best research house by *BusinessWeek*, before the advent of the *Institutional Investor* rankings. Our competitors were Donaldson

Lufkin & Jenrette (DLJ), Smith Barney, Auerbach Pollack, F.S. Smithers, Rothchild, Cowen & Co., Faulkner, Dawkins, and the like. None of these firms did any degree of investment banking; most did precious little trading—and none catered heavily to private retail clients. Profits flowed from institutions paying fixed commissions of $0.80 per share. Today, commissions are a penny a share. The big wire houses that dealt with retail individuals, such as Merrill Lynch, E.F. Hutton, Dean Witter, and Shearson, did no in-depth research. Firms like Goldman Sachs, Morgan Stanley, and Salomon Brothers did investment banking and trading, but no research. With essentially no investment banking influence, research was more impartial.

Investment opinions in the 1970s were longer range. There was less emphasis on quarterly performance by the mutual fund industry. Daily trading volumes were low, under ten million shares a day on the NYSE (compared to three billion today), and there were no NAS-DAQ price updates—those stocks were "over the counter," and yesterday's prices were found in the Pink Sheets. Hedge funds had no influence, and quarterly corporate results were of only minor importance. Analysts not only had the time, but also were expected to provide in-depth, thoughtful, and balanced reports and investment opinions. In my most bullish company reports, I still detailed all the negative risks. And institutional investors actually had time to read these longer reports, unlike today. My Automatic Data and EDS reports contained lengthy discourse balancing positive and negative points, long assessments of current operations, and a forecast of the outlook over the next couple years. The content had shelf life. It had to; the report was distributed by U.S. mail, and the reader might not review it until a month later.

Analysts in those days were more professionally qualified. An analyst spent a decade or more getting seasoned. Serious, career-minded, early-stage analysts like me were persuaded to undertake the arduous three-year CFA program. Receiving a CFA designation is similar to earning a CPA in accounting, passing the boards to become an MD, or passing the bar exam to qualify as an attorney. It is the pinnacle of an analyst's professional education.

Research delved more deeply into the guts of a business. Management access in those early years was easy, but had mixed consequences. It was a snap to obtain informal meetings with executives in order to review the business and better understand the operations. This presented a stellar opportunity to develop the ability to judge management, their character, and their effectiveness. There was not as much quantitative data or as many specific internal forecasts for corporations to divulge. Financials and detailed earnings models played a minor role. Discussions were broader and pertained to operations, developments, and competition.

Executives had more time to meet with investors and analysts. There were markedly fewer of us. Executives had fewer demands on their time. Casual meeting opportunities abounded. We would spend the morning seeing executives at NCR in Dayton, Ohio, and they would join us in the afternoon at the top-ranked NCR South golf course. More executives were out at the practice putting green at lunchtime than we had spotted all morning at the headquarters. Analysts took field trips to Nice on the French Riviera to meet with the heads of U.S. companies' European operations over several glasses of Bordeaux as they profusely spilled the beans.

Analysts had time to observe managements and penetrate the facades. IBM was so formal in white-shirt attire and demeanor during that period that puncturing its facade became a diversion for analysts. I remember the debut of its new PC that was to be distributed through Sears, a stunning new tactic for this computer-mainframe juggernaut. During the analyst marketing presentation, a wag asked, "Will they be stacked on the floor next to lawn mowers or washing machines?" On another occasion, the chairman of a major technology firm made the keynote address to the computer services industry trade association. Computer services were an all-domestic business at that time. His staff prepared a formal speech on international trade, which he read off in 25 minutes. He then cut and ran, avoiding any questions. The whole show was exasperating, vastly missing the mark. I realized he was out of touch.

Beginning in the mid-1970s, Wall Street went through a massive consolidation, and investment research began its metamorphosis. The profitable partnership structures of most firms on the Street collapsed quickly after May Day 1975. That was the end of fixed commissions; they quickly shrank to 10¢ a share. My first-year bonus of $2,000 had melted to $100 four years later. Research boutiques folded and merged, no longer able to afford to do research without trading or investment banking revenues. Commissions from big institutional investors, such as mutual funds, began to underpin research budgets. And analysts eventually became beholden to the forces of institutional investors, investment banking, and trading.

Securities Analysts Reach the Major Leagues

In the 1980s, Street research started to transmogrify. It dawned on big Wall Street brokerage firms that respected, authoritative, potent research could enhance their business almost across the board—in institutional sales, trading, and investment banking. Brokerage firm top managements were paying attention to research and expanding budgets there. In only a few years, they bought all the leading analysts, enticing them away from smaller boutique brokerage firms. The new wave pushed the leading firms to the top research tier on the Street. Morgan Stanley led the charge. We had respect and status within our firms. This was the early phase of analysts becoming important on Wall Street and to brokerage firms' bottom lines.

Research analysts steadily built teams and their coverage gravitated toward greater specialization. The initial *Institutional Investor* poll in the early 1970s, which ranked the best Street analysts, had fewer than 25 industry categories. By 2002, there were 77 sectors. That first year, the category encompassing essentially all of high tech and the computer industry was termed "electronics." During 1985 to 1995, I narrowed my own coverage from the computer industry to software/services and finally to just computer services. Even within the last group, I concentrated specifically on transaction processing and outsourcing, leaving consulting/professional services and a few other segments to my teammates.

The road that led to the spoiling of research had begun. When analysts were clearing real money, around a half million annually, their egos inflated in line with the pay. Our attitudes reflected our newly vital role within the business. Investment bankers, traders, and management started conferring with us. Analysts felt important. We were in demand by the press and having our names in print boosted our cachet. There followed television interviews, further goosing our exalted status. Our ability to access CEOs surged as they realized our sway over their stock. Company user groups, trade associations, and industry conferences all stepped up requests to have us speak at their forums.

Even as the heavyweight brokerage firms became research leaders, analysts still maintained a modicum of impartiality. There were almost no bureaucratic encumbrances or compliance oversight, and analysts could shift opinion ratings on a dime, could express views fairly freely, and had little investment banking inhibition. They were not bothered by having to be in contact with the traders. There were even some last vestiges of service and care for the retail private client—that is, the individual investor. I took the time to help found the Software/Services Analyst Group on Wall Street (comprised of all the Street analysts who covered the sector) and served as its first president.

It was still a period when analysts concentrated most of their efforts on conducting research rather than marketing. I made trips to Europe and Japan, not to meet with investors, but rather to visit computer company managements, and to survey the international competition. During my first tour to Tokyo, the yen was king. Translating my car-service tab from the airport to the Okura Hotel into dollars, I was sobered to realize the price was $500. Our travel agent had blundered and sent me off without a Visa, so I had to jam my meetings and speech to the Japan Society of Security Analysts into the maximum 72-hour transit limit. I was whisked through passport control with 30 minutes to spare, the Narita Airport officials all doing double takes that a transfer, which normally took a few hours, lasted three full days.

During this period of my career, probably reflecting my hyperactive nature, I got into long-distance running. I had run cross-country on the track team in college, so when jogging first came into vogue, I knew it was a sport in which I could excel. Running was a stress release and gave me time to quietly ponder things, away from the maddening work setting and the two kiddies at home. And it quickly led to my running the Boston and New York marathons in 1980. On a cold day during the New York City Marathon, my running glove was snatched by a delinquent in Brooklyn. When I was running out of gas after the 20-mile mark in Harlem, the bystanders cajolingly cautioned, "You better not stop in this neighborhood!" At the finish of the New York Marathon that autumn, 3 hours and 35 minutes after the starting gun, I winged it to Monterey, California, for an annual high-tech conference, flaunting my medal prominently around my neck at all the meetings. Rupturing my Achilles tendon the next year, I saw my racing days come to an end. I often think all the racing and training helped me to take a disciplined, hardworking, and patient approach to my career.

I was an analyst at Salomon Brothers covering the computer stocks in the early 1980s. Several associates there later became notable industry leaders. Lewis Ranieri was the pioneer of mortgage-backed securities and created a massive new market. He was a wild, pen-chewing, driven powerhouse. John Meriwether was lurking in fixed income. Later he spawned Long-Term Capital Management with other industry luminaries. Before long, it became a cropper and almost dragged the entire market under, amid notorious controversy. There were other stalwarts such as Henry Kaufman and Michael Bloomberg.

The General Motors acquisition of EDS in 1984 marked a turning point in my career. Doron Levin's book *Irreconcilable Differences* recounts the captivating story of the GM-EDS deal. I was part of the drama. To further the banking relationship with General Motors, noting its new-found inclination to diversify, a Salomon banker put together a list of five acquisition ideas. GM's treasurer Courtney Jones jumped at the suggestion to buy EDS, and an offer was made to Ross Perot: $1 billion to him personally in realizable net worth. That was real money in those days. Ross sold EDS and obtained a fabulous no-risk convertible security in addition to the cash, but then proceeded to maintain full operational control of the EDS subsidiary. He stopped the GM auditors at his Dallas headquarters' gates, refused to open his books, and proceeded as if the company had never been acquired. The battle with GM's chairman Roger Smith was joined.

Salomon was a trading firm and also a major investment banking force. Research there was viewed as a back-office support function, and though managed somewhat autonomously from banking, we analysts were second-class citizens. This dawned on me when I was told that my total annual compensation including bonus for 1984 would be unchanged from the prior year, despite my playing a key role in the GM deal that generated $7 million in fees to the firm, a gargantuan sum in those years. I grasped that, regardless of my contributions, the prospect to make it big as an analyst at Salomon was limited.

EDS's relationship with GM remained combative; the forced surgical EDS implant was being rejected by the GM bureaucracy. Despite the negative impact of this culture clash, GM's colossal new computer-processing business tripled the size of EDS. As the leading Street analyst on the stock, I had to walk a tightrope. This was an early hint of the research conflicts with investment banking that were to manifest in the 1990s. Within a couple years, Perot, a GM board member, was excoriating GM's chairman Roger Smith publicly: "Until we nuke the GM system, we'll never tap the full potential...." And by the end of 1986, Ross and his key management compatriots were bought out of their $750 million convertible securities and walked dazed but lucratively away from the heavily guarded EDS campus barricade for good.

When my son was ten years old and had a passion for railroad trains, we took off on EDS's plane with Paul Chiapparone, a senior executive (and, incidentally, one of the two EDS hostages sprung in the 1979 secret Iranian raid) to tour GM's locomotive engine manufacturing plant in Canada. We operated a newly minted diesel railroad engine on the test track; Justin got six turns in the engineer's seat, and I could barely nudge him out for one go at the controls. He flew copilot on the EDS jet heading back home to New York. Not a bad day for a ten-year-old.

Digging for Skeletons and Pumping Executives

Doing good research meant sometimes acting as an investigative reporter. This means digging out information about companies that executives are unwilling to disclose. Usually it is negative. They voluntarily give out only the glowing side of their story. Sometimes this necessitates some honest thievery. Analysts are always on the lookout for the fat three-inch-thick company binders marked for internal use only, sitting in an airport lounge or a hotel conference room, containing all the statistics on dozens of divisions and tons of other facts and information, such as a list of clients. This gives analysts a fix on aspects that executives would never willingly divulge.

Creative insight and clever probing have always been hallmarks of good research. In the 1970s and 1980s, the only way to discover what was happening inside a particular company I covered was by piecing together information from lower-level employees. In 1973, at my two-day public-speaking course in uptown New York, I was startled to see that most of the other participants were junior salespersons from that firm. All of their five-minute practice speeches pertained to current sales issues and challenges. Keeping my identity under wraps, I took copious notes and zipped my lips. It was an incredibly insightful inside assessment. Always be aware of and listen to people around you.

I also recall a flight in which a Computer Associates salesman, not realizing I was a Street analyst, told me all the games and gimmicks that the software company played to create a revenue mirage, a practice I had long suspected but had had difficulty pinning down. I never trusted them again. Eventually management was charged by the SEC for fraudulent accounting and pleaded guilty to a federal indictment. Some of the best information sources are middle-level executives who banter like jocks in a locker room. The analyst's role is to put this gossip in the proper context, weighing it against other public information, recognizing that it might be myopic, isolated, or unimportant. But it might also generate sensitive questions to lob at top executives. Their reaction can be telling, because broaching these vulnerabilities usually catches them off guard. Executives strive mightily to prevent outside investors and analysts from peering at internal dirty laundry. Although individual investors are unlikely to have this opportunity, they can pay attention to how management reacts to analyst questions on conference calls or in press interviews. Analysts might be bringing a skeleton out of the closet.

Investors need to be critical of what they hear from executives. Direct, incidental contact and information can be a unique source of research, but you also need to do your homework. Never take an isolated conversation as the sole basis for an investment. The company must check out on numerous other counts. Even if you have a close executive relationship, say your neighbor or old school friend, remember that the insider perspective is not necessarily accurate. A risk of having close executive relationships is that though they might aid understanding, they also give you a favorable bias. Analysts on Wall Street too have certain personal relationships with corporate executives that give them an invaluable source of information and access, but the friendship might be motivated by the desire to obtain preferential treatment.

Through an organization that I am still actively involved in, the Business Executives for National Security (BENS), I had some perfect opportunities to schmooze with certain CEOs. The chairman of Automatic Data Processing, Josh Weston, invited me to join an Air Force tanker refueling mission en route from New York to the Strategic Air Command (SAC) base in Nebraska. The trip renewed my tie with the military, because I had spent three years aboard a Navy LST ship out of Norfolk as an operations officer in the mid-1960s. On subsequent outings with BENS—aircraft carrier night flight operations, nuclear submarine dives, Army tank battles, and an F-16 flight—I bonded with other company chairmen. I had a renewed buddy-ship with one CEO who had earlier bad-mouthed me to other analysts. There is nothing like being strapped in a four-way harness in a seat facing backward on a Navy transport plane, violently hitting the deck and arresting gear wires while landing on an aircraft carrier, to help you bond with the executives onboard. Subsequently, I have been to Iraq and Afghanistan with such company.

For me golfing was another good way to build personal relationships with executives. After kidding around for four-and-a-half hours, competing for whopping $5 or $10 stakes, and downing a couple beers, you become friends. After that, business is personal. Later, if I called up the CEO, he was ready to chat, mostly about golf, but it always gave me an opening to broach business topics. The chairman of a company I covered introduced me to Arnold Palmer before we contested a round at Bay Hill. He also hosted me at the 2000 Masters Golf Tournament in Augusta. Such camaraderie diminishes the normal barriers between executives and analysts. I was not particularly privy to sensitive inside information, but I did get a better sense of leanings and direction on key issues.

Another time, one of a firm's biggest contracts was about to expire and Wall Street was uncertain whether the client would be resigned. Somewhere along in a round of 18 holes that I was playing with a member of the management, I gathered the impression that a successful renegotiation was imminent. There were no details. But it was enough to assure me. I took a positive stance, and it was validated shortly thereafter. It is not always golf. Events like the 1996 Atlanta Olympics, which I attended with another company's executives, similarly helped me to establish close relationships. When the same firm shocked the Street that autumn with news of an earnings shortfall, I knew which members of management I could trust to give me the straight scoop.

Talking to executives is an art. As an investor, you must decide whether what you hear makes sense. Does it stack up? Does it ring true? Analysts have a thorough understanding of the industry, competitors, users, and trends. And they have an in-depth grasp of a company's business, past record, issues, and management. We should be qualified to gauge executives' remarks. Still, it is not easy. We can be fooled. In any casual conversation you might have with executives or when tapping into conference calls, you need to be on guard.

Regulation Fair Disclosure (Reg FD), implemented in 2000, requires full company disclosure to the public of any material information that could influence stock prices. This new requirement has had the effect of muzzling executives in the past few years. They are now unable to give any selective forecasts, guidance, or broad indications of expected future progress. Still, things dribble out in phone conversations. Street insider awareness is enhanced by posing questions usually to the CFO or head of investor relations (IR). Most analysts have direct access to these two company representatives. It is rare for them to have an entree with the chairman or CEO. The advantages in being an analyst for so long were my age and industry standing. Several chairmen viewed me as a peer, which aided my reception. I played golf with these company leaders, dined at their homes, and attended the symphony with them, all occasions for serious bonding. Younger analysts had no such relationship. Investors need to be aware of the experience of analysts covering any particular stock. Be skeptical if they have not been in place at least ten years. Most Street analysts today are junior, do not have access to top-level executives, and do not have a seasoned perspective.

There are many facets to interacting with management effectively. If we take no notes, they speak more freely. Still, most analysts
scribble frantically. Sticking to important, broad topics is key when
talking with a chairman. You cannot expect an executive at that level
to know the capital-spending budget for next year or the nuances of
percentage-completion accounting. CFOs are the source for financial
matters. Do not presume they have anything helpful to offer on
aspects such as products, manufacturing, or research and development. Rapid response is another measure. Leading analysts who have
the most influence on a stock get rapid answers. When a callback lags,
it is a warning that something major is about to be announced. I once
downgraded my opinion at the end of a quarter on a company that
was unresponsive. Usually the company was quick to call me back. I
read a pending earnings shortfall disclosure into such an uncharacter-
istic pause, I forewarned investors, and the stock price sank. It was a
mistake. Everything was fine, but the company never failed to return
my calls promptly after that.

Reading Executive Body Language

Most companies hold meetings at least once a year for Wall Street
institutional holders and securities analysts. These are usually annual
affairs lasting from three hours to one-and-a-half days. Executives are
paraded onto the podium, audiovisuals are flashed on the screen, and
bulky notebooks are handed out with copies of all the slides. We
scrawl voluminous notes and ask endless questions. But the best
information is revealed during informal coffee breaks. Onstage, there
is a lot of temporizing; the remarks are planned, canned, always given
with an optimistic spin. Although important disclosures are rare, it is
still imperative for analysts to attend. We can detect an overall tone,
read body language, sense any hesitancy, observe confidence levels,
and get an impression of both the executives and the attitudes of
investors in the audience. Usually the stock moves that day in concert
with the tenor of the session.

These meetings are normally mundane and tedious. But not always.
Once, at the yearly Microsoft gathering in Seattle, the scheduled meeting was shifted to a convention hall near the Navy piers following a

bomb scare. But Bill Gates had the idea to corral the 250 Street professionals onto an aircraft carrier tied up nearby. Even the U.S. Navy made way for Bill Gates. Chairs and audiovisual equipment were arranged on the hangar deck, and all the analysts calmly embarked, enthralled by the imposing military venue. We never determined whether it was all a setup or whether it was truly spontaneous. EDS once held a Texas barbeque on its ranch outside Dallas and gave the attendees helicopter rides. On another occasion, I observed a stern, proud executive at a trade association meeting take two steps backward from a raised lectern and crash three feet down into a heap. Disappearing from view, he whimpered, "I think I'm alright." Afterward, he pleaded with me to keep the matter from his fellow executives back in the home office, lest he become a laughingstock.

The content of meetings, however, is usually predictable; rarely are there any newsy or dramatic developments. Microsoft always lowballs the outlook, reducing expectations. Analysts disregard it. Sometimes, though, forecasts can be alarming. Computer Sciences once put forward tepid revenue guidance, the shares were creamed, and it was the beginning of a several-year-long industry-wide downturn in consulting and outsourcing. EDS once astounded a group with the bullish revelation that it was bidding on a contract some 25 times the size of any previous deal. That started a 16-year run in the stock. These are exceptions.

Conference calls have taken research to yet another level of detail. In the years before the orchestrated group calls, analysts chatted with executives for no more than 20 minutes to understand the just-reported results. Now everyone can listen in for an hour or more. On the downside, all parties monitoring these calls get the same spoon-fed executive hogwash, and all Street research reports reflect this similar information—another reason for the less and less distinctive, original, or creative research analysis. The Street research reports parrot executive explanations, churning out what was said on the call. If you listened in on the call, you do not even need to read the reports.

Conference calls usually accompany news flashes or press releases. Events such as earnings shortfall pre-announcements, contract awards or losses, acquisitions, and management changes often demand that an investor make a judgment. An immediate impression is usually the correct one under such pressured conditions. This is where a certain feel comes into play. Often you must do a fair amount of guessing based on your prior understanding of a company or an industry. Your knowledge of the companies you own is the key to putting most breaking announcements in the proper context. Remember to avoid an emotional reaction. Make a detached, impartial conclusion even when engulfed in a firestorm. Do not bend a new development to fit your ongoing investment position. Do not be blinded by unconditional faith. Although normally the best course is to sit tight until calm is restored and a reasoned opinion can be reached, once in a while the turn of events is a dramatic enough catalyst—a Black Swan event—to shift your investment view. Such events should be the exception, but never be oblivious to the possibility that all of a sudden it might be a whole new ball game.

Most analysts hold annual industry conferences, featuring the sector's company executives. Competition to draw investors to these forums is fierce. My strategy was to be the first one of the year, so we scheduled our conference in early January to one-up my rival analysts. My format was also unique, having only casual Q&A breakout sessions, no dreary stage presentations. And we held these events off-site, in plush Florida resorts such as the Ritz-Carlton on Key Biscayne. There our audience was captive for two-and-a-half days. We always teed up colorful industry-related characters—H. Ross Perot, a NASA astronaut, and the like—to entertain at the dinners held at intriguing sites such as museums or mansions. Our shindig became the best annual conference in the sector. My decades of rapport with the companies in the industry brought out more senior executives, chairmen, and CEOs than any of my competitors' gatherings.

Individual investors are not invited to these meetings. But do not worry—not much in the way of surprising news or major developments is ever disclosed. In this era of required full disclosure, executives are muzzled, confined to PR pablum, and if there is any real company news, it is put out in a press release. There is only one sell-side brokerage analyst at such a conference—the one giving it. And he is consumed with running the show. Do not expect much research comment from his firm other than pro forma BS. These conferences are basically a marketing ploy to butter up institutional investor clients and gain brownie points with executives. If there is any material effect on the stock of the companies presenting, it is because the major institutions in attendance decide to buy a stock after hearing the story. This can push up the price for a short time.

The Numbers Sing but Keep Them in Perspective

Numbers and data might be boring, but they are vital to making investment choices. Elaborate, extensive earnings models have become a dominating aspect of research. These are multiple-page charts of quantified data. They start at the top with sales and revenues and filter all the way down to earnings per share. But they also extend to cash flow statements, balance sheets, and other data such as order-rate bookings. Models are built sedulously, mostly by junior analysts.

My philosophy has always been that the numbers sing. Models dive down into minute quantitative levels. Executives collaborate with the Street in the forecasting aspect when analysts develop and update these models. The end product is a measuring tool to monitor scores of different financial elements each quarter. They virtually tell the whole story of the health of a company. By analyzing recent financial patterns and trends with these models, analysts acquire a reasonable grasp on potential future results. The only problem I had was that I never knew how to build such a model on a personal computer. I entered Wall Street way before the PC era, never used computers in school, and, despite close brushes with technology, somehow managed to remain a Luddite. My kids, of course, are the opposite. At a press conference in the 1980s where I spoke about my book on the computer industry, my daughter Laurel, just starting elementary school, was asked if she was learning to use computers in school. She quipped, "No, we're just programming in Basic!"

The use of models has altered the research landscape. Corporate financials are always under massive scrutiny. Earnings spreadsheets have led to an environment where analysts are harder to please each quarter. They invariably find certain items that are wide of the mark, causing questions and forcing corporate executives to be defensive.

The Street can always find fault somewhere in the quarterly income and cash flow statements or balance sheet. This level of scrutiny is probably healthy.

That said, be skeptical of research that overly weighs models in the analysis. Concentrate on the broader scenario and the factors that shape the general outlook. Do not get entangled in exhaustive earnings model minutiae. Even professional Street portfolio managers do not have the time or skills to get mired in such mathematical detail. Individual investors cannot be expected to grapple with these quantitative monsters.

The prominence of models has detracted and displaced the ancient art of undertaking original investigative legwork—talking to customers, checking with former executives, spending time with competitors, or meeting with outside experts. This unbalanced, highly quantified, stay-in-the-office, model-driven mathematical research produces an environment like a medical laboratory. A patient needs a doctor with experience and big-picture awareness for a proper diagnosis, not just lab results and statistics. Models are altered constantly, tend to be based on consensus with little "forecastive" value added in, and are of limited use to investors and portfolio managers. Put them in the proper perspective.

Regardless of models, street research is still not focused enough on financial and accounting matters. Analysts often become enamored of a new technology, drug, or other promising prospect that is all futures. There is no substitute for earnings, cash flow, and strong finances. If any of these is lacking, it is a highly speculative stock. When these factors are downplayed or explained away, do not buy into the thesis. Equity analysts' understanding of financials is modest compared to that of credit and fixed-income analysts. Most stock research fails to delve deeply into the latter disciplines—balance sheets, cash flow, working capital, liquidity, and accounting and financial disclosure practices.

Do not think Street earnings estimates connote any real degree of accuracy. Precise earnings forecasts imply a ridiculous level of accuracy and mislead investors. Estimates change several times throughout the year. Analyst earnings estimates tend to be as favorably biased as their investment ratings. Rarely is there a forecast of a decline.

Consensus Street estimates for the S&P 500 have not predicted an earnings decline in more than 20 years. *The Wall Street Journal* pointed out that in July 2007, according to Thompson Financial, Street analysts estimated banks and brokerage firms (a heavily covered sector) in the S&P 500 index would expand profits by 9% in the third quarter. Ugh! Actual earnings slid by 27%, as reported three months later. Estimates move in reaction to news, not in anticipation of it. Companies are under artificial demands to meet or exceed a specific quarterly earnings expectation. Stock price volatility is exacerbated by quarterly results that vary by as little as 1¢ from a Street consensus expectation. Estimates, both annual and quarterly, should be in ranges to properly portray their inexactness, leaving room for movement.

Research Buttressed Investment Banking in '90s Bubble Era

By the 1990s, the value of analysts and their enhanced rapport with the CEOs of companies they tracked was beginning to be recognized by investment bankers. Commonly the analyst had better access to the chairman or CEO than the banker. The analyst entree became important in gaining banking assignments. Although analysts actively participated in banking deals in the late 1980s and early 1990s, they were not beholden—no entrapment yet. Investment banking was not yet an outsized, massive contributor to brokerage-firm bottom lines as it would become later in the '90s Bubble Era. Banking's role was still balanced, and analyst research maintained some measure of autonomy.

The '90s Bubble Era "was the best of times, it was the worst of times." Professionalism suffered. Analysts in the 1990s produced biased, distorted research. It was analysts gone wild, the ruination of credible research. I was a 25-year veteran at the time and old-fashioned enough to just not get it. The more professional, rational analysts like me were called relics. It felt good to be back in style later, after the bottom fell out of the Internet stocks. Always beware of investments tied to an assumption that we are entering a new era. They rarely work out.

The Internet boom/bust stories are legend. It was all about absurd expectations, a chimera. Heed the lesson.

That incredible period was bountiful for an extremely wide group of people. Virtually everyone seemed to embrace the wildly bullish times, from Fed Chairman Greenspan to the Chairman of the SEC, individuals to corporate CEOs, venture capitalists to analysts, the press to the government, car dealers to real estate agents. My airport taxi driver bragged about his wife sitting at home day trading. Governments, corporate pension funds, and charity endowments saw tax receipts, surpluses, and portfolios bulge. The disproportionate federal- and state-tax collections stemmed mainly from the exercising of capital gains and stock options. They all seemed to think that it was the result of their own astute policies and, even more unbelievably, that it would be permanent.

It even dawned on my daughter that there was money to be made in stocks. She was coming of age, just entering college, and I salted a few stocks into her own brokerage account. As the stocks climbed, all of a sudden she had more regard for my business. I told her that stock-price appreciation was called capital gains. Her retort was, "Dad, I like capital gains! Can you give me more of them?" Later I attempted to entice this college graduate, who had majored in archaeology and art history, to a career on Wall Street. Fat chance. I sat her down for an afternoon at our sales and trading desk in San Francisco. Anticipating that this experience would spark interest in the investment field, I inquired about her reaction. She was underwhelmed and quipped, "Those guys up there are cute!" This woman was headed in a totally different direction.

The roar from Wall Street produced a buoyant economy, soaring real estate prices, and abundant jobs with Internet start-ups for kids just out of college. Street professionals basked in the light of their influence and enjoyed their compensation, and so did venture capitalists, fund managers, bankers, and treasurers. All these groups benefited regardless of, or maybe because of, the abundance of improper Street practices, later to be uncovered.

In research, budgets were flush and analysts had the freedom to build their teams. Firms hired research assistants with only undergraduate degrees. Office spaces bulged. With such resources, teams produced lengthy tomes, phonebook-size industry studies and reports. Quarterly industry reviews proliferated; user surveys mushroomed. Investors and portfolio managers never had time to pore over all this tedious detail, but corporations and executives in those industries were pleased to have these industry research publications float in over the transom for free. The thicker the magnum opus, the more our expertise shined, like a college term paper.

As public interest surged, analyst stature reached unimagined heights, rivaling that of Hollywood celebrities. Crazed, star-struck, new-generation analysts—actually "cheerleaders"—were awarded three-year guaranteed contracts. Bonuses skyrocketed. On marketing trips instead of one-on-one appointments, a dozen or more portfolio managers filled meeting rooms. Analysts had the ear of CEOs, and obtained instant access to top management of the companies under coverage. They created revenues for their firms and wealth for investors. Investment recommendations and price targets ignited stock prices. Stock Buy ratings turned out to be "fabulous ideas," surging upward. *Institutional Investor* magazine has an annual feature profiling "home-run hitters," an analyst whose Buy opinion moves up 100% or 200%. In the late 1990s, it took stock surges of more than 1000% for a stock idea to make that list.

Charles Kindleberger, an academic expert on economic bubbles, manias, panics, and crashes, defines a *"bubble"* as an increase "in asset prices in the mania phase of the cycle...over an extended period of 15 to 40 months that then implodes." Robert Shiller, in his book *Irrational Exuberance,* characterizes a "speculative bubble" as "a period when investors are attracted to an investment irrationally because rising prices encourage them to expect...more price increases." In *The Panic of 1907,* Bruner and Carr mention several conditions that are almost always evident during economic bubbles: "entry into the market by naive, inexperienced, and unsophisticated investors; talk of a 'new paradigm' rendering long-standing investment maxims invalid; aggressive financing; and media hype and considerable popular interest." Sounds like the 1990s to me—and the real estate market around 2005–2006. It is good to keep these past bubbles in mind in order to identify such a state in the future.

There are many historical parallels to the 1990s, such as the mid-1800s railroads, which were the growth stocks of that era. They sprang up in months, went public quickly, and were chased by investors at a feverish clip. Almost all of them soon were acquired for a few cents on the dollar or went bankrupt. I have collected more than a hundred old railroad stock certificates from that period, a fraction of the thousands of publicly traded names during that time.

Another historical example is the incredible 1980s Japanese stock market explosion when many sectors, such as textiles and shipping, saw price-to-earnings multiple valuation levels top 100x. Understated earnings, cross shareholdings, and world economic leadership were reasons used to justify these radical heights. And, as with the U.S. Internet bubble, Japanese investors rewarded market-share expansion rather than profit growth. Real estate prices in Japan leaped off the charts, and the Japanese chased trophy properties around the world to places like Pebble Beach and Rockefeller Center. The stock most typifying that bubble was Nippon Telephone and Telegraph (NTT). Its shares sold at a price-to-earnings multiple of 200x and it reached 3,000,000 yen before capitulating 80% to 500,000 yen in the early 1990s. And Japan's Nikkei index rolled over from 40,000 to 15,000 in the same time frame.

John Rubino, author of *Main Street, Not Wall Street*, says that bubbles are most likely to happen when new technologies, new business practices, or new leading companies emerge. In the Roaring '20s, the stock price of Radio Corporation of America (RCA) soared from under $10 to $100, then sank below $10 in the 1930s. In the 1920s, preexisting standards of value, such as net-asset value or dividend yield, were tossed out. There was a proliferation of automobile, telephone, and aircraft manufacturers, the new technologies of that era. The 1990s Internet explosion also resulted in thousands of IPOs, newly public companies with wildly excessive valuations. And compared to the manufacturers of the 1920s, there were essentially no capital requirements. The 1920s was called as an era of limitless prosperity. Even an influential Yale economist talked about the market reaching a "permanently high plateau." In the recent epoch there were books that forecast that the Dow would reach 36,000. Both eras inspired an investing mania. In the 1920s, shoeshine boys were plunging into the market; in the 1990s, waiters were day trading.

The '90s Bubble Era rewarded corporate market-share gains and intriguing conceptual business plans rather than profit improvement. Traditional valuation measures such as price-to-earnings (PE) ratios were discarded in favor of imagined future discounted cash flows. That is because PEs became infinite for the plethora of Internet start-ups running red ink. In early 2000, Yahoo!'s market value was $105 billion, greater than the combined automobile and auto parts industries! Laws of economics were temporarily suspended, and profits were deemed unnecessary; the focus was on concept, market share, sales, futures, or any number of enticing mirages. In the 1990s, the S&P 500 index tripled in five years; in the roaring 1920s bull market, the Dow Jones Industrial Average quadrupled in six years.

The shocking stock market excesses of the 1920s decade-long bull run ended in the massive collapse of the 1930s and led to radical stock market reform measures under Joseph P. Kennedy and the new, Roosevelt-created SEC. It took a decade to offset the 1920s excesses and install necessary reforms. Some 25 years passed before the stock market recovered to the previous highs of 1929.

Internet Euphoria Perverts Street Research

In the '90s Bubble Era, derisively known as the "dot-com" era, companies with hundreds of millions of venture capital to blow and no prospect of ever earning a profit became the "New Economy." It was the rise of the great American money machine called the new paradigm. Internet start-ups went public and saw their stocks reach triple figures. The magazine of choice was *Red Herring*, with more than 300 workers and a circulation of 275,000, for news about Internet and tech IPOs. The mutual fund managers wanted "the new stuff," such as Priceline.com. That stock surged to $162. Computer services companies that I covered, such as EDS and First Data, with a fast revamp of their PowerPoint presentations and a change in logo, became eCommerce B-to-B eBusinesses because it helped their stock prices.

Green analysts were abundant during the '90s Bubble Era and the quality of their research reflected their immaturity. These bull market babies, who became Wall Street analysts amid the flourishing economy and soaring stock market, had no appreciation of a potential downturn. Reckless analysts and investors all propounded the theory that the old rules did not apply anymore; they thought elephants could fly. And they did, but not for long.

eToys peaked at $84 and sunk to zero. Webvan launched its IPO at $35; its trucks were seen scurrying all over San Francisco and a few other cities. In the end, $1.2 billion in capital was burned. A billion here, a billion there—it seemed like play money at the time. Pets.com went public a month before the March 2000 market climax, peaking at $14. Later that year, it announced plans to liquidate and shut down. Mp3.com shot up to $105, reaching a market value of $5.6 billion, before its demise. DrKoop.com top-ticked at $45, a market cap of more than $1 billion, before capitulating at the end of 2001. Theglobe.com went public in late 1998, roaring ahead 60% on its first trading day to close at over $63. Two-and-a-half years later, it was delisted from NASDAQ and traded for 16¢.

It was not only Internet names. Some shooting stars were in telecom network equipment. Redback Networks was a wonder of a public offering in 1999, the stock reaching its apex of $191 in March 2000, then going into Chapter 11. In late 2003, the shares were worth a few cents. Losses over its short life span amounted to $5.4 billion, which was serious red ink for a tiny firm whose revenues never surpassed $278 million. Not all the disasters were publicly traded stocks. There were scads of private companies like Miadora.com, the best online retail jewelry site. It raised $51 million in venture capital, burned through it, and closed down, all within 15 months.

Then there are the "winners" that still exist today, whose stocks continue to trade albeit at a staggeringly discounted level. iVillage's zenith was $130 before it was acquired in the single digits. Openwave Systems launched its IPO in mid-1999 at an equivalent of $48, and shot up to $624 the following year at the height of the NASDAQ bubble before collapsing to $1. Wave Systems did its IPO at $15 in 1994, topped $143 in 2000, and was trading below $3 in 2006. Akamai Technologies launched its IPO at $28 in 1999, peaked at $345 in 2000, and fell to 57¢ by 2002. Yahoo!'s IPO was at $1.38 adjusted; it doubled its first day and shot up over $120 before plunging into single figures.

Amazon.com, the champion, did its initial offering at $1.50 adjusted and saw its stock trade all the way to above $110, before tanking to below $6. Japan's Internet-related wonder company, Softbank, saw its shares dive a daunting 98.5%, from 198,000 yen to under 3,000 yen. The granddaddy holding company that ruled the Internet universe, CMGI, ascended to $163.50 before being hammered to a low of 28¢. Countless '90s Bubble Era executives in the end created no value and drove their stocks to zero, yet a few lucky ones walked away with hundreds of millions or even a billion dollars.

During this time, analysts were inundated with requests by institutions to track, even endorse, these flashy new-wave Internet entrants. Their ringmasters were youthful leaders who acted like Hollywood moguls, with overconfident and mostly off-putting attitudes. At investor conferences their sessions were packed, given the mania for such risky high-beta upstarts. The critical investment factors—real earnings, finances, and cash flow—were forgotten during that period. The new stocks had absurdly high prices, tenuous business models, deficit prospects, and promotional management. So I viewed them as extremely risky speculations. Such oversight sometimes still happens today.

Historically, 8% to 10% annual stock market returns have been the norm. In the late 1990s, the world turned upside down and market participants anticipated doubles, triples, and more, as characterized by the astounding, irrational stock price pinnacles. In the aftermath, although there was some sobering atonement, investors still anticipated at least 10% to 15% yearly gains. This presumption was not in line with past long-term results. Assume that the market might appreciate only 5% to 10% over time

Part and parcel of the absurd euphoria during that time was the annual November Comdex Conference in Las Vegas, by far the most outsized trade show in the country. At its peak in 2000, attendance reached 211,000. It was impossible to move around the strip; taxi lines snaked endlessly; stars such as Bill Gates, Larry Ellison, Michael Dell, and John Chambers filled 5,000-seat theaters with at least that many being turned away. The number of corporate exhibitors crested at 2,337. What was once a personal computer forum had broadened to cover everything from consumer electronics to the Internet, computer services to semiconductors. There was free entertainment by rock bands and vocal celebrities. Along the way, Comdex (originally termed Computer Dealers Exposition) was sold for $860 million in 1995 to a Japanese entity. That Japanese firm must have been caught up in the same ecstasy as Wall Street and its investors. The conference's demise paralleled the bursting of the bubble. As a public company, it declared bankruptcy in 2003, and the entire Comdex trade show was canceled in 2004. The end.

Research Runs Amok

Research coverage and stock Buy ratings in the 1990s did not differentiate between extremely speculative equities with red ink and little revenue, and established, stable, blue-chip firms that had proven profit records. Analysts made no allowance for differing degrees of vulnerability among stocks they recommended. Investors were similarly indiscriminate. The lesson is that companies with proven profits and assets should be valued accordingly. Investors must weigh the risks of firms whose outlook is vague. This element is paramount. In the 1990s, investors sought what was perceived as the best opportunity for the biggest gains from the sexiest, emerging, new-wave companies. Analysts felt pressure from the sales force, trading, management, institutional clients, and retail investors to oblige with recommendations. Long-standing, formerly leading companies such as General Electric, ExxonMobil, Wal-Mart, and Johnson & Johnson were thought boring. And there was little discretion with regard to market capitalizations. As an individual, pay careful attention to stock valuation and risk. They are still often disregarded by the Street.

Reports during the '90s Bubble Era were suddenly all positive. No longer did the Street put negative concerns or risk factors into research commentary. Compliance stopped noting the absence of pessimistic topics in the reports. Stock recommendations were all hype, promotion, and favorable prognostications. Lofty stock-price targets helped tout the flattering story. When a PE ratio was not possible due to red ink, elevated price goals were justified by quantifying such things as number of website visitors, market shares, and revenue multiples.

The pathetic quality and blatant partiality of research of the time was elegantly portrayed by Roger Lowenstein of *The New York Times* in a 2006 article on the Adelphia management scandal. His description of the research on the company during that era is revealing: "But what stands out from the analysts' reports is less the hype than the utter superficiality. Nowhere does a reader gain a feeling for what distinguished Adelphia—its cloistered weirdness, its familial obsessions, its precarious capital structure and persistent deficit of free cash flow. The analysts beat their breasts over minutiae, they obsess over stock charts, they deliver pages upon pages of spread sheets crammed with figures, yet nowhere do they scrutinize or even critically question the convenient company projections on which the numbers are based."

Research was further damaged by widespread arrogance during the 1990s bubble. Analysts, portfolio managers, and investors could not imagine that their unrestrained enthusiasm might be wrongheaded. Their only fear was the possibility of missing out on the upside. Analysts lost touch with reality. There was no historical perspective, no balance, only an effort to keep up with the bullish herd. They accentuated the pizazz. It all went together—loss of objectivity, haughtiness, and indiscriminate promotion.

Today a measure of the hubris has subsided but not totally dissipated. The exit of characters such as Grubman and Blodget sharply reduced analyst compensation. Extensive layoffs in 2009 helped reestablish some humility. Curtailed or tightly controlled press contact has also contributed to the return of modesty. But there is still an overconfidence that exacerbates mistakes and wrong opinions.

The brief career of Henry Blodget is a good example of how attitude can be destructive. He was of the new breed of analyst, with no track record or seasoning. He had no MBA or CFA and was typical of the flock of novices that charged into the business in the 1990s. A youthful, collegiate, but also glib and precocious new arrival on Wall Street in 1994, Blodget became an overnight sensation in late 1998, placing a $400 price target on Amazon.com, which was then trading at about $240. It zoomed above his outrageous goal within a month. The press heralded him as an oracle of the New Economy, and for a while he basked in the limelight.

His Internet stocks propelled him into an über-analyst. Blodget also covered Internet Capital Group. It reached $212 before its steep plummet. His rating was still positive at $15. His recommendation on

24/7 Real Media was favorable, while his internal email portrayed it as a "piece of s—," according to the legal evidence used against him. Its price swooned from over $60 to under $1. The news headline when he finally capitulated and reduced his opinions was "Now He Tells Us." In a settlement with the New York State Attorney General, Blodget is now banned forever from the securities industry. Separately, in 2003 his firm settled 20 class action lawsuits alleging false or misleading research reports, some by Blodget, for $133 million.

Fame can be intoxicating. The power to move stocks up or down sharply with a shift in a recommendation, in addition to all the corporate executive and media attention and high poll rankings, makes analysts feel omnipotent. When they start to believe that they are superior, that is when the most egregious errors are committed. Distrust analysts who appear in the media too often. They are focused on pumping up their image and probably are not spending enough time doing research. Investors should put more credence in humble, unassuming analysts.

Events and Consequences of the Bubble Era Are Still Relevant

The bigger the party, the worse the hangover. By October 2002, the NASDAQ Composite had crumbled some 78% from its high in March 2000. Cisco Systems, a substantive, quality, technology leader, crashed 92% from $82 to $6. Tech leaders such as Intel dove 81% from $75 to $14, and Microsoft cracked by 64%. Trust in Wall Street was broken in the 1990s aftermath, and further destroyed in the 2008–2009 debacle. Even the New York Stock Exchange was sued. Mutual funds were discredited. Individual investors suffered massive wreckage. At home, day traders had to abandon their temporary retirement and find real jobs. A friend of mine who is a therapist had to forgo retirement and again take on a full slate of patients. Given the market nosedive, he had no trouble filling up his client list. As tax receipts plummeted and deficits amassed, government spending was suddenly faced with a reduction in proceeds.

The crash, a term rarely used on the Street, led the exuberant and arrogant new-wave analysts to their demise. In my view, some of them should have ended up in federal detention, like Mike Milken did after that sorry 1980s phase of pushing the junk bond envelope. But that did not happen. The end of boosterism and hawking brought a lot of other Wall Street interests down with it.

After the market was punctured, all the transgressions of the Bubble Era surfaced fast. Committees were established, procedures were formalized, compliance oversight ballooned, brokerage management changed, rumors ran rampant, anxiety mounted. As revelations erupted, heads rolled. The market plunge halted banking deals and damaged commission revenues. Research budgets got whacked, partly from cost scrutiny, and exacerbated by the loss of credibility and the absence of support from investment banking. Its cost was shifted from banking to sales, trading, and general corporate overhead. That led to an even sharper examination of research's merit. Management quickly determined that an adequate product could be generated a lot cheaper by middleweight and junior analysts. Layoffs ensued. Many of the more senior, higher-paid analysts (like me) proved expendable in the new period of economic constraint.

Almost none of today's analysts were in the stock market business like I was during the 1970s bear market. Current analysts typically arrived in the 1990s. They have no recollection of the 1972–1974 market swoon. Before that there was euphoria over conglomerates, one-decision stocks and the Nifty Fifty. Growth stocks such as Avon, Polaroid, Xerox, and Sony, expanding at a 15% to 20% clip, sold at PE ratios in the 50x range. The first company I ever covered as a Wall Street analyst in 1971 was Automatic Data Processing (ADP). Since its growth rate was 25% to 30%, its PE was 100x. This was not considered abnormal—it was in line with others—so my initial rating was Buy. Extreme valuations were as much of an aberration then as they were in the 1990s. The stock market became more rational after the latter bubble burst, but excesses during howling bull markets often take more than just a half-dozen years to wring out. The bear market that commenced in 2008 completed the job.

Warren Buffett missed the incredible appreciation in Internet, tech, and telecom stocks during the late 1990s. Buffett is value-oriented and invests only in companies he trusts and understands. A Luddite, he was boggled by the absurd valuations. For a few years, he had to excuse himself at his annual meetings for missing the boat, not participating in the hysteria. Sticking to his guns, he became an idol again during the capitulation.

You too have the freedom to avoid extremes and dodge the debacle that always follows a bubble. Institutional investors, most of who must always be fully invested in stocks, do not have that luxury. Street analysts are similarly compelled to recommend stocks to feed insatiable institutional demand. You can stand aside during euphoric periods or when certain stock sectors get overheated. Extreme market swings are unsustainable and always adjust precipitously. In this decade there has already been a real estate bubble, the credit bubble, and assorted other bubbles that have busted. *The Wall Street Journal* puts it succinctly: "Big bubbles tend to end badly, take time to unwind, and claim a lot of victims." Sobriety, soundness: Investors must reflect these qualities. The extremes so evident in the '90s Bubble Era are relevant to your investment decisions in the future. Never forget the events and consequences of those years.

Research today is a shell of what it represented before the bubble burst and prior to the adoption of Reg FD. Analysts can no longer gain as extensive access to executives to develop insightful, unique research. They now tend to take publicly available information and put it into a research format. Brokerage firms have lower-paid analysts to cover the waterfront, even using MBAs in India to generate cheap, generic research. Morningstar is an independent research firm typifying this trend. It has some 100 analysts covering 2,000 stocks. This is what Street research has become, wide-ranging but more superficial.

The point of all this is that you need to grasp how Street analysts do research and how they have operated historically. With this awareness, you can conduct research like the insiders without the baggage, the biases, and the distractions. As an individual investor, you can investigate stocks on your own, listen to executives on conference calls, review earnings models, and act like a research analyst. Even though you cannot call the CEO or attend a brokerage institutional investor conference, you can benefit from understanding how analysts orchestrate these research functions. It pays to put yourself in the shoes of analysts in certain instances. Other times you can profit by doing exactly what they do not do.

8

Reforming Research to Level the Playing Field

Various elements of Street research are detrimental to individual investors. There needs to be an array of alterations in the manner in which brokerage firms conduct research, to make the game fairer and to put individuals on par with professional Street insiders. The system that went so awry in the 1990s will not be corrected until all parties involved in the investment business have altered their practices. The necessary research reforms should be spearheaded by the SEC. Bodies such as the NYSE and NASD could also be effective as catalysts for improvement. Although individuals do not have the power to effect these changes, their voice is powerful, and they should make their grievances known at every opportunity. Following the economic meltdown caused in fair measure by Wall Street, the federal government seems bent on major reform of financial institutions. The research and individual investor functions need to be a part of new regulations.

Analysts hardly have time to conduct true research. They manage a team, grind out or massage intricate earnings models, tune in to incessant conference calls, attend meetings to deal with the bureaucracy, and scramble to respond to scores of telephone calls and emails from institutions, the sales force, and the press. Exigencies abound. On the road, their schedules are booked solid with institutional client meetings all over town, with no time even for phone calls. As budgets are slashed and junior analysts proliferate in the ranks, analysis is being demoted, even outsourced, since it is of little benefit to the investment banking department or traders. Having lost credibility with individual investors, research has become only a commoditized service for institutional investors.

Research Should Be More Autonomous

Analysts' loss of objectivity is the fault of the entire system and less a question of individual misdeeds. A whole new research model is required. There should be more separation, not just from investment banking, but also from the sales force, corporate executives, and institutional investors. Although analysts can no longer be paid directly for or be involved in obtaining or executing investment banking business, guess what? Research opinions are still skewed in favor of investment banking clients.

Analysts confront an assortment of demands; it is impossible to serve all the groups effectively. They attempt an absurd balancing act. The brokerage-firm trader on the desk gets the first call from the analyst, as traders scramble to make a few cents per share on a stock trade in an hour or two. The institutional sales force covering the portfolio managers at such places as SAC Capital, Putnam Management, or T. Rowe Price want the analyst's insight to generate a short-term commission-producing transaction that day. The director of research emphasizes analyst poll rankings in an effort to look good with upper management. The analyst is always aware of all investment banking relationships the firm has with the companies he covers, another factor subtly influencing the research. Retail brokers (sometimes termed financial consultants or account executives) dealing with individual investors need objective research and effective stock picking. Brokerage firms should step back and reconfigure all research to properly address each constituency.

Street research needs more autonomy. Analysts should be shielded from being bulldozed by buyside clients and in-house salespeople, traders, bankers, and management. They should be akin to auditors, judges, and sports officials. Their role as impartial advisers must be restored. We need built-in safeguards to enable unbiased views and to prevent recourse if recommendations are unpopular. At present, analysts are overly hesitant to adopt pessimistic opinions, fearing backlash from all the research constituencies and corporate executives.

Analysts generate commission dollars for the firm. Institutions allocate stock trades and orders to a brokerage firm in return for valuable input or research help from the analyst. Research is a value-added service rendered to the client, but buyside payment to brokerages for this service does not go directly to the research department. Transactions go to the institutional and private-client salespeople. They get credit for the revenue. The research budget is defrayed by sales. Research leaders then bow to sales force demands. And these are just the conflicts originating from within the analyst's own firm.

Analysts are susceptible to the demands of the institutional sales force, who provide a major portion of the research budget and whose motive is usually to generate immediate trades. Institutional and retail clients represent two disparate research audiences, each having distinct requirements. The institutional sales force conducts an annual analyst evaluation, which in turn determines analysts' compensation. It is a conflict, because analysts strive for good marks in this popularity poll by providing short-term, trading-focused ideas rather than considered, longer term, investment-oriented research. Twisted to please all research users, the product becomes ill-suited to any one of the audiences.

Outside of the firm, institutional clients want industry and company insight, forecasts, and analysis of trends. Major buyside institutions' in-house security analysts consume hours of brokerage analysts' time, using them to obtain a more thorough understanding of companies. These insiders are only mildly interested in stock recommendations. Hedge funds, by contrast, are always angling to shape analysts' opinions to their short or long positions. And it is the hedge funds, and the other major institutional clients, that generate the bulk of commission revenues to brokerage firms. Because hedge funds trade so actively, their hot money holds undue sway over research analysts. The hedgies and big gorilla institutions demand special treatment from analysts. They expect analysts to behave like consultants. The rest of the clients and investors make do with a written report or commentary on a mass conference call.

A new model to pay for research will be necessary in the future. Investment banking no longer renders financial support. Commission rates are diminishing, dropping 18% annually in the U.S. in recent years; the price for an institutional trade is now only a penny or two per share. Fidelity demands a rock-bottom "execution only" price, in order to forgo paying for research it does not want. Electronic institutional trading commissions are less than a penny per share. Commission revenue allocated to research has been cut by more than half over the past seven years. The Street is reducing research budgets, outsourcing, and downsizing analyst staffs. Research has become a backwater. Prudential Financial closed down its stock research department altogether in mid-2007, laying off about 420 people.

Institutional investors have been spoiled by receiving all brokerage services in a bundle, including research. They will not pay for such services separately. So brokers have shifted toward hiring junior-level analysts at modest pay levels, just bodies to cover vast numbers of stocks. Research has been spread a mile wide and an inch deep. The goal seems to be to cover numerous names with less-seasoned analysts, just in case some banking business comes along. Obviously, a firm is not in the running for an investment banking deal unless there is research coverage, despite the cleanup after the 1990s bubble. Regardless of attempts to uncouple banking from research, conflicts of interest remain.

Research should be a separate arms-length entity, as brokerages have made their investment management and mutual fund units. Analysts need more distance from the sales force and traders, and from the executives of the companies they cover. The Eliot Spitzer–required independent research provided by several Street firms was not the answer. Many of these entities offered the same three or four pages of data on a stock, slapped on their own cover page opinion and conclusion, and pushed that out as research. It was basically just boilerplate.

Research departments should charge hard-dollar fees just like any consultant or other professional service. This would aid objectivity and enhance quality. Only the best research would attract paying clients.

Pure competition would result. Analysts would not be ranked according to popularity and intensity of communications. Payment for research should be required of the institutional sales desk and retail brokers of the parent brokerage firm. Many brokerages might even eliminate their research departments and use the research entities of others, which would result in more independence.

Research Should Be Less Expensive and More Tailored

Wall Street has always been absurdly overcompensated. Its denizens earn several times what counterparts gross in other industries. That includes doctors, attorneys, and corporate executives such as CFOs. Their compensation compares to that of sports figures, entertainers, and certain CEOs. An analyst's education, training, and professional qualifications are minimal compared to those of these other vocations. Junior analysts get paid $150,000 to $500,000. Senior analysts who have been in the business a decade or so, and are *Institutional Investor* ranked, can still clear $1 million annually, although that is down from $2 to $6 million during the '90s Bubble Era.

Research must become less expensive. The mind-set of most Street firms in the past was to maintain a stable of all-stars who rack up votes in the *Institutional Investor* poll rankings. So the tendency over the years has been to hire ranked analyst teams at excessive prices and lock them in for two or three years under a guaranteed contract with no commensurate performance requirements. The analyst is under no commitment to achieve milestones. No bonus incentive is dependent on attaining any preestablished goals. All the analyst has to do is stay employed. Firms are vulnerable to the mercenary jumping ship after the contract is finished. Sharply higher compensation attracts prominent analysts to come onboard. But embarrassing disparities develop with the comp level of similarly distinguished analysts already at a firm for several years. Analysts who remain with a firm for a decade or two sometimes are not paid at a level commensurate with a new hotshot hired from another firm. There needs to be a greater premium on analyst loyalty and longevity.

This old method of maintaining an assortment of stars has degenerated, sending research into disarray. When an established analyst departs, it is difficult for a firm to afford a similar replacement. They still desire to rank high on the *II* poll, by hiring leading analysts, but the means to pay for these heavyweights is gone. As a result, emphasis is being placed on cultivating new talent internally. A few firms like Goldman Sachs have successfully done this, but most brokers are of the old school and have found it frustrating to develop junior analysts. Research management is hard-pressed to recognize their progress and reward them with appropriate incentives. The economics of developing minor leaguers inside a firm until they reach the major-league level are compelling but necessitate a long-term view, foreign to most research directors.

Analyst compensation is not based on accuracy of investment opinions, earnings estimate precision, or other calculable measures. Unlike the brokerage sales force that can be judged on the commission dollars it generates, the research analyst's performance is judged more qualitatively. It is almost a popularity contest. One of the more precise, quantitative outside assessments of analysts is the Greenwich Survey, but because it is low profile, it has only a minor influence on firms. A key ingredient of analyst remuneration is effectiveness with major institutional clients. This translates into grants of commission business. The institution commits to do a certain amount of commissions, say $10,000, with a brokerage firm each quarter to pay for the help of a particular analyst. And there are also sales-force and institutional investor surveys and similarly flawed peer-group cross-evaluations. But analyst pay is still largely a judgment call. Revamping compensation and tying it directly to the accuracy of analysts' advice would be a giant leap forward to ensure objectivity. Analysts would never permit other influences to color their views if their compensation depended on their opinion accuracy.

Investment research is conducted to determine which stocks will outperform and which will underperform over the long term, the long term being at least a one- or two-year span. If the charter is *investment* research, the research needs to look out one or two years. If that is the goal, the bulk of an analyst's compensation should be based directly on the precision of these calls. Accurate Sell recommendations should be valued just as highly as correct Buy opinions.

Firms that utilize research to produce short-term trading ideas will judge analyst calls perhaps on a quarterly basis, which is an entirely different type of security analysis. Even the pay of mutual fund portfolio managers is misaligned, because it is heavily based on assets under management. What a surprise it was to see Janus's new chief investment officer overhaul its reward structure a few years ago, keying it more to "competitive performance, first and foremost."

Research must be tailored to a specific audience. Analysts cannot serve two masters. Securities research should be structured similarly to retail merchandising—that is, wholesale sells to institutions, retail to individuals. This might require separate research departments and different analysts. The push has been in the opposite direction, to equalize the research product for all audiences, so individual and institutional investors have access to the same product. But the needs of each group are vastly different. Research for individuals should be thematic, with long-range investment objectives, clearly indicating degree of risk, always assuming that the user is a naive, uninformed consumer. This audience should not be misled with stock-price objectives. Notable, bold-print warnings similar to those on a cigarette package should be in these reports, alerting small investors to the fallibility and variability of the research recommendations.

More Time Is Needed to Conduct Research

After I became a seasoned analyst, I was probably typical of most analysts and spent about 20% of my time actually conducting research. *Institutional Investor* magazine published an article several years ago on the "Secrets of the Superstars." It listed analyst work priorities by importance, and communications with clients ranked much higher than research. This priority indicates the upside-down emphasis of marketing over research analysis. And there were other misplaced preoccupations: staying in companies' good graces, juggling investment banking demands, providing global coverage, and working with junior analysts. Finding time for research was ranked last!

The October 2008 *Institutional Investor* All-America Research Team survey revealed that institutional investors sought from analysts skills such as responsiveness, management access, and services—mechanical, administrative, and communication capabilities. Research-related activities such as written reports, idea generation, financial models, and earnings estimates ranked in the bottom half of their list of the 12 most important attributes. No wonder actual research is such a low priority. Even if conducting the research is a more central goal, analysts need to focus and concentrate on fewer stocks. I noticed in a typical healthcare industry research report from a major brokerage firm that the analyst covered 28 companies in the sector, from big to small. It is impossible to do quality research when attempting to track that many names.

Institutions make constant demands on analysts, insisting that they bring company executives to their cities for meetings, requiring exclusive one-on-one executive meetings at conferences, and pressing analysts to call them first with insightful tidbits and nuances. Analysts are sucked into this vortex. An institution's every whim is made a priority. We are called securities analysts, but a more apt moniker would be research communicators. Analysts spend double or triple the time on investor/client contact compared to research analysis.

Analysts chew up most of their day talking to key clients and the sales desk, and in other marketing activities. Travel is incessant. While based on the West Coast, I made 18 trips to the East Coast one year, a personal best. Often analysts head out on Sundays and do not get back until Friday night. Weekends are frequently disrupted by business trips. In the office, we scramble all day, reacting to stock-price moves, rumors, press releases, accusations, and news. We constantly get inquiries from institutional analysts and portfolio managers, institutional and retail sales forces, traders, the press, and others. We spend time in discussion with the other analysts and support staff in our groups. Our handheld Blackberry email devices, cell phones, and laptops go with us everywhere. I did not bother shutting down these electronics on airplane flights as requested, because sometimes there was reception at 30,000 feet.

At some point, the Street started to put speed ahead of everything else. And institutional investors began to demand an instant comment on almost every situation. No reaction or even a delayed one is not an option. Street research analysts are under a constant barrage of pressure, always reacting, scrambling, and on the move.

Their travel, 24-hour on-call communications, instant analysis, and speed—and the trading mentality of their major constituents—leave precious little time to conduct quality, thoughtful research.

Former Analysts Are Ill-Equipped to Manage Research

A big problem with research is that it is customarily supervised by former analysts. Sector leaders are almost always analysts and have minimal background in how to be effective heads of a unit. They frequently lack the proficiency to encourage, empower, support, direct, mentor, or inspire other professionals because they have never managed an organization. The ex-inmates are running the asylum. And just try to organize a flock of arrogant, highly paid rock stars. Analysts are like consultants or professional golfers: basically loners who have never had any experience in playing on a team or directing an organization. More professional leadership, with farsighted vision, is needed. Powerful, established, competent analysts cannot be managed. They need to be empowered. Instead, these days, they are being constrained by heavy oversight. This is another reason I and countless other senior analysts have exited the business.

Until the 1990s bubble burst, there was a less burdensome management structure. Established analysts had freer reign. That was before research mushroomed into an uncontrollable morass. When the markets tanked and legal issues came to the forefront, management muscled up—as if on steroids—despite analyst layoffs. A decade ago, about the only internal analyst reporting tasks were annual reviews of staff and cross-evaluations among peers. Now a host of requirements have been added, such as annual business plans, mid-year plan reviews, mid-year staff reviews, twice-a-year investment committee assessment, opinion change committee sessions, recommended list oversight group meetings, mandatory legal compliance briefings, organized training classes, departmental meetings, monthly group leader sessions—you get the idea. I estimate that all these internal requirements now take at least 10% to 15% of analysts' time compared to less than 1% in the less bureaucratic times.

Research management is cautious by nature, and these days it is hogtied by new regulatory and legal guidelines. There is a labyrinth of committees and approval processes if analysts plan to alter an investment rating or initiate coverage of a company. Meetings and directives abound. Leaders are protecting their backsides from being dragged into more lawsuits. All this supersedes the real analyst job of producing quality, forthright, useful, timely research.

Before the 1990s, most firms had one director of research. There was one sole decision maker, and it was clear who was responsible for all research matters. At the same time, the management style was hands-off. It was not possible for one person to overmanage dozens of analysts. And it worked well, before the hoard of unqualified, out-of-control analysts beholden to investment banking flooded into research during the frothy 1990s bull market. Now it is common to have several research managers in a single firm. Having multiple managers means no one makes a decision. Analysts often do not know whom to contact on any given issue. Most managers avoid making definitive decisions. The right hand frequently fails to communicate with the left hand. Policies at brokerage firms shift constantly, almost arbitrarily. The hoops analysts must jump through take time away from research. There ought to be clearer delineations of authority.

Management turnover further diminishes analyst productivity. Management new to the scene does not remember what was promised or decided the year before, regarding such things as compensation, staff, conferences, and other plans. Analysts often need to start over from scratch, briefing the new leaders and readjusting to trifling new procedures.

Investment committees are another dysfunctional aspect of Street research. These brokerage-firm management groups review opinions and potential rating changes with analysts, sitting in front of stock charts armed with only snippets of understanding and information on any particular company. These committees are influenced by recent stock price actions, and have little long-term vision. Such clumsy group oversight is an impediment to crisp decisions and steady, consistent investment recommendations.

Greater Research Accountability Is Necessary

Professional credentials should be required of analysts. Every other profession demands mandatory licensing of its practitioners: Accountants earn CPAs, attorneys pass bar exams, medical doctors pass their state boards, and architects and engineers have to pass exams and adhere to strict requirements. There are no such prerequisites to be a Street securities analyst. Incredibly, the CFA is voluntary. Even an MBA degree is optional. Back in 1971, I needed an MBA just to get interviews on the Street. Such standards should still be the norm now. All new analysts should pass Level 1 of the CFA, or perhaps fully obtain the charter, before being given the authority to establish stock opinions and recommendations. I believe that initial Level 1 should be compulsory for all analysts within, say, three years of their entry into the business. And the Level 3 full CFA title should be obligatory for all senior analysts.

The security analyst profession should be like that of a neurosurgeon or heart specialist, wherein leading experts in the field are not household names. High TV visibility and too much press, quotes, and media exposure tend to displace thoughtful, behind-the-scenes, quality research. It is more fun to be famous and blab to reporters and interviewers than to grind away in the office or in the field. And it is an ego trip. Brokerage firms should put extreme limits on analyst contact with the media. Analysts must act in a more professional manner, like CPAs, rather than sports figures and movie stars.

Analysts should assume fiduciary responsibility for the objectivity and thoroughness of their research. Because analysts render authoritative advice that has major financial implications, there should be a more formal, legal trust established between them and investors just as there is for investment managers. It is my opinion that analysts should be subject to malpractice suits in cases of misconduct. I am suggesting that they should have a legal responsibility for professional conduct, not accurate findings. The French company Moët Hennessy Louis Vuitton sued Morgan Stanley over errors in research that unjustly denigrated it. Analysts must be held to professional standards.

One baby step toward higher accountability was the requirement that research reports include a statement certifying that the analyst's written opinion is truly his own personal view. But it is not enough. Like medical doctors, attorneys, and CPAs, analysts must have a fiduciary obligation to conduct their business in a *professional* manner. Why are investment managers held liable for their conduct and not security analysts, who often have a much broader impact on corporations, investors, and stocks? A more precisely defined professionalism would add more gravity to Street behavior; it is sorely needed in the aftermath of the 1990s bubble market absurdities and the multitude of wrong or poorly considered investment opinions during the 2008–2009 bear market.

Accountability should also be demanded of the upper levels of management. There are glaring conflicts of interest in most brokerage firms. Instances in which the CEO or other top executives of a firm have reached down to analysts to influence coverage, investment ratings, and the tone of commentary are widespread. Perhaps the most notorious case was at Citigroup, when Sandy Weill urged Jack Grubman, at Citi's wholly owned Salomon Smith Barney entity, to take a "fresh look" at AT&T just before that firm chose its bankers for a lucrative underwriting deal. According to a story in *The New York Times*, in another egregious act, the Chairman of Bank of America attempted to influence objective investment research. A few weeks after the announcement of BofA's acquisition of Merrill Lynch, he was on a conference call encouraging Merrill brokers to promote BofA stock to their clients. Not only was this bad advice, it was biased. Any communications between brokerage management and analysts or any other employee who advices investors, should be treated similarly to investment banking contact—that is, done in the presence of legal compliance. This would curtail coercion, questionable deals, and biased research.

Brokerage executives should be barred from corporate boards of directors. This constitutes a massive conflict of interest, raising potential inside information issues. Goldman Sachs no longer permits its executives to serve on outside boards. At the very least, research coverage should be prohibited of any company where an executive from the brokerage firm serves on the board.

Research should also be disconnected from corporate investment banker selection. A paragraph should be required in every deal prospectus certifying that executives chose the investment banking firm based on considerations that completely excluded research factors. The analyst's coverage and investment rating during the period the company was making its banker selection should be stated in that paragraph. This disclosure would make any cozy analyst relationship with company management obvious to investors. The clause should also detail the analyst's communications and involvement with the corporate executives regarding the investment banking association and any direct contact regarding the deal.

Security analysts are often not isolated enough from the corporate clients of the investment banks at which they work. If they cover a company with whom the bank completes a stock offering or major merger or acquisition deal, research is only suspended temporarily. The restricted period is just 40 days following an offering. Company executives expect that the analyst will reinstate coverage at the end of this limited time span with a positive opinion. The restricted period should be at least six months or even a year. That would discourage corporate executives from expecting enthusiastic support from the analyst as part and parcel of the investment banking relationship.

Institutional Investors Should Play by the Same Rules

Reforms are necessary not only for sellside brokerage-firm research but also in buyside institutions. Certain practices of mutual funds, investment managers, insurance companies, banks, pension funds, and hedge funds are detrimental to the individual investor. An enjoinder on buyside institutional investors is necessary to balance out the system. The Spitzer-induced modifications to brokerage-firm and mutual fund practices have not affected the unregulated Wild West ways of the hedge funds. And the money comes not only from wealthy individuals making speculative investments. Massive state pension funds, college endowments, and corporate retirement assets have been poured into these risky, unfettered investment pools that don't play the game by the standards established for the rest of the market.

You would be amazed at the advantage mega-institutional holders have in gaining access to corporate management when sitting with a multimillion-share position. Buyside meetings with executives at headquarters should be open—or at least Webcast—to other attendees, buyside and sellside. One-on-one confabs with management at analysts' conferences should also have an open door. For at least 48 hours after they conclude a meeting or a full-blown conference call with any corporation's executives, buyside investors should be prohibited from conducting transactions involving the stock of that enterprise. The inordinate influence that big holders have over executives must be restricted. Buyside access to exclusive information must be curtailed.

Other unsavory tactics should be forbidden by the SEC: Institutions should be prohibited from verbally promoting a stock that they are currently selling and from making comments to drive a stock lower in order to purchase it cheaper. Since sellside analysts cannot hold or communicate opinions contrary to their published recommendation, the buyside must also be held to the same standards. Hedge funds should be barred from bad-mouthing companies in which they hold short positions. All self-serving commentary to boost the price of an existing holding should be banned.

Broader disclosure should be required by major stockholders. Currently, only shareholders owning more than 5% of a company's stock must report their position in an SEC filing. Corporations disclose these biggest holders in their annual proxy statements. Typically, there are only one or two large holders, if any, so there is a no way of knowing anything about holders owning 1% to 5%, who might very well have undue influence on executives. Any owner of more than 1% or maybe 2% of a stock should be revealed by corporations and holders in their filings every quarter. More detailed reporting of major stockholders in a company would reduce the executive tendency to play favorites with select buyside institutions. Institutional holdings and changes should be reported more often. Currently, mutual funds reveal their lineup of stocks quarterly. Hedge funds are never required to publish their positions. In the interest of greater transparency, institutional investors should be required to report their trades within days of each transaction. Greater exposure would discourage a lot of connivery.

Institutional portfolio managers should not be allowed to personally own any stocks that are held in the funds they manage. Likewise, buyside analysts should be prohibited from investing in any stocks they cover. They need to be held to the same standards as sellside analysts. The compensation of portfolio managers and senior analysts should be disclosed. Top corporate executives' remuneration is reported annually in proxy statements. It is subject to the review of shareholders. The same should hold true for all institutional portfolio managers and senior analysts at brokerage firms and institutions. It would encourage greater restraint. The constituencies, such as mutual fund holders and sellside research users, would have more influence if there were more scrutiny. Absurd compensation levels would generate skepticism, and require justification. And a little bit of daylight might bring moderation, even sanity, to the business.

Corporate Executives Are Part of the Problem

Investment research reforms must also extend to public corporations and executives. There has been a transformation in publicly held companies from traditional owners' capitalism to the current era of managers' capitalism. Executives now operate as if they own the company rather than as employees, which is properly their position. Excessive compensation, stock options, over-the-top perks, and absurd efforts to boost immediate profitability all come at the expense of long-term public-shareholder interests. Although founders who still own sizable stock positions in their public company should be allowed some leeway, too many CEOs act as though they started up the business. The problem this presents for securities analysts and investors is that executives expect them to serve their own personal financial interests. Executives attempt to manipulate their stock price by biased embellishment of upbeat news and favorable factors and nondisclosure or underemphasis of gloomy aspects. Company managements must be prevented from engaging in self-serving practices to persuade analysts and investors of their stock's favorable prospects.

The individual investor is more profoundly affected by Wall Street's failings than the professional institutional insiders. New approaches are necessary from research management at brokerage firms. Buyside institutions (such as mutual funds and hedge funds) and publicly held companies must also change their ways. The attitude of all these parties toward the individual investor has been phlegmatic. Reforms, such as separation of research, and analyst compensation based on opinion accuracy, could vastly improve the current discredited state of research. But to revamp, an entire new research model might be required. The Street needs to approach research more creatively and more professionally. Until that happens, individual investors will just have to work around the Street, learn its ways, exploit it, and in the end be responsible for their own investment decisions.

Afterword

Overhaul your approach to investing. Invest the right way. Revamp your practices. Realign your investing strategies. Separate babble from substance, regardless of whether the source of that blather is Wall Street, the media, or companies. Do not rely on the Street. Alan Abelson's stance is that "Selling, not analysis, has always been Wall Street's strong suit." And as Warren Buffett says, "Never ask the barber if you need a haircut." By digesting the observations and exhortations in this book, conscientious investors should now understand how Wall Street really operates, be able to avoid the Street's traps, and improve investment performance.

Use information from the Street the same way you would employ *The Wall Street Journal,* or a friend's investment suggestion. What does a brokerage opinion of Neutral or Hold indicate? The term is meaningless. Yet this type of jargon is what comes from the Street. View the Street as just one among many sources of information pertaining to potential investment strategies and opportunities. The information it offers is only a starting point—not a final conclusion.

Do not take Wall Street literally. Put it in the proper perspective. *Use its information and its research content, not its conclusions or recommendations.* Most professional portfolio managers who run mutual funds have mediocre investment performance records. Street analyst opinions are even worse; analysts cannot pick stocks. "In a bull market, you do not need them," Gerald Loeb says of securities analysts. "In a bear market, you do not want them." Research reports are never complete, forthright, balanced, or objective. They are good for background, but they are not actionable. Corporate management should be utilized in the same manner as Street analysts—for gaining an understanding of a company and industry trends, but not for investment guidance.

I am often asked about my daily investment regimen. Since I no longer have to work at the office from 6 a.m. to 5 p.m., I tune into CNBC and Bloomberg Television every morning with my first cup of coffee. After poring over the sports page, I study *The New York Times* business section and *The Wall Street Journal.* Then I sit down at my computer to peruse my holdings and any pertinent company or industry sector news. On the weekends, I cannot live without *Barron's. Forbes* arrives every two weeks and I read relevant articles in other investment or business magazines online. I tap into conference call replays in my car if I have a drive of at least 45 minutes. And on an Excel spreadsheet, I track key data on my stocks: date of purchase, original price, estimated dividends, yield, and gains and losses. My brokerage accounts are online, so I can monitor them easily. Day-to-day and week-to-week I strive to keep up with the market, but my best thinking occurs while I'm secluded on an airplane or at a vacation resort, pondering and strategizing. This is when I can get away from watching the daily ripples, and take a long view on the market's ebbs and tides.

Invest for the Long Haul; Be Patient and Realistic

Since retiring from the Wall Street cauldron, I have become an individual investor, free from the constraints that entangle most insiders and the influences that bias the Street. I make time to read the financial press, assess the markets and my stocks online, chat with investor friends, and periodically review my investment strategy and portfolio. My approach is to always be open to tweaking my investment positions, but on guard against the urge to make a trade based on a short-term catalyst. The advice of John Bogle, founder of Vanguard, is this: "Learn to ignore most of the everyday noise." Invariably, doing nothing is a sounder long-term approach than making a lot of shifts in your holdings. Resist the temptation to react; do not pull the trigger every time you learn something new. In other words, *stand there, do not just do something.*

As an individual investor, you are free to do the right thing. But that freedom also enables you to make foolish, elementary mistakes that professionals tend to avoid. Ray DeVoe, the market observer, contends: "Good judgment comes from experience, and experience comes from bad judgment. But bad judgment is just a polite term for stupidity." I hope this book helps you avoid the latter.

I have been away from Wall Street now for six years. This distance allows me to combine an insider's knowledge with an outsider's perspective. Having read this book, you possess the same advantage— not only an awareness of the strange Street practices but also the ability to make your own detached investment decisions. My investing has improved since I exited Wall Street. I have the time to devote to my portfolio. While I was a securities analyst, my investments were almost entirely in the computer-services stocks that I covered. My position precluded active buying and selling, and I was required to hold the stocks for many years. Fortunately, the computer services business was exceptionally stable and consistent, while expanding at a healthy clip. The industry was an ideal growth stock sector at that time. The long-term nature of my holdings necessitated patience in my personal investment practice. This attitude has become even more pronounced now that I am no longer exposed to all the Wall Street noise and distractions.

Perseverance must be accompanied by realistic performance goals. Aim for a 5% to 10% annual total return including dividends; 15% would be spectacular. Be patient and long-term oriented, and have reasonable expectations. The sobering lesson of the 2008–2009 bear market train wreck is that the primary investment objective should be protection of capital rather than maximization of capital gains. Overreaching for growth and capital gains exposes investors to excessive risk. Reduce greed and lower risk. In some years, such as 2008, no return or even a loss of 10% to 15% is a glorious victory. Take heed of the recent bear market damage and rein in your investment return target to limit risk.

In the mid-1980s, EDS, a stock I covered intensely, was merging with General Motors. One member of management, a Texan who was one of EDS's first employees and had played an integral on-scene role as a part of the company's harrowing Iran hostage rescue, decided to opt out and start up his own oil-drilling company. He hung up his business suit and started wearing blue jeans to his modest office. What surprised me, when I inquired about his new venture, was his limited objective. He was aiming to achieve a mere 10% to 15% annual return. I was from Wall Street and therefore accustomed to 20% to 30% growth stock targets. His business plan was to buy up small, remote wells, maintain a low-cost overhead, and attain profitability even if the price of oil was just \$5 to \$10 a barrel. The price of oil moved from the teens to \$20, and after a few years, he and his handful of private investors began to generate some robust returns. But the ongoing aim remained a 10% to 15% return. The oil price was below \$20 for much of the 1990s but, given the new company's low-cost structure, it was not a problem. Now, more than 20 years later, with the price of oil per barrel two or three times the original level, just imagine the gains!

After I dropped off the Wall Street payroll, my investment strategy shifted to an emphasis on consistent, reliable, income-producing securities. My priority became protection of capital and income generation, not capital gains. The first major position in my portfolio was an oil pipeline and storage royalty trust that was listed on the NYSE and carried a dividend yield of around 7%. The business was consistent and predictable. Oil flows through the pipelines and is stored in tanks, creating ongoing revenue regardless of oil price fluctuations. All I wanted was to take home my 7% dividend and keep risk to a minimum. A humble attitude is a characteristic that is as important for investors as it is for corporate executives. And *voilá,* over the ensuing four years, I watched with delight as the dividend was boosted by almost 50% and the share price doubled.

If you are at my stage in life, living on a mostly fixed income, you face the investment question of growth versus income. High-yield value investments should constitute the bulk of a senior person's stock portfolio; no more than 20%, maybe even as little as 10%, of such a portfolio should be devoted to growth stocks. Growth stocks are risky and volatile. They might be a thrilling pursuit if you need excitement, but the rush will quickly vanish if they are decimated in a bear market. Growth stocks such as Intel, Cisco, Google, and Goldman Sachs were sliced in half or by two-thirds during 2008. The impact of that on an investment portfolio is devastating, and could take years to make up. I do not concur with the thesis that growth stocks are necessary to keep pace with the overall market and economy. Low PE-multiple income stocks perform just fine in a rising market.

Dividend and interest income should be derived from both bonds and stocks, with at least half attained from the former. I feel strongly about shielding capital, especially at this point in life. Obtain higher yield with income stocks, royalty trusts, limited partnerships (LPs), limited liability companies (LLCs), and master limited partnerships (MLPs) that are listed on the NYSE, or even preferred stocks. Income stocks can generate dividend yields above 5%, sometimes close to 10%. But be careful.

Heightened risk accompanies yields in the 10% range. There is no free lunch. A few years ago, I coasted along with Calpine (a California utility) bonds that were paying more than 10%. My assumption was that electrical utility firms never go bankrupt. What a surprise when this one did! My losses far exceeded all the interest I had earned in the prior years. The conservative avenue to maximizing income is to seek quality stocks yielding around 5% that have good prospects of raising their dividends in the future. That way, based on the original purchase price, there is the potential to obtain a 10% yield down the road.

Exploit Your Status as an Individual Investor

Conduct your own research. Observe. Read. Listen. Overhear. Ponder. Anticipate. Predict. Analyze. Question. Judge. Be skeptical. Avoid being overconfident. Be different and unafraid to go your own way. Steer clear of the herd instinct, the market tendency toward imitative behavior. When evaluating companies as potential investments, seek out specialty firms—they do it better than generalists. The business should be relatively simple to understand. Financial strength is paramount. Gauge the value of a company's assets. The five- or ten-year earnings record is important. But nothing is perfect. Some variation in earnings performance is natural and inevitable. To assess corporate management, scrutinize quality, character, values, and attitude. An important trait in a company's executives is humility. Steer clear of arrogant executives. Be wary of spin and self-promotion.

Invest long-term; do not trade. Look for value. Seek dividends. Do not spread yourself too thin; limit the number of stocks you own so that you can pay proper attention to each one. Keep it simple, nothing too exotic. *Preserve your capital.* If you can avoid material shrinkage in your overall portfolio, performance will take care of itself, and you will achieve excellent long-term results. It is not what you make, it is what you keep. Investment risk (the possibility of permanent loss of capital) and price valuation are critical factors when looking at a stock, but they are usually overlooked in the pursuit of big gains from "new era" investment ideas. Consistency is more important than absolute appreciation. Do not be fooled by the Street. You are no longer an amateur playing against professionals. Invest intelligently; take advantage of the Street; and outflank the experts to make money in the market.

Go to **www.stephentmcclellan.com** for my blog, recent articles, appearances, interviews, and my current investment views.

Glossary

'90s Bubble Era   The years during late the 1990s ending with the March 2000 stock market decline when euphoria reigned, especially in high-tech, Internet, telecom, and a few other stock sectors. Investment bank brokerage firms went wild with initial public offerings (IPOs). Analysts lost all sense of objectivity in promoting speculative, excessively priced stocks.

10-K report   An annual filing to the SEC required of publicly held companies that includes extensive financials and commentary on the business. Widely available to the public.

10-Q report   A quarterly filing to the SEC required of publicly held companies, less detailed than the 10-K, that includes financials and commentary on the business. Widely available to the public.

Accounts receivable turnover   The average period a company is owed funds from its customers for sales transactions. Granting of credit extends the time of collection. Ninety days is a standard. The time is calculated by dividing annualized revenues by average accounts receivable, and dividing that into 365 days.

ADR (American depository receipt)   A certificate in the holder's name indicating ownership of a non-U.S. company's stock; the actual shares of the foreign company are held at a U.S. bank's foreign branch.

Annual report   A publication by a publicly held company discussing the year's results, including extensive financials (sometimes contains the 10-K report) and often reviewing the company's business and outlook.

Axe (in a stock)   A Street analyst with the reputation for doing the best research and being the most knowledgeable on a given stock.

Balance sheet   A financial statement that includes assets (such as cash and accounts receivable) on one side, and liabilities (such as debt) and stockholders equity on the other.

Bear market   A material, enduring decline in stock prices of at least 20% over a period of more than one year. Broad-based investor pessimism and negative sentiment. Ten bear markets have occurred since 1946, according to S&P, with the average drop of more than 30% during a span of 16 months. On average, it required 22 months to recover completely. The most notable bear markets were the 1930s, 1967–1982, and 2008–2009 periods.

Big/large cap stock   A company with total shares outstanding having a value or capitalization of at least $5 to $10 billion in the stock market.

Black Swan event   A highly improbable event that has an extreme impact, readily explainable after the fact, but always a surprise, as defined in the book *Black Swan* by Nassim Taleb.

Blackberry   A portable, hand-held e-mail, phone, and Internet device (PDA) used by many Wall Street analysts and professionals like me.

Bloomberg Television   A cable channel that broadcasts stock market and investment programming all day long.

Bonds   A debt investment security usually issued by a corporation or government (normally a long-term borrowing tool), promising to repay the principal upon maturity and paying stated interest at regular intervals.

Brokerage firm   A Wall Street investment banking firm dealing in stocks, bonds, and other financial investments, acting as both principal and agent, usually catering to institutions and individuals, providing investment banking services and securities trading and transactions.

Bubble Era   *See* '90s Bubble Era.

Bubble years   *See* '90s Bubble Era.

Bull market   A period of rising stock prices of more than 20% over at least a one-year time frame. Widespread investor optimism. The 1990s represented one of the most notable bull markets in history.

Buyside   Institutions, such as mutual funds, hedge funds, pension funds, endowment funds, banks, insurance companies, and other major organizations, that do substantial investing. They "buy" stocks from and utilize Wall Street brokerage firms.

Buyside analyst   Securities analysts employed by institutional investors to cover stocks internally that the firm owns or may be interested in buying. In-house portfolio managers are the audience and users of this internal research.

Call option (call)   An investment instrument, a contract giving the owner a right to purchase usually 100 shares of the attendant stock at a fixed (strike) price until a specific (expiration) date. A speculation that the related stock price will rise. It allows participation in the stock price move of a large number of shares for a modest outlay. Can be highly volatile.

Capital gain   The profit that results from the appreciation of a capital asset over its purchase price.

Capital gains tax   The U.S. federal tax rate on profits or appreciation upon the sale of a stock or an investment holding, currently 15% if the position is held at least one year or the normal (higher) personal income tax rate if less than one year.

Capital spending   The corporate expenditures on property, plant, and equipment. Not recorded as an immediate, upfront expense but rather depreciated over a period of usually 5 to 20 years—the depreciation expense incurred on an ongoing basis.

Capitalized software   Corporate computer software that, although purchased, is not accounted for as an upfront cost, but instead is depreciated over a period of years, enhancing current profitability.

Cash flow   Corporate after-tax profits, plus other noncash expenses such as depreciation/amortization. The inflow of cash to a company minus real, immediate, out-of-pocket expenses. The cash received and spent by a business during a fixed time frame. An ultimate measure of a company's performance.

Cash flow statement   One of the three principal financial statements required of all public companies, detailing the numbers that determine cash flow.

Cash generation   *See* Cash flow.

CEO   A company's chief executive officer.

CFO   A company's chief financial officer.

Chairman   A company's head of the board of directors, the most senior position, above that of CEO or president.

Chart   *See* Stock chart.

Chartered Financial Analyst (CFA)   The professional designation for financial analysts by the CFA Institute. Requires four years' working experience in the investment business and the successful completion of three extensive examinations over a period of years. Indicates a high degree of professional qualification and standards.

CNBC   Cable channel owned by NBC, devoted almost exclusively to the stock market and investment content; programming runs all day.

Collateralized debt obligation (CDO)   An asset-backed security, a portfolio of fixed income assets containing various levels of debt based on risk, the debt having the most risk receiving the highest interest rate. Heavily composed of subprime mortgage debt, grossly misrated by rating companies, assigning in many cases AAA status to CDOs containing junk-level debt, typical of bubble market excesses. Holders of these instruments were unclear on the amount of risk being sustained, were reaching for unnaturally or unsustainably high returns. Like bubbles that have gone before, this has ended up in a plethora of massive losses and write-offs in 2007 by institutions such as Citigroup.

Commercial bank   The major banks used by a company for its corporate banking requirements (such as line of credit and short-term borrowing).

Commission   The fee charged by an investment bank brokerage firm for buying and selling securities on behalf of its clients. The transaction charge to a major institution to trade a sizable block of stock can be as little as a few pennies per share.

Compliance (legal)   Attorneys and other legal personnel at a brokerage firm that ensure that the firm adheres to securities laws and regulations. Involved in overseeing security analysts' research.

Computer services   The industry sector I covered as an analyst. Composed of companies providing data processing services to corporate clients, such as payroll processing, datacenter outsourcing, credit card processing, and consulting.

Conference call Normally, this refers to a broadcast and Q&A session by a company via telephone and/or Webcast to Wall Street analysts and institutional investors. Conducted quarterly or at other intervals to discuss earnings results or to detail material news. Open to the public on a listen-in-only basis.

COO A company's chief operating officer; usually ranks below CEO but above CFO.

Correction Euphemistic, misleading term commonly used to describe a stock market decline of less than 10%. The Street abhors negative references, preferring expressions that put a favorable face on gloomy investment elements.

Credit Default Swap (CDS) An insurance-like contract purchased by a bondholder to protect against losses if a debt issuer goes into default. CDSs have become major vehicles for speculation, allowing investors to bet on future changes in a particular entity's credit quality. Financial firms sold these in great quantity and are now faced with potentially massive payoff requirements.

Dead cat bounce Even a dead cat, if it falls far enough, fast enough, will bounce upon hitting the ground. This refers to a stock that descends precipitously in price and then experiences a modest rebound. Do not think of the bounce as the beginning of a prolonged recovery.

Debt Short- or long-term borrowings by a company, from drawn-down bank lines to long maturity bonds. Payment of short-term debt is due in less than one year; long-term debt, beyond a year.

Debt-to-capitalization ratio A company's long-term debt as measured against the total of long-term debt and stockholders' equity. Indicates the extent of debt leverage on the balance sheet—less than 20% is modest, and over 50% may be too high.

Deferred revenue A company's sales that, for accounting purposes, are deferred into a future period and recorded later, diminishing immediate sales but enhancing future revenue.

Depreciation/amortization Depreciation is the allocation of the cost of property, plant, and equipment over a period of years while the asset is being used to generate revenue. Amortization is the same, but pertains mainly to intangible assets such as goodwill, copyrights, patents, and trademarks.

Divestiture   Sale or disposition by a company of a business segment or division.

Dividend   Cash or stock paid by a company to its shareholders; normally an established amount consistent each quarter. Any revision is usually done annually.

Dividend payout ratio   The percentage portion of a company's net income paid out to shareholders in the form of dividends.

Dividend yield   The annual dividend amount per share as a percent of the current stock price.

Dow Jones Industrial Average (DJIA)   The most commonly used U.S. stock market index, comprising 30 large capital companies, widely held stocks, price-weighted, the components occasionally removed and replaced to keep the index representative. Some of the current stocks in the index are 3M, American Express, ExxonMobil, Intel, Merck, Procter & Gamble, McDonald's, and Wal-Mart.

Earnings estimates   Security analyst forecasts of a company's earnings per share (EPS), usually for the current and next year, and each quarter of the current year. Published in virtually every research report and widely available over the Internet.

Earnings guidance   Corporate management forecast or direction pertaining to the expected results for the current and sometimes following year. Often disclosed publicly on conference calls or in earnings report press releases.

Earnings model/spreadsheet   An extensive, detailed, computer-generated company income statement as expected by a security analyst, usually for the current year and the following year, on a quarterly basis. Specifies assumptions on each line item (such as revenue, expenses, taxes, and share count) to derive earnings per share (EPS) estimate. Published in most research reports.

Earnings per share (EPS)   A company's net income divided by total shares outstanding, reported, or forecast on an annual and quarterly basis.

Earnings reports   Statements released each quarter by publicly held companies disclosing financial results for that period. Usually accompanied by commentary, spin, and a lot of rationalizing.

eBusiness   Internet-related businesses, sometimes referred to as eCommerce; a sexy term bantered widely during the '90 Bubble Era to hype stocks.

Economists   Experts employed by brokerage firms and banks to forecast future trends in the economy that may have an impact on the stock market (such as employment, GDP growth, interest rates, and the Consumer Price Index [CPI]—inflation). Their influence on Wall Street has steadily diminished.

Emerging market stocks   Stocks in companies from rapidly developing countries or newly industrializing regions of the world, such as China, India, Brazil, and Southeast Asia.

Emphasis/recommended list   A brokerage firm's list highlighting its best stock ideas, and touting the strongest Buy opinions.

Equity   Stock or shares representing ownership in a company.

Exchange traded fund (ETF)   Open-ended mutual fund, continuously traded in the market throughout the day (like a stock), precisely tracking various stock market indexes, sectors, stock groupings, or commodities. Low costs, actively traded.

Ex-dividend (date)   A stock trades on this basis, that is, excluding the declared dividend, four days prior to "stock of record date" that determines which holders are entitled to the dividend. The price opens that day lowered in price by the amount of the dividend. Be aware of this date when selling a stock.

FASB (Financial Accounting Standards Board)   A private, non-profit organization, originally stemming from the American Institute of Certified Public Accountants, with primary responsibility for establishing generally accepted accounting principles (GAAP) in the U.S. The SEC has designated the FASB to set accounting standards for publicly held U.S. companies.

Financial Analyst Journal   The magazine published by the CFA Institute that features detailed academic studies and analyses on investment topics.

Financial consultant   *See* Retail broker.

Financial reengineering/restructuring   Extensive balance sheet revamping; financial alterations. Activities, such as paying down debt, divestitures, stock repurchasing, and off-balance sheet financing, that often have the effect of enhancing earnings results.

Financials   A company's income, balance sheet, cash flow statement, and other accounting statements.

Fortune 100   The top 100 U.S. corporations, ranked by gross revenues, as listed in the well-known Fortune 500 annual ranking.

GAAP (generally accepted accounting principles) earnings
Earnings results reported by publicly held companies conforming to the accounting standards established by FASB. These are strict, conservative principles. It is common for companies to also present enhanced results by excluding certain expenses that are not FASB-compliant, termed as "normalized" or pro forma.

GDP (gross domestic product)   Measurement of the size of a country's economy; market value of goods and services produced by a country in a specific time frame (normally a year).

Growth stock   The stock of a company that is expanding rapidly, whose stock price should climb in sync with the company's progress. The cash it earns is reinvested in the firm's internal development. Little or no dividends are paid out.

Hard dollar fees   Payment to a brokerage firm for various services in actual dollars, rather than through commissions (soft dollars) from stock trades.

Hedge fund   Private investment funds, such as DE Shaw, Bridgewater Associates, and Farallon Capital, that are available to select, qualified high-income individual investors and institutions. They normally charge a 1% to 2% fee and keep 20% of annual gains. Losses must be recovered before the 20% takeout restarts. They are largely exempt from regulation by the SEC and other bodies. Highly flexible investing strategies: short sales, futures, swaps, derivatives, almost any type of investing activity.

II **All-America team rankings**   The annual ranking by *Institutional Investor* magazine of leading Wall Street brokerage firm security analysts, broken down by industry sectors, based on polling of buyside institutional investors.

Income statement   A company's profit and loss statement, reported quarterly, containing revenue (sales), various expenses, taxes, net profits (income), shares outstanding, and earnings per share. Indicates a company's operating progress. Foremost financial statement influencing the stock price.

Income-producing investment   An investment that returns a regular cash payment to the holder, such as a dividend-paying stock or interest-bearing bond.

Index fund   A mutual fund that tracks a specific stock market or other financial market index such as the S&P 500, Dow Jones Industrial Average, and Wilshire 5000. Carries low fees.

Individual investor   A person performing his or her own investing; overseeing a personal portfolio; not acting on behalf of an investment institution.

Initial public offering (IPO)   A company's first sale of its shares to outside investors, to be traded in the stock market. Usually raises capital for corporate use (primary), sometimes insiders selling shares (secondary). Provides liquidity for previous holders; the shares can be bought and sold in the open market.

Institution   *See* Institutional investor.

Institutional investor   An organization such as a bank, mutual fund, hedge fund, pension fund, insurance company, foundation, or money management firm that makes sizable stock market investment transactions.

***Institutional Investor (II)* magazine**   The sophisticated, expensive, monthly publication aimed at Wall Street institutional investors, widely read by Street professionals, featuring investment-related topics such as research, money management, mutual funds, brokerage firms, investment banking, and leading personalities.

Institutional sales force/desk   A brokerage firm's sales personnel responsible for major institutional investor clients: transmits research information, takes orders to buy and sell stocks, assists in major trades, helps sell offerings and investment banking deals. Office location where these salespersons are clustered is often referred to as "sales desk."

Interest income   A fixed, guaranteed fee paid to holder of bond or other fixed income security; compensation to lender, paid out at specific intervals, usually every six months. The percentage of principal that fee represents is the interest rate.

Investment bank A brokerage firm that assists companies and governments in issuing and selling securities to raise capital; offers merger and acquisition advice and makes markets in and trades stocks, bonds, commodities, and other instruments. Federal law was altered in 1999, enabling these firms to provide many commercial banking services.

Investment banker A professional who works in the investment banking department of a Wall Street brokerage firm. Typically has corporate finance or public agency expertise. Assists organizations in raising capital/issuing securities and merger/acquisition activities.

Investment banking Services provided by a department of a Wall Street brokerage firm, pertaining to raising capital, strategic merger and acquisition consulting, and corporate finance. *See* Investment bank, Investment banker.

Investment opinion/rating A brokerage firm security analyst's recommendation on a stock, such as Buy, Hold, or Sell.

Investment research committee Various research management members, often including the market strategist, technician, legal compliance, and Director of Research, who review and sanction analyst opinion changes.

Investment risk The possibility of permanent loss of capital. Prospect of losing money in an investment.

Investor relations (IR) The department at a company that is responsible for contact with institutional investors, brokerage analysts, and individual investors. Provides information on the company that is of interest to investors, such as current business progress, order rate bookings, profitability, growth, and financial trends.

January effect A stock market indicator; the direction of the stock market during the month of January, usually an accurate forecast of the trend for the entire year.

Limit order Order to buy or sell stock at a specific price, effective for the day or good until canceled (compared to placing an order at the prevailing "market" price).

Lock-up period The time frame following an initial public offering when management, employees, and insiders are forbidden from selling their shares in the open market. Specified in the offering prospectus, usually a six-month span.

Long-term   The general Wall Street consensus of an investment holding period of more than one year. In my view, this time frame should be at least two or three years. Federal capital gains tax of just 15% for securities held one year or more.

Margin (account)   A brokerage account allowing the client to borrow from the broker up to 50% of the value of the securities held in the account. Can be drawn down to purchase more stocks or for personal use.

Market strategist   An expert usually employed by brokerage firms to provide research and commentary on the overall stock market trends and direction, offering insightful investing observations and big-picture orientation.

Marketing   A security analyst function of communicating research via telephone and direct one-on-one meetings. Travel to different cities to meet with institutional clients is termed "marketing."

Model   *See* Earnings model.

Morning call   The daily brokerage firm conference call over an internal squawk box system, usually around 7 or 8 a.m. Eastern Time. Security analysts and other research professionals present their opinions, observations, and findings to the sales force, traders, and retail brokers.

Mutual fund   An investment pool with specific standards, goals, and strategies. Available to public investors; investment decisions made by a portfolio manager; value calculated at the end of each day (net asset value per share). Different types are growth, dividend yield, big cap, small cap, or industry sector focused. Offered by companies such as Fidelity, Vanguard, and American Funds.

NASD   National Association of Securities Dealers, a securities industry organization responsible for the self-regulation of the trading of stocks, corporate bonds, futures and options, and the activities of more than 5,000 brokerage firms.

NASDAQ   The name derived from National Association of Securities Dealers Automated Quotation system. The largest U.S. electronic screen-based equity securities market, encompassing some 3,200 stocks formerly known as over-the-counter (OTC) stocks, which are not listed on the NYSE or American Exchange.

Net income   A company's earnings after subtracting all costs and expenses (including taxes) from revenue. Sometimes referred to as the bottom line because it is at or near the end of the income statement. Earnings per share is net income divided by shares outstanding.

New York Stock Exchange (NYSE)   The largest listed stock exchange in the world, with more than 2,700 actively traded securities. These are mainly bigger capitalization stocks and more established companies than those traded on NASDAQ. NYSE stocks are generally more conservative investments than NASDAQ securities due to high listing standards.

Nikkei index   Nikkei 225 is the main stock market index in Japan; the Tokyo stock exchange, price-weighted, similar to the Dow Jones Industrial Average and/or S&P 500 in the U.S.

Off–balance sheet financing   Debt or asset financing that is not indicated on the balance sheet. Often pertains to activities such as leases, loan commitments, derivatives, letters of credit, and sometimes subsidiary liabilities.

Operating cash flow   The cash provided from a company's business operations before depreciation and amortization, excluding financing expenses such as interest and taxes.

Operating income   A company's income before depreciation and amortization, interest, and taxes.

Operating profit margin   A profitability measure of a company's basic business operations: operating income divided by revenue— that is, operating income as a percentage of revenue.

Organic growth   A company's internally generated revenue expansion, from the sale of goods and services, as opposed to acquisitions.

Outsourcing   An element of the computer services industry I covered as an analyst on Wall Street. The business of running an organization's computer datacenter, back office processing, and other data-processing activities, by an outside services firm.

PE multiple   Price-to-earnings ratio: the price of a stock divided by current or next year estimated earnings per share. Putting every stock on a similar basis allows value-price comparisons. The higher the PE, the more expensive the stock. Available in virtually every research report.

Pension fund   Retirement funds such as state and municipal employee pension plans that are major institutional investors with sizable stock holdings.

Portfolio manager   The professional at a mutual fund, hedge fund, pension fund, and so on who is responsible for management of an institutional investment portfolio or other sizable investment assets. Duties involve stock selection, asset allocation, financial analysis, investment monitoring, and other investment management functions.

Preferred stock   A class of stock senior to common stock, with superior rights in bankruptcy liquidation. Dividend is fixed over its life; no voting power; some similar characteristics to bonds.

Pre-tax profit margin   A company's income before taxes as a percentage of revenue—that is, income before tax divided by revenue. A common measure of profitability among companies.

Primary offering (issuance)   An issuance of shares by a company to raise capital, as opposed to a secondary offering. Can be an IPO or a follow-on offering.

Private client   *See* Individual investor.

Private equity   An investment fund open only to select high-income individuals and institutional investors; high initial investment requirement, normally above $100,000; limited partnership interests; invests in private companies, often purchasing publicly held firms, taking them private. The eventual gains on privately held companies via an IPO or sale to another company. Some leading firms are Blackstone, KKR, and Texas Pacific Group.

Pro forma earnings   A company's GAAP income adjusted to exclude nonrecurring and extraordinary expenses such as restructuring costs and investment losses. Companies egregiously overuse this practice to sweeten the reported profit picture.

Profit   *See* Net income.

Proxy statement   A company's annual disclosure to shareholders pertaining to voting in the election of the board of directors. Includes background information on board members and management, executive and board compensation, and shareholders owning more than 5% of the stock.

Publicly held stocks   A company's shares that have been issued to the public, usually via an IPO, and are freely traded in the open market.

Put option (put)   An investment instrument; a contract giving the owner a right to sell usually 100 shares of the attendant stock at a fixed (strike) price until a specific expiration date. A speculation that the related stock price will decline. Allows participation in the stock price move of a large number of shares for a modest outlay. Can be highly volatile.

Recurring revenue   Continuous, predictable sales by a company generated from ongoing clients each quarter, year after year, from assured repeat business or long-term contracts. A highly visible revenue stream.

Reg FD (Regulation Fair Disclosure)   An SEC mandate that publicly traded companies disclose to all investors simultaneously, material information that might impact the stock. Eliminates some of the past selective disclosure to certain privileged institutional investors and security analysts but has inhibited executive communication with investors.

REIT (Real Estate Investment Trust)   Company that invests in real estate; must distribute at least 90% of net income to shareholders and thus pays no corporate income tax. Shareholder pays normal income tax rate on dividends. The investment structure is similar to mutual funds.

Restriction period   The SEC-required 40-day quiet period following an IPO during which the underwriting firm and insiders are prohibited from disclosing any information about the company that was not revealed in the prospectus. Security analyst at the underwriting firm cannot initiate research coverage on the stock during this span.

Retail broker   Sometimes has the title of financial consultant or financial advisor. The salesperson at a brokerage firm who focuses on individual investors (private clients, retail clients). Individual investor clients' main conduit to a brokerage firm's stock research.

Retail investor/client   *See* Individual investor.

Retail producer   *See* Retail broker.

Return on Equity (ROE) A company's annual net income as a percentage of the average level of stockholder's equity during the year. An important measure of return on stockholder's ownership interest—that is, a company's capability to generate earnings from net assets. Widely available in research reports.

Revenue The funds a company obtains from sales of products/services in a specific period, disclosed quarterly and annually in the income statement. Sometimes termed "top line" (of income statement), often broken out by regions, products, or operating groups.

Revenue recognition A method of recording revenue. The main accounting treatment is accrual basis: revenue recorded when service is performed or product is sold, even though payment may be in the future. Becomes more unclear with long-term contracts (percentage-of-completion accounting), deferred revenue, and installment sales.

Road show Meetings with prospective institutional investors on a multi-city tour set up by an underwriting firm for corporate executives to pitch their story and entice participation in an offering. A similar outing is sometimes conducted, with no attendant offering, to boost the stock price (nondeal road show).

Royalty trust Similar to REIT, usually in oil and gas or mining; pays no corporate taxes but is required to distribute at least 90% of its profits in the form of dividends. Investors pay personal income tax on dividends. Offers high dividend yields.

S&P 500 Standard & Poor's widely published broad stock market index that contains 500 large cap stocks. Several index funds and exchange traded funds track this index and are vehicles for investors to participate in the broad market.

Sales desk *See* Institutional sales force/desk.

SEC (Securities Exchange Commission) Federal agency responsible for enforcing U.S. securities laws and regulating the securities industry and stock markets. Enforces public company disclosure standards and requirements to submit quarterly and annual 10-Q and 10-K reports.

Secondary offering (issuance) The sale of management and insider stock to the public, endorsed by the company; sometimes part of an IPO but usually comes later.

Securities   The term referring to investment instruments in general, such as stocks, options, mutual funds, and bonds.

Security analysis   Research on companies and industries to determine the best, most appropriate stock investments. Evaluation and assessment of stocks to form investment recommendations such as Buy, Hold, and Sell.

Security analyst (investment analyst)   A professional at an investment bank brokerage firm, or on the buyside at an institutional investment firm, who conducts research on companies and industries to determine the best, most appropriate stock investments.

Selection committee   The brokerage investment bank's professionals who decide which stocks will be placed on its emphasis/recommended list, highlighting its best investment ideas. Usually composed of director of research, market strategist, technical analyst, and other such members of research.

Sellside   The investment banks and brokerage firms that "sell" investment securities to institutions and individuals. They act as agents in trading securities, and sometimes as principal, when trading for their own account.

Shareholder   The owner of company's stock. Shares can be held in the Street name at a brokerage firm or retained directly in the owner's name in certificate form.

Short position/sale   The trading tactic that bets on a decline in a stock price. Stock shares are borrowed from a brokerage firm and sold, with the requirement to repurchase and return them later, presumably at a lower price, generating a profitable trade. The short seller must pay the stock dividend to the brokerage firm so that it can pass it on to the owner whose shares have been borrowed.

Short-term/near-term   The general Wall Street consensus of an investment or trading holding period of less than one year. The federal capital gains tax on securities held for under one year is a normal personal income tax rate.

Small cap stock   A company whose total outstanding shares have a value or market capitalization of under $5 billion. Sometimes small cap is defined as a $250 million to $1 billion valuation. Micro-cap is under $250 million, and mid-cap is $1 billion to $10 billion.

Squawk box   The brokerage firm's intercom broadcast system linking personnel, desks, and offices throughout the organization. Used often throughout the day to inform employees on business matters.

Stock appreciation rights (SARs)   A seldom-used corporate executive and employee incentive compensation plan that provides a cash bonus payment based on the rise in stock price on a specific number of shares during a stated period (usually one year).

Stock buyback/repurchase   An action by a company to purchase its own outstanding shares, usually in the open market. The shares bought back are normally retired or retained in treasury for reissuing. The practice has risen dramatically in recent years. It is a temporary financial tactic to boost earnings per share and aid stock price.

Stock chart   A chart depicting company or market stock price trends and patterns, and trading volume, over specific periods.

Stock options, employee   A widely used corporate employee compensation incentive program giving the holder the right to purchase a specific number of the company's shares at a preset exercise price (normally the market price the day it was granted). Usually there is a vesting period of one or a few years before the employee can exercise. Recent scandals involved illegal management backdating of the grant date at lower stock price, providing an immediate gain.

Stock recommendation   *See* Investment opinion/rating.

Stock split   When a company expands the number of shares in the float, while at the same time reducing the price on an equivalent basis, to enhance liquidity. A 2-for-1 split doubles the number of shares and cuts the price in half. There is no benefit to the holder though the shares usually react positively to the news because it underscores that the company is experiencing robust performance and is often accompanied by a boost in the dividend.

Stop loss order   Investor order with a brokerage firm to buy or sell a specific security when a stated price is reached. Often used to protect a gain achieved in a stock by limiting the downside. In this case, once the limit price is hit, it triggers a market order to sell the shares.

Street, the   *See* Wall Street.

Tax rate   The corporate income taxes paid, specified on the income statement. Ranges as high as 39%. An expense deducted from revenues in determining net income. Derived by dividing tax expense by income before taxes.

Technical analysis   The use of charts in the study of stock and market price trends to predict future price direction. Presumes an efficient market that discounts all known factors in stock/market price. No consideration of fundamentals or business. Merits are controversial.

Technician/technical chartist   A Wall Street professional who performs technical analysis to formulate conclusions on future price movement.

Trader   The Wall Street brokerage firm or institutional investment professional who executes large-sized stock transactions, and who buys and sells securities on an extremely short-term basis (sometimes only seconds or minutes) to exploit small price changes and generate gains for the in-house account.

Trading desk   Location in a brokerage or institutional investor firm where traders are clustered. A noisy, chaotic, wild scene of intense activity and high-pressure dealings.

Tranche   A portion or slice of a series of securities. One of a number of connected securities or a class within a security series, an installment of a securities issue.

Treasuries   U.S. government debt to finance deficits: treasury bills (T-bills) have a maturity of under one year; notes, from one to ten years; and bonds, more than ten years. Guaranteed interest rate; the lowest risk investment. Current interest rate on widely traded ten-year. Treasury note is the most common indicator of interest rate direction in the economy.

Turnaround   A company's efforts, following negative setbacks and disappointing performance, to reverse the course and reconfigure the business to reestablish a positive earnings trend. Usually encompasses new management, layoffs, divestitures, financial restructuring, and PR hoopla.

Unbilled revenue   A company accounting policy that records earned revenue that, under contract terms, the customer cannot yet be billed for. A liberal accounting technique, broken out on the balance sheet.

Underwriting   An investment bank brokerage firm's action of undertaking the risk of issuing (selling) stock or bonds on behalf of a company or government. After a price has been agreed to at the time of issuance, the investment banking syndicate guarantees the proceeds to the issuer.

Value stock   Shares that appear to be trading at a discount relative to other stocks—underpriced or inexpensive based on fundamental analysis. Often carry a low PE multiple or price-to-book value ratio, and/or high dividend yield. Sometimes defined as stock selling below intrinsic value or at a "sensible" price.

Venture capital (VC)   A limited partnership fund that invests in high-risk start-up companies. Because of the speculative nature, the start-up is unable to borrow major sums from banks or obtain equity financing from the public with an IPO. A VC fund obtains a sizable equity position with a goal of gaining a big return on invested capital.

Volatility   A specious term often used to describe a declining stock market. Rarely utilized in characterizing a rising market.

Wall Street (the Street)   Refers to the broad securities business; sometimes a more narrow term depicting New York–based investment banking and brokerage firms.

Webcast   A broadcast by executives over the Internet of a company's quarterly results; commentary and Q&A with Street institutional investors, security analysts, and the public.

Wire house   A brokerage firm predominantly focused on retail, individual investor clients; not serving big institutional investors or providing investment banking services.

Write-off   An accounting action reducing the value of an asset or investment on a company's balance sheet (taking a loss) because the expected return has diminished or vanished.

INDEX

private lives of executives, 140
pro forma earnings, 107
professional stock
　recommendations, 85
profit margins, 60
promotion, 117-119
purchase dates, 78

Q-R

quarterly earnings conference
　calls, 83
quarterly earnings press
　releases, 83

Radio Corporation of America
　(RCA), 166
Ramada Inns, 91
*A Random Walk Down Wall
　Street* (Malkiel), 70
Ranieri, Lewis, 153
ratings
　conformity of opinions, 28-29
　misleading nature of, 11-15, 43
　overstated opinions, 21-22
　reluctance to downgrade,
　　19-21
　unique opinions, value of,
　　30-31
　unreliability of, 9-11
RCA (Radio Corporation of
　America), 98, 166
reading executive body
　language, 158-161
realist executive style, 128-129
realistic performance goals, 193
recommendations. *See* ratings
Red Herring, 167

Redback Networks, 168
reforming research
　accountability, 185-187
　autonomy, 176-179
　executive influence, 189-190
　expense, 179-181
　institutional investor
　　advantages, 187-189
　management and supervision,
　　183-184
　overview, 175
　time constraints, 181-183
**Regulation Fair Disclosure
　(Reg FD), 157**
reports. *See also* research
　incomplete nature of, 15
　stock price targets, 24-25
repurchase programs (stock),
　119-120
reputation of executives, 140
research
　conformity of opinions, 28-29
　corporate executives' impact
　　on, 53-56
　earnings models, 161-163
　effect of *Institutional Investor*
　　poll rankings, 49-50
　executive body language,
　　reading, 158-161
　via executive relationships,
　　155-158
　focus on institutional clients,
　　38-41
　growth of securities analysis,
　　33-38

important for background understanding, 29-30
individual and small team research, seeking out, 31-32
investigative reporting, 154-158
need for reforms
  accountability, 185-187
  autonomy, 176-179
  executive influence, 189-190
  expense, 179-181
  institutional investor advantages, 187-189
  management and supervision, 183-184
  overview, 175
  time constraints, 181-183
overconfidence, 32
overview, 35-37
research trends in 1970s, 148
unique opinions, value of, 30-31
rising industry sectors, 65-66
risk management, 64
Rubino, John, 166
Rochdale Research, 31
Rukeyser, Louis, 2, 38, 148

S

Sallie Mae (SLM Corporation), 120
Salomon Brothers, 35, 153
Salomon Smith Barney, 18, 186
Satyam, 72
Sears, 120
secular shifts, identifying, 27-28

securities analysis, growth of, 33-38
securities analysts
challenges, 8
compensation, 11, 180
day in life of, 5-7
growth of security analysis, 33-38
investment ratings
  conformity of opinions, 28-29
  misleading nature of, 11-15, 43
  overstated opinions, 21-22
  reluctance to downgrade, 19-21
  unique opinions, value of, 30-31
  unreliability of, 9-11
job function of, 3
job qualifications, 3-4
overconfidence, 32
professional credentials, 185-187
reports, incomplete nature of, 15
research. *See* research
rewards and job perks, 7-8
role in brokerage firm investment banks, 4-5
  in 1970s, 148-151
  in 1980s, 151-154
  in 1990s Bubble Era, 163-174
unreliability in stock picking, 9-10
youth and inexperience of, 41-43

V

value stocks, 67-68
Vanguard Group, 16, 68, 192
visionaries, 125-126
volatility, 17

W

Wall Street
  big company bias, 22-23
  conformity of opinions, 28-29
  inability to spot secular shifts,
    27-28
  misleading practices
    access to selective
      information, 50-51
    corporate executives'
      impact on research
      opinions, 53-56
    deletion of coverage, 46-47
    disregard of market
      strategists and technical
      analysis, 44-45
    effect of Institutional
      Investor *poll rankings on*
      research, 49-50
    focus on institutional
      clients, 38-41
    hedge funds, 51-53
    lack of coverage, 47-48
    lack of credibility of Buy
      ratings, 43
    leaping ahead of upgrades,
      48-49
    neglect of small cap stocks,
      45-46
    youth and inexperience of
      analysts, 41-43

positive bias of, 16-19
research. *See* research
short-term orientation, 25-27
The Wall Street Journal, 10,
  83, 192
Wall Street Week, 2, 38, 148
Wang, Charles, 127
Washington Mutual, 112
Wave Systems, 168
Webvan, 168
Weill, Sandy, 186
Weiss Ratings, 10
Welch, Jack, 125
Weston, Josh, 128, 156
Whole Foods, 110
worrywart executive style, 129

X-Y-Z

Xerox, 115-116, 126

Yahoo!, 128, 168
Yang, Jerry, 128
youth of securities analysts,
  41-43

Zacks Investment Research, 18

FINANCIAL TIMES

In an increasingly competitive world, it is quality
of thinking that gives an edge—an idea that opens new
doors, a technique that solves a problem, or an insight
that simply helps make sense of it all.

We work with leading authors in the various arenas
of business and finance to bring cutting-edge thinking
and best-learning practices to a global market.

It is our goal to create world-class print publications
and electronic products that give readers
knowledge and understanding that can then be
applied, whether studying or at work.

To find out more about our business
products, you can visit us at www.ftpress.com.